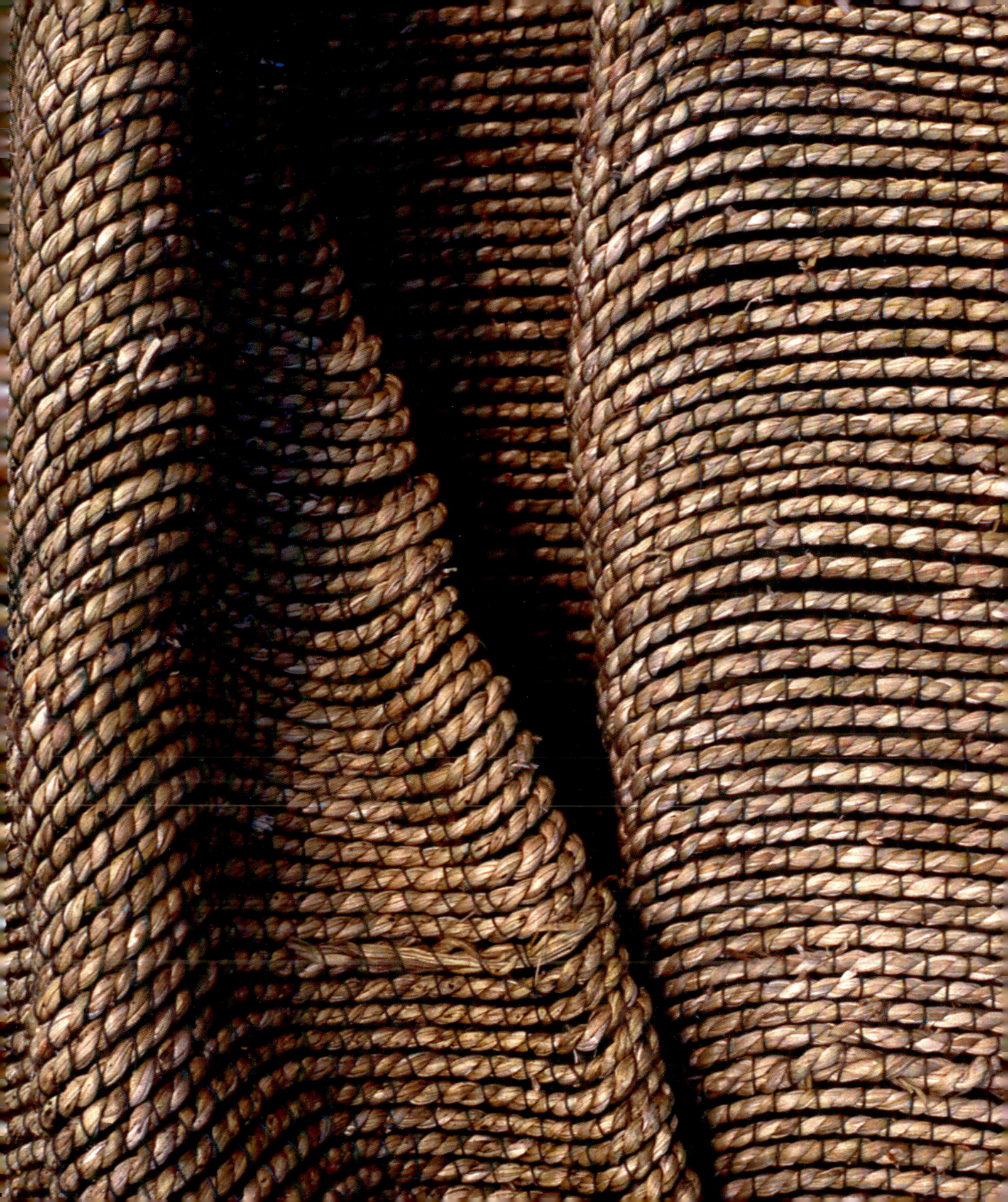

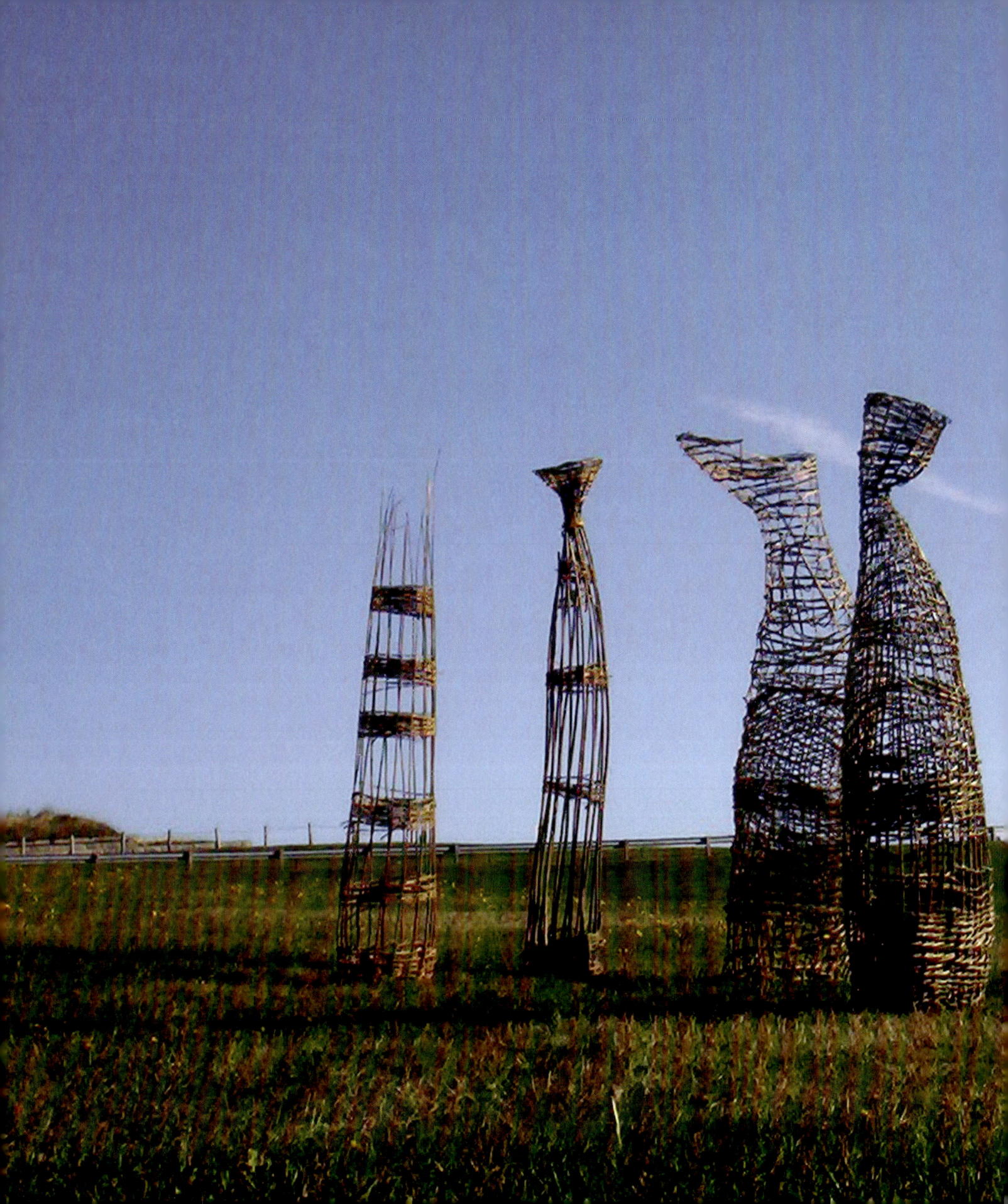

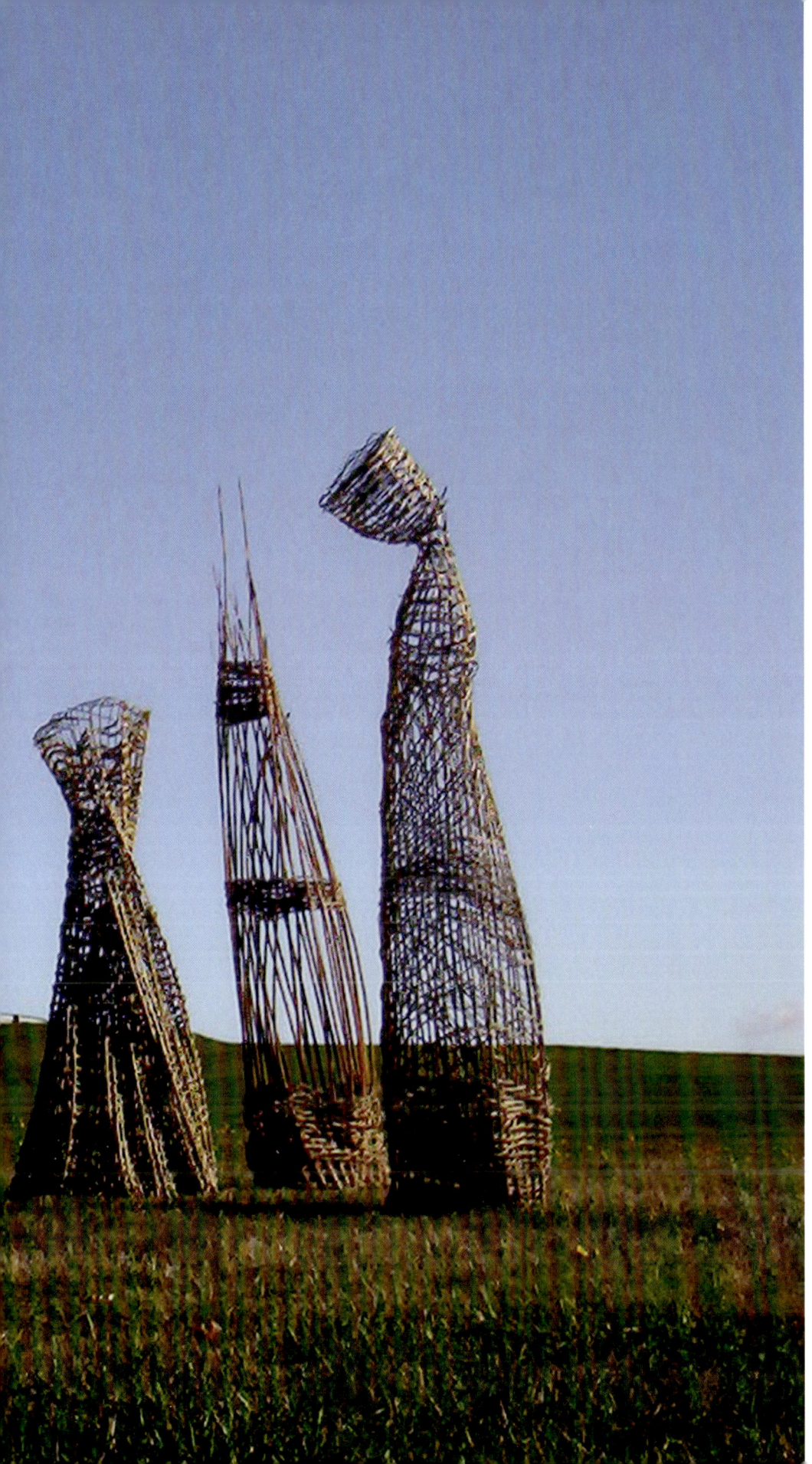

Return to Delos, 2004
Timeless Forms series,
1995–2002
twined willow and seagrass
and *Timeless Figure* (centre),
c. 1996
bronze, cast from twined willow
140–170 cm high
Installation at Citadel Hill,
Halifax, NS

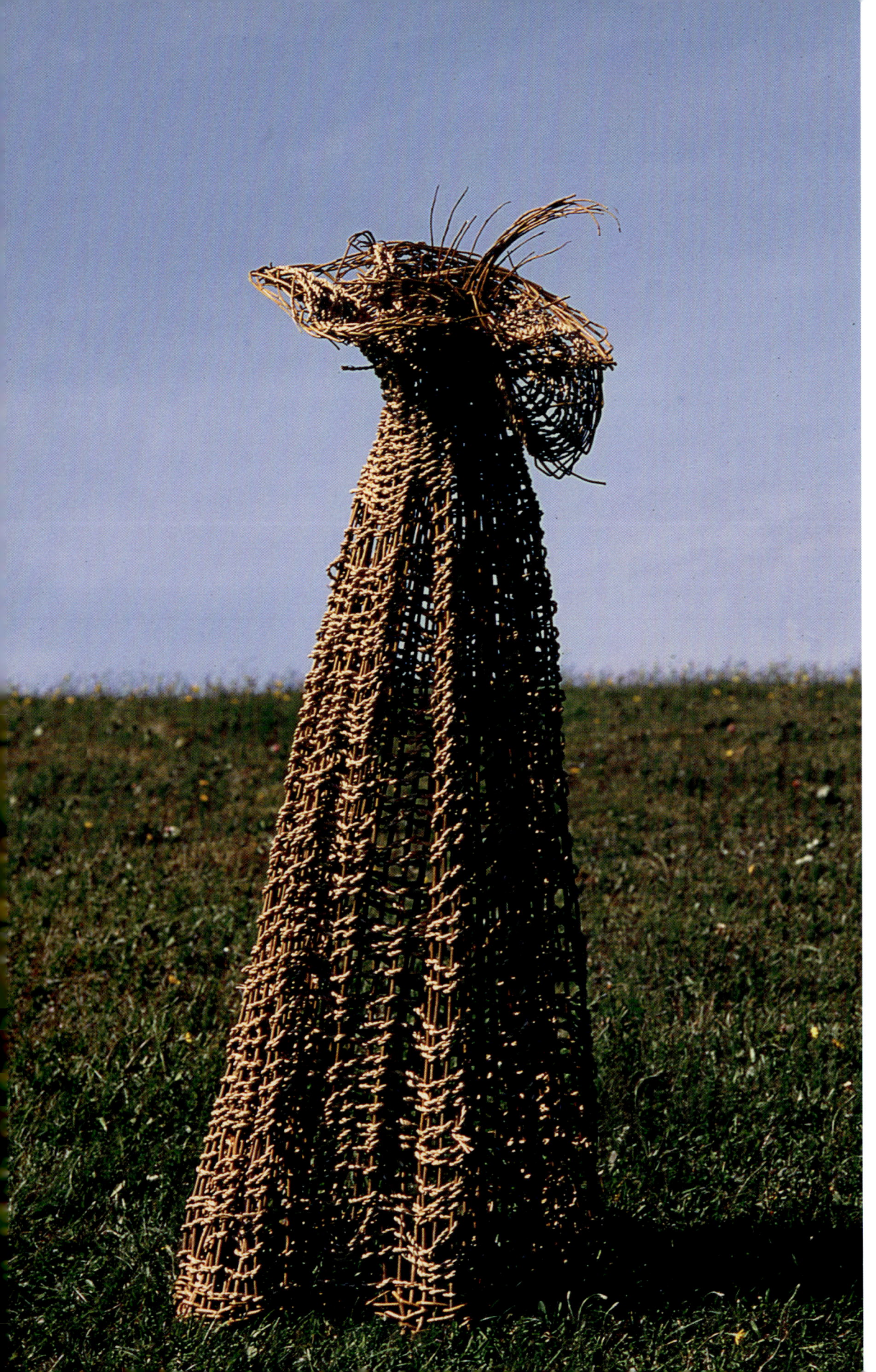

Timeless Form, 1995
twined willow and seagrass
135 × 64 × 64 cm
Citadel Hill, Halifax, NS

Timeless Forms

Dawn MacNutt

MSVU Art Gallery | Owens Art Gallery

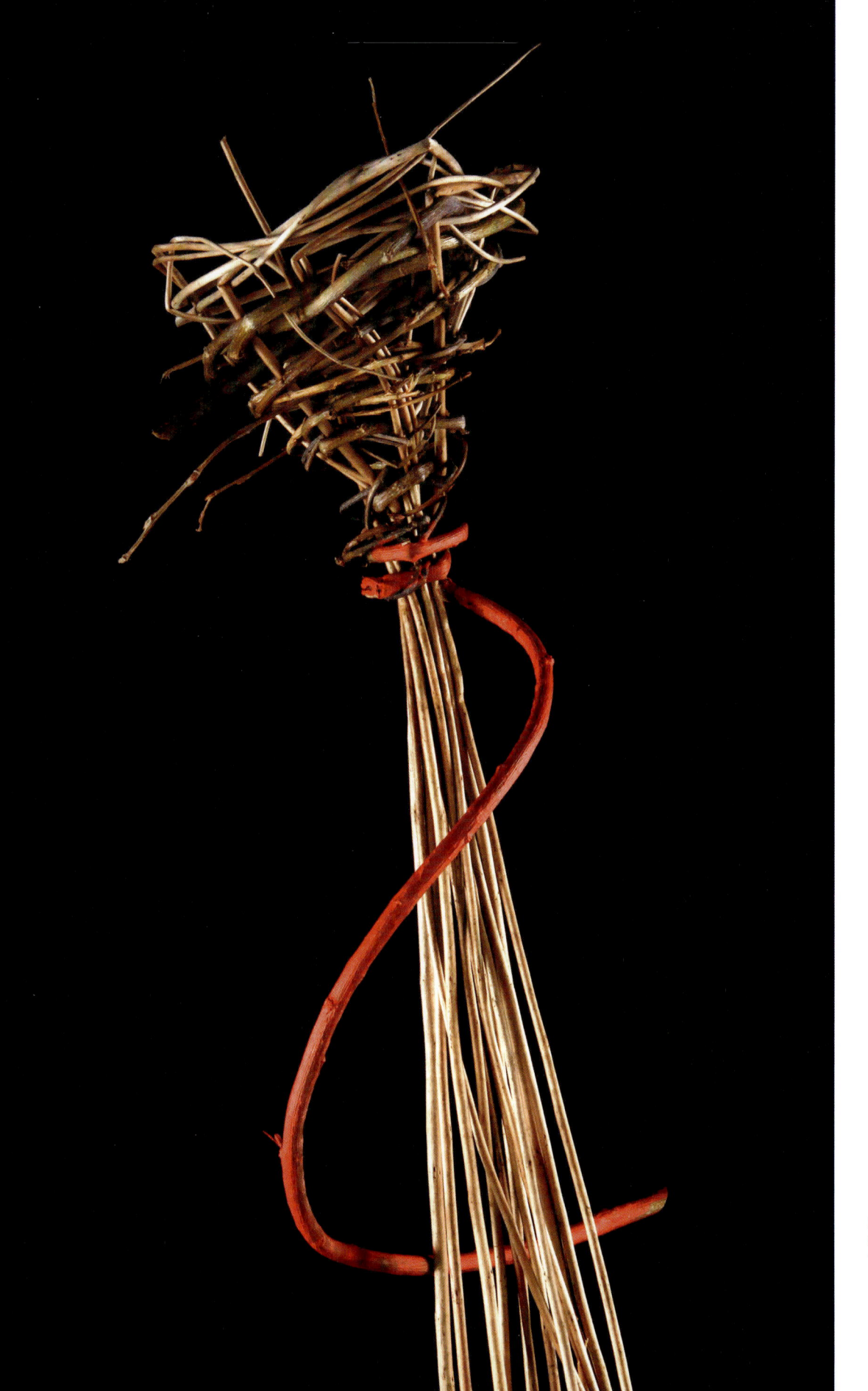

Free Spirit (detail), 2009
twined willow, acrylic paint
142 × 38 cm

Contents

11   Preface

15   Beginning

23   Fortunate Adversity

31   The Mount Allison Years

41   Once Upon a Time

47   Kindred Spirits

61   Love

71   Vytaiemo

75   Courage

79   All the Ancients Walk Inside Us

89   New Horizons

99   Illumination

113   Caring

119   Spirits

127   Lost

133   Bright Colours on a Dark Background

137   Muse

147   Acknowledgements

151   List of Works

159   About the Artist

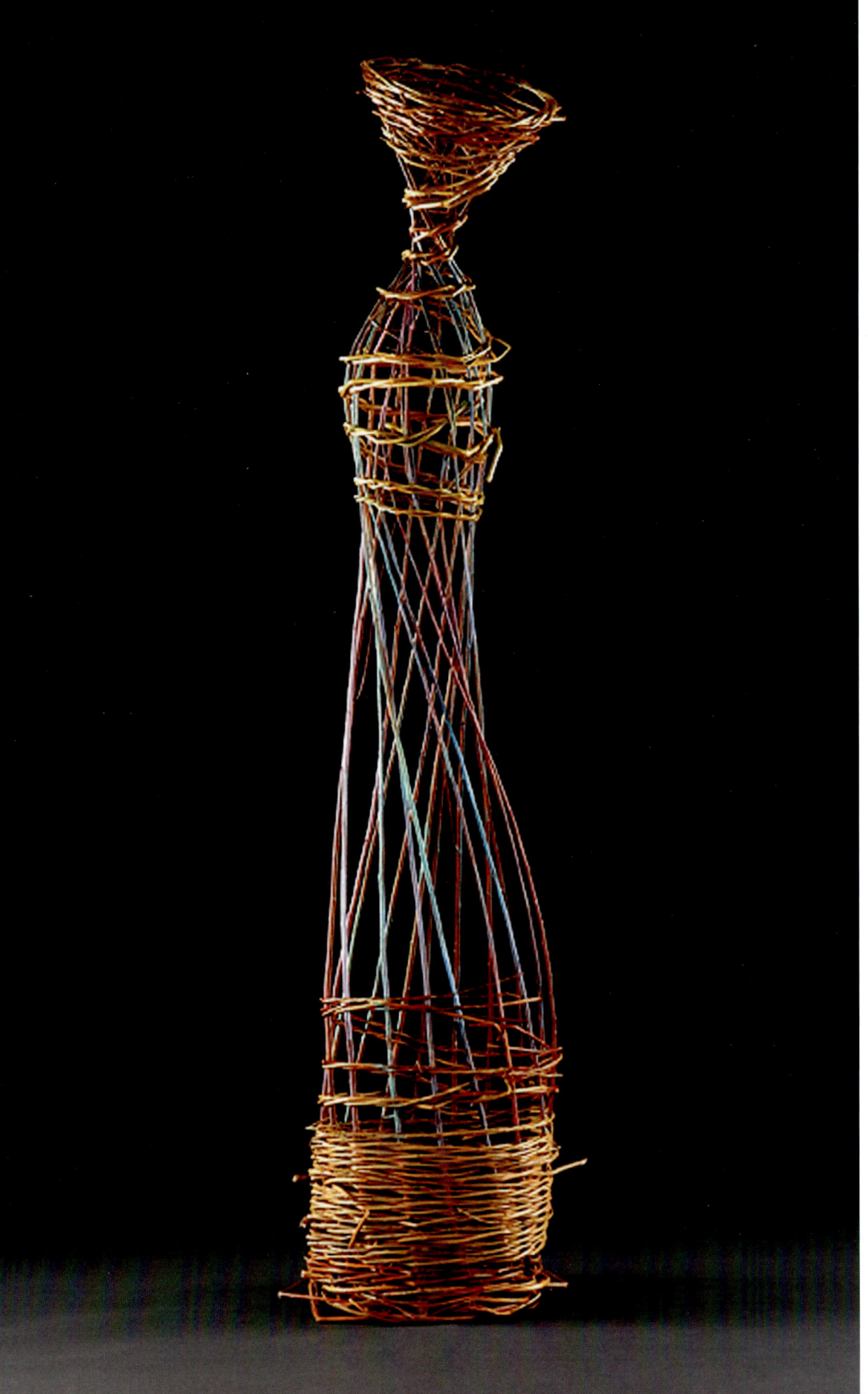

Summer Stroll, 2008
twined willow, acrylic paint
150 × 40 × 40 cm

opposite:
Summer Stroll (detail), 2008

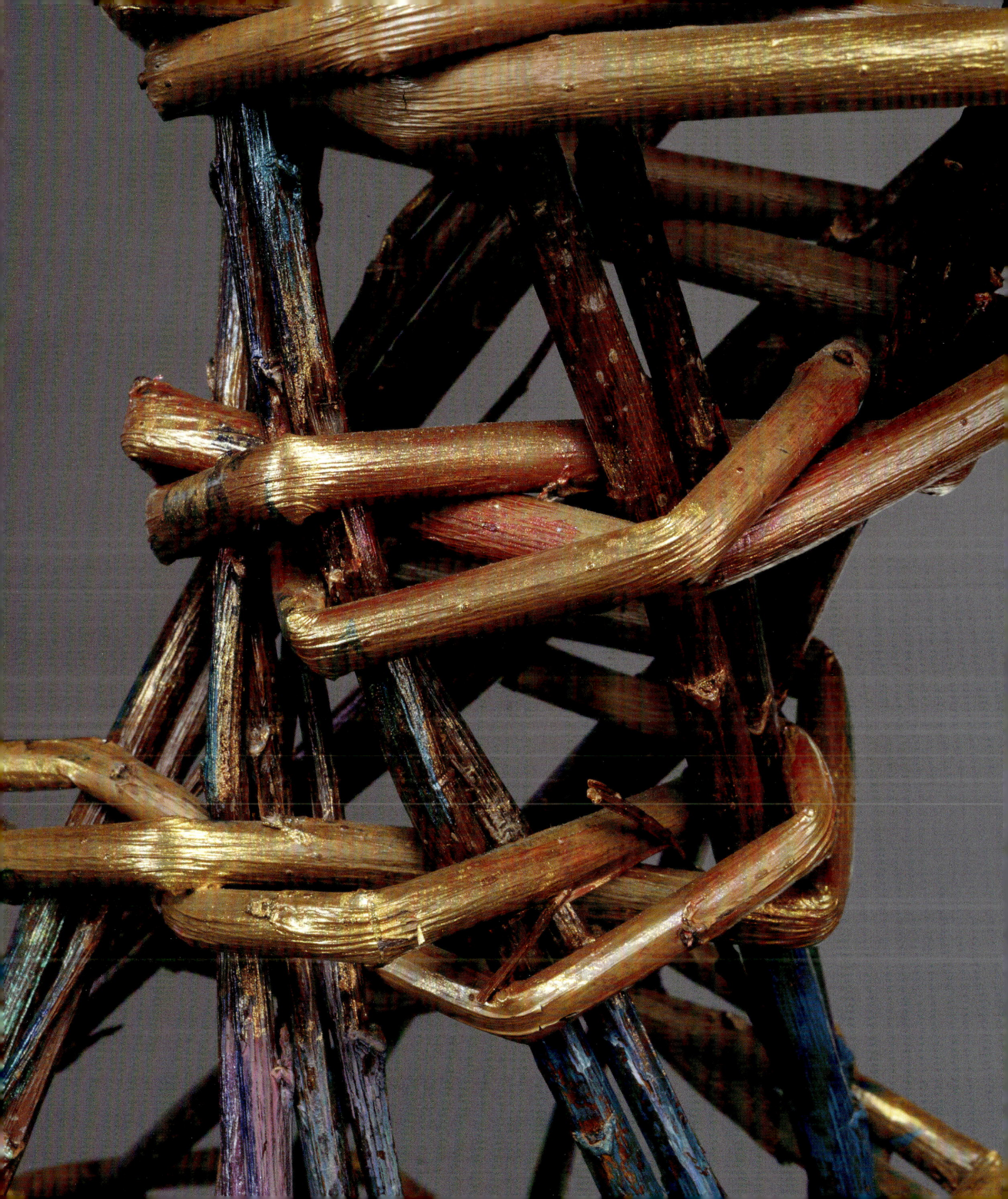

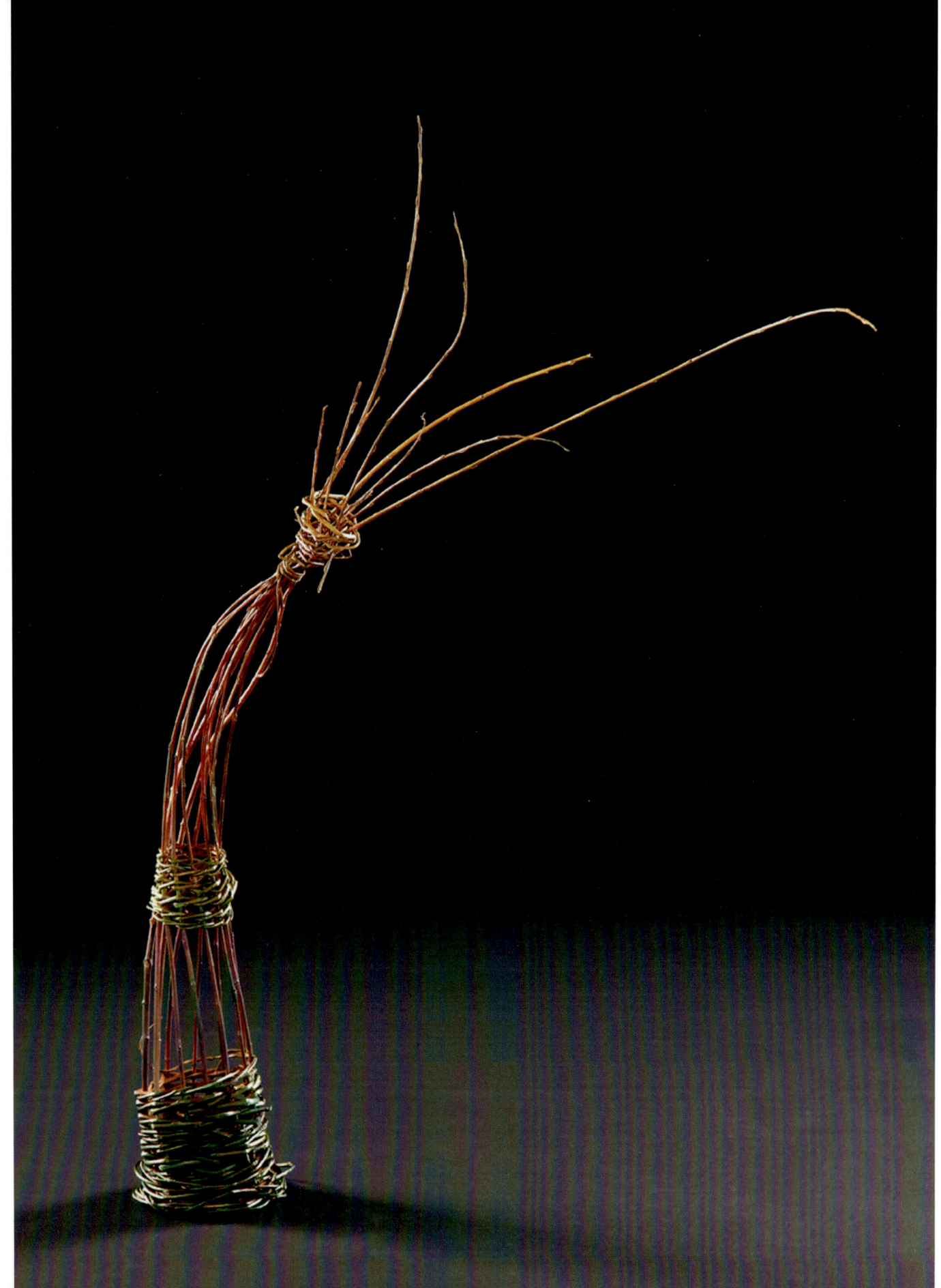

Preface

Dawn MacNutt is a singular artist with a deep appreciation for life's contradictions and the creative energies they contain. As the pages of this book reveal, her life and artistic practice have been shaped by "fortunate adversities" and various other paradoxes. Guided by creative intuition and a profound curiosity about the complexities of human experience, she has made living sculptures, woven delicate fabrics from metal thread, and created enduring bronze installations from tender willows. Throughout her career, she has celebrated both the strength and fragility of human life, creating poignant pieces that serve as tributes to loss, mourning, and resilience. Over time, her work has grown ever more complex and nuanced, shedding some of the innocence of earlier pieces while remaining true to the spirit of artistic play and exploration.

It was a privilege for us to work on this book, which precedes a solo retrospective of MacNutt's work that will be presented at MSVU Art Gallery in 2025 and the Owens Art Gallery in 2026. Together these two projects align with our galleries' mandates, which prioritize Atlantic artists and spring from a long history of supporting women's education. As both a graduate of Mount Allison University (class of 1957, LLD 2014) and a recipient of an Honorary Doctorate of Humane Letters from Mount Saint Vincent University (2005), Dawn MacNutt is an important part of this legacy.

On behalf of MSVU Art Gallery and the Owens Art Gallery, we would like to thank Dawn MacNutt for her passion and commitment to art and artistic life. Working with her on this book was both an honour and a pleasure, and we look forward to curating her retrospective exhibition. We are also extremely grateful to the Honourable Margaret Norrie McCain, who has supported MacNutt's practice for many years and who very generously funded this book. We are delighted to work with Goose Lane Editions on this publication, and we would like to offer particular thanks to Julie Scriver, Alan Sheppard, and Alison Taylor

Against All Odds, 2013
twined willow, acrylic paint
92 × 75 × 40 cm

for their support. The manuscript for this book was spearheaded by Margaret Kashmir, whose efforts we sincerely appreciate. A myriad of other individuals helped make this book possible, including Peter Barss, Gerry Farrell, Maxine Krawczyk, Bruce Murray, and Laura Ritchie. We are grateful to Dawn's husband, Merle Pratt, who ensured our visits to Little Harbour were nourished with food and laughter. Finally, we would like to sincerely thank the personnel working at both the MSVU Art Gallery and the Owens Art Gallery — your ongoing support makes this work possible.

Melanie Colosimo, Director, MSVU Art Gallery
Emily Falvey, Director/Curator, Owens Art Gallery

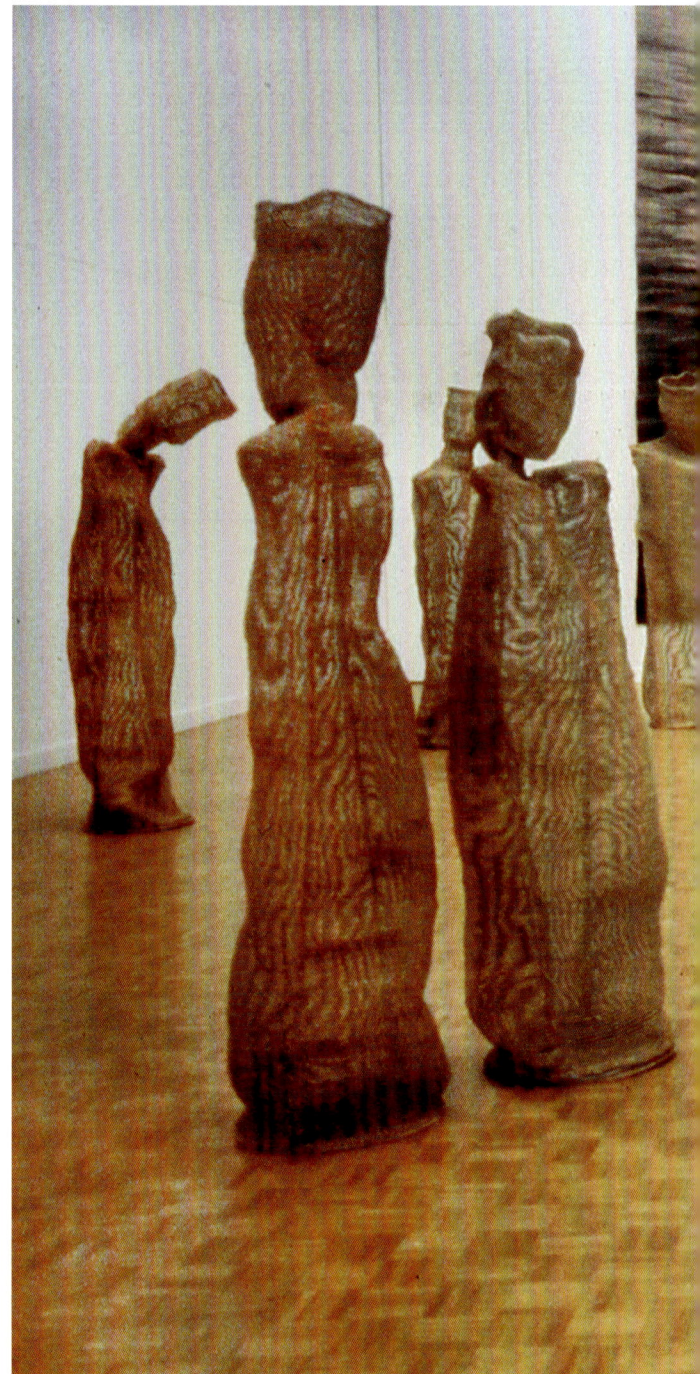

Woven Forms (freestanding), 1984
welded, wrapped metal armature
dimensions variable
and *Rhythms* (on wall), 1984
loom-woven wool tapestry
304 × 304 cm
Exhibition at MSVU Art Gallery

12

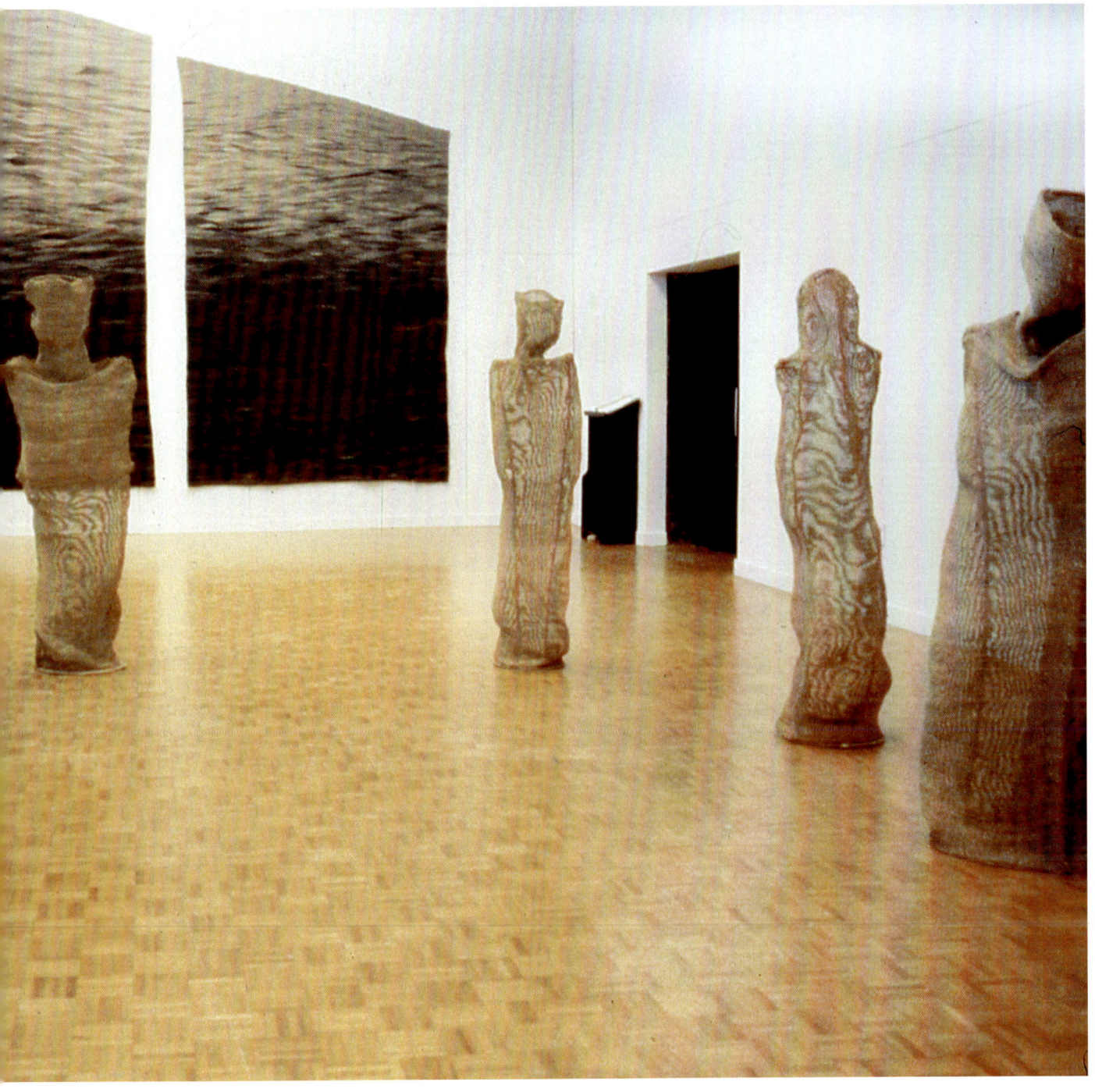

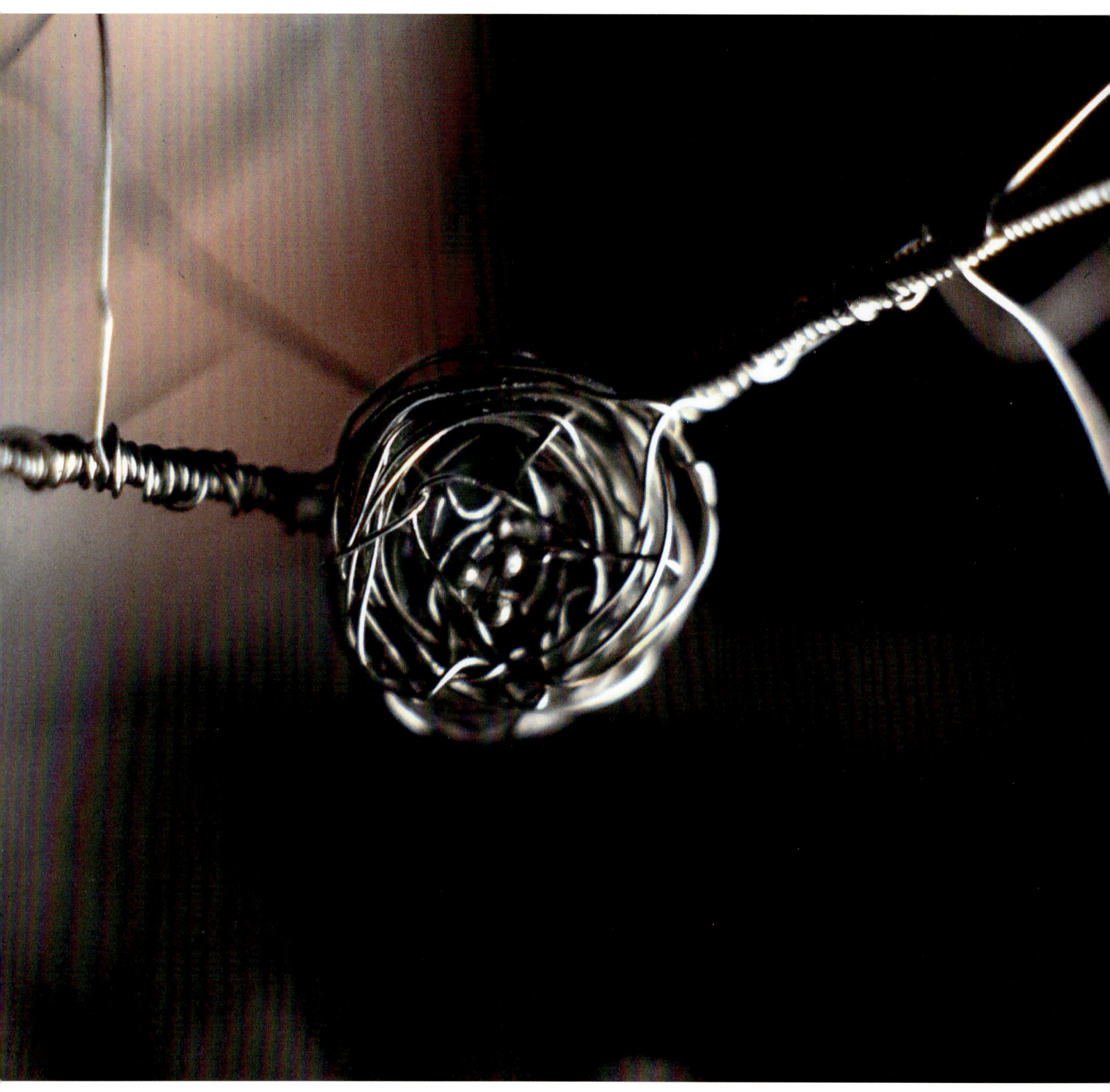

Beginning

The farmhouse on the hill, where I was born, still stands — just a mile from where I now live, along the ragged rural coastline of Nova Scotia. Even though eighty-seven years have passed, it looks much the same. I have no desire to go back inside. It is the outside that lingers in my memory, influencing many of the works that have emerged from my head and hands over the years.

The evocative scents of clover, cornflower, and cosmos. The elegant Queen Anne's lace that tickled my nose as I weaved through the tall grasses. Delicate robins' eggs nestled in a mound of hay. Lady's slippers, collected and placed in a glorious satin glass vase, filling the room with exotic perfume. The pungent smells of salt water, oil, and eelgrass. Fishing at dawn from a motorboat, rolling in the waves, my father's sturdy hand on the steering paddle.

I was two when war broke out in 1939. My fisherman father learned how to weld so he could be of service in the emerging Canadian shipbuilding industry, and we moved to Quebec so he could work in a shipyard. I was three or four, and I vividly remember the train trip. My mother was wearing the most beautiful dress I had ever seen. I was transfixed, and the fabric's print embedded itself in my brain: black silk crepe with a vibrant multicoloured pattern on the bodice. Bright colours on a dark background — a combination I still find beautiful, and one that has served as a metaphor throughout my life and work. Happiness is more vivid against a backdrop of sorrow. There is always hope in the darkness.

When I was five, we moved back to Nova Scotia to live with my grandmother in New Glasgow. World War II raged in the background during these years. There were restrictions on what groceries were available, and food stamps rationed sugar, butter, and meat. But the war brought out thoughtfulness in the people of our community, and generosity with what little we had to share.

Silver Thaw (detail), 1981
wrapped and melted silver wire
4 × 4 × 2 cm

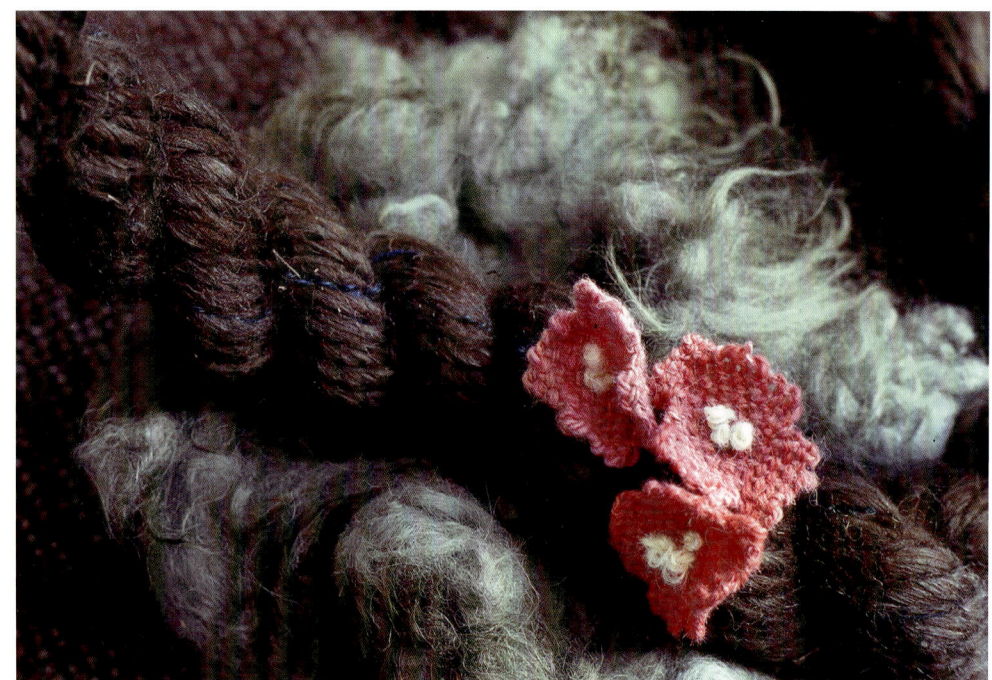

Tangled Garden (detail), 1979
felted, dyed fleece, plied wool
yarn, hand-spun, naturally dyed,
needle-woven flowers
25 × 20 × 2.5 cm

Kindred Spirits (detail), 1984
seagrass woven on copper wire
warp loom, sculpted, welded
metal armature
dimensions variable

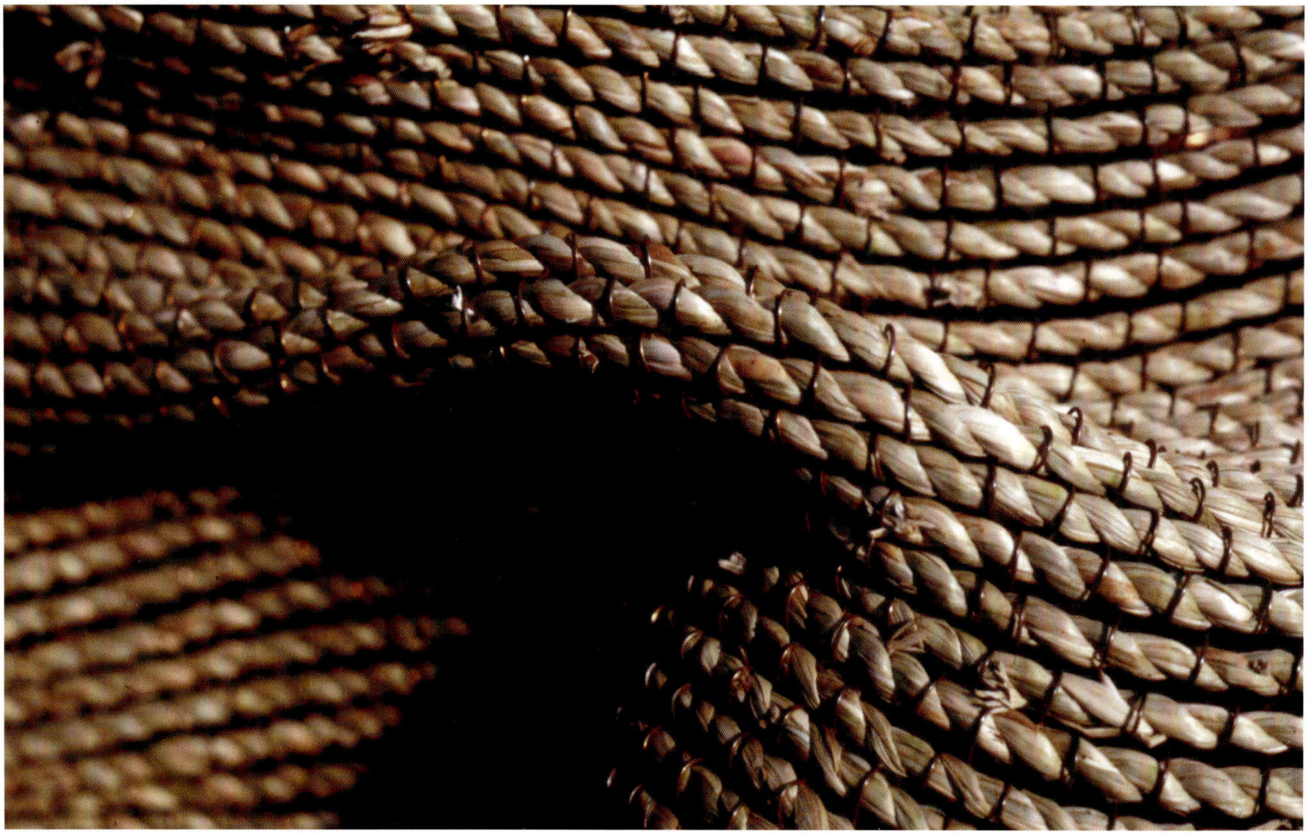

With no imported food, we grew a Victory Garden in the backyard. My curiosity was the bane of existence for my uncle Chapin, who had planted the garden and visited frequently. He would scold me, "Don't touch!" But I couldn't walk among the flowers and plants *without* touching, crushing, smelling, and tasting.

The snowball bush demanded I squish its smooth, white berries to see what was inside. I squeezed wild cucumbers until their soft centres yielded a cool wet substance that became curiously sticky. I separated grasses into threads, and rubbed the centres of flowers until pollen dyed my fingertips saffron orange. I compared each petal of daylily, nasturtium, and petunia for texture, aroma, and juiciness, then used them like pure pigment — blended with a little spit — to create paint. These sensual pleasures awakened my love of colour and the tactile joys of exploring and working with my hands.

Before long I moved on to fabric and "learned" to sew. I don't recall any instruction beyond threading a needle, so I just explored, making many wrong turns and mistakes. Instruction can be a wonderful thing, but it can also thwart adventure and invention. Nothing I produced was perfect, but it was very freeing — and resulted in the most peculiar doll clothes!

It was also at this age that I "discovered" weaving. I had precious scraps of printed silk, bequeathed to my mother by her aunt, who had worked in a silk factory in Boston. I remember one scrap that was green-and-fuchsia shot silk. In childish curiosity, I pulled apart the weft from the warp of the fabric and observed that the green threads ran in one direction while the fuchsia threads travelled in the other direction, running over and under the green. The result was a shimmering, changing fabric, shining in tones of rose, sliding into subtle green, and back to a valley of neutral. It was magical, and I was just as enchanted many years later when I learned how to weave such magic.

I remember my favourite spot in my grandmother's house was on the stairway landing. The corners of the window held geometrical stained glass inserts of red, blue, amber, and green. I loved to sit on the stairs and daydream, mesmerized by the light shining through the coloured glass. In those trancelike moments, I wondered

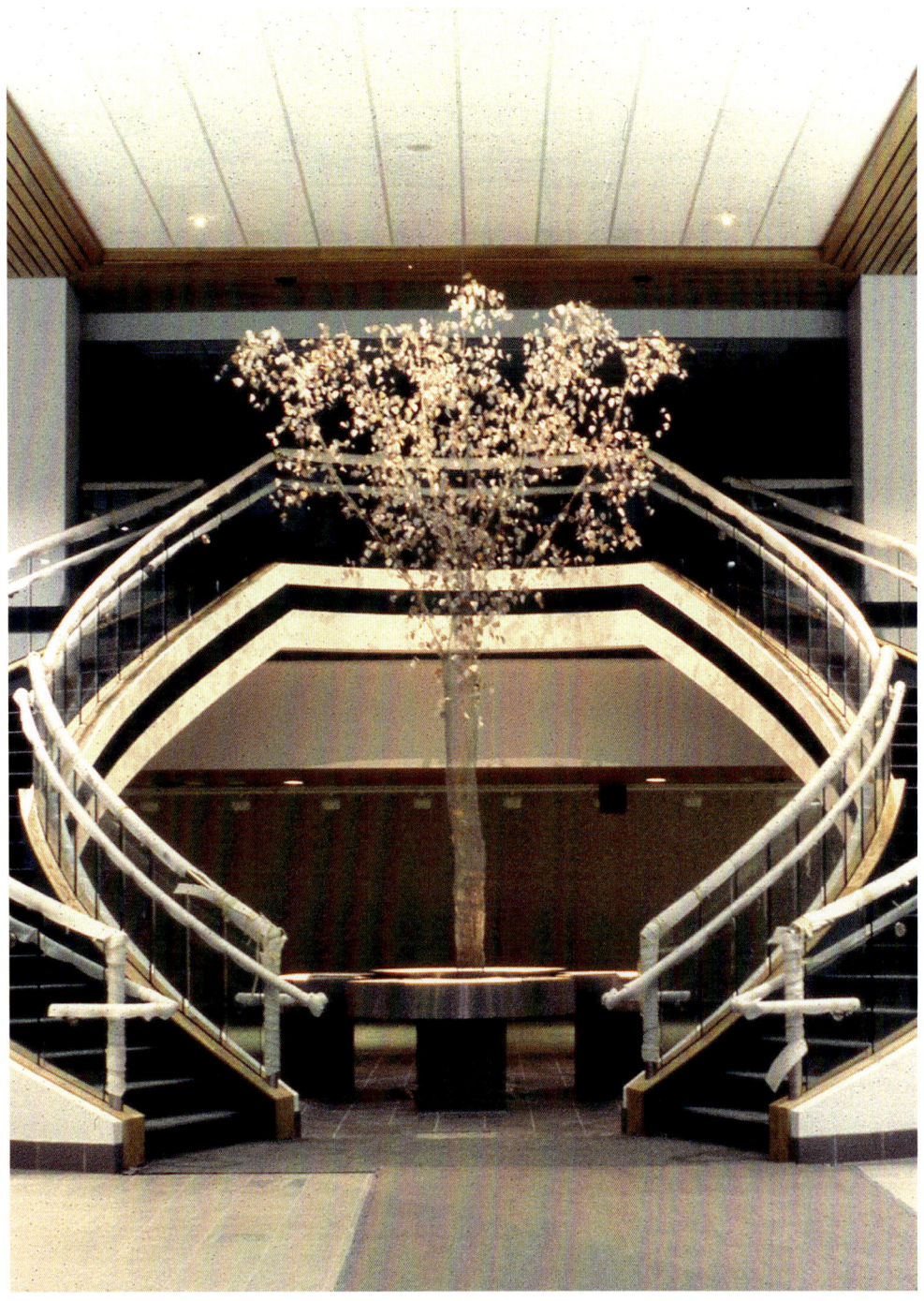

Together We Stand, 1989–1990
stainless steel wire woven
on loom, branches wrapped,
hung from the ceiling; leaves
hand-cut from Moonbeam and
Eclipse fabric, aluminized knitted
polyester attached to the tree
with fine wrapped stainless steel
610 × 457 × 457 cm

opposite: *Together We Stand*,
1989–1990 (detail)

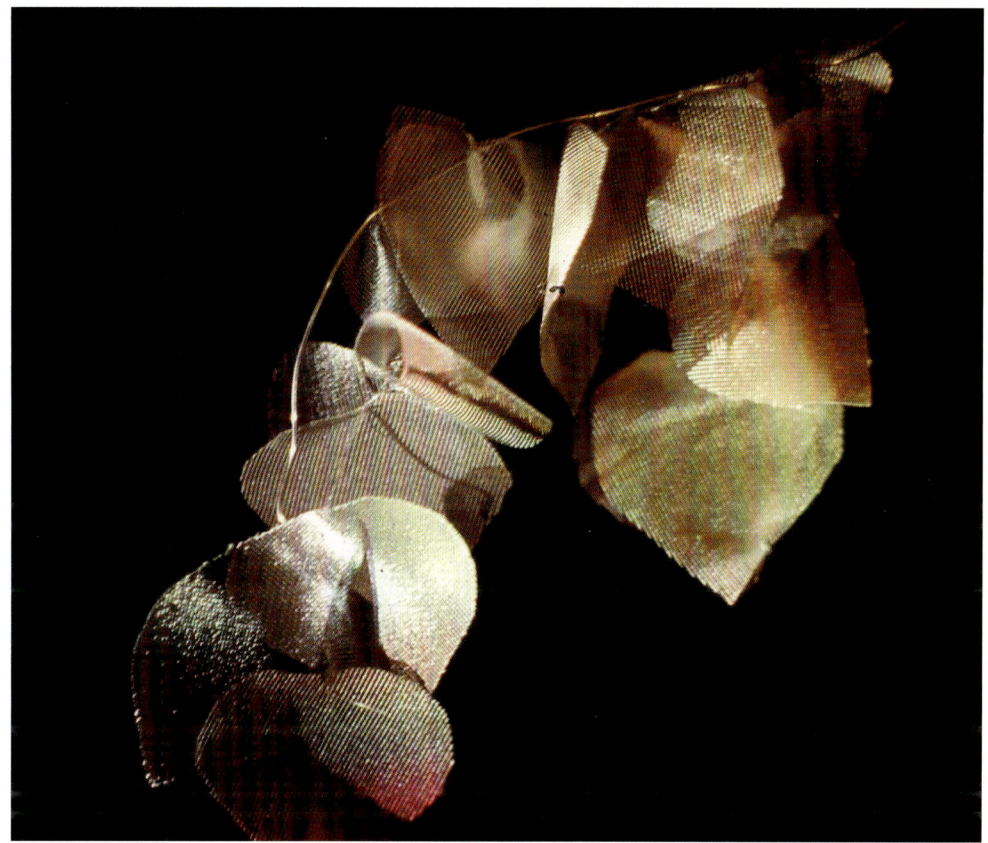

at the personal nature of perception — that I could see and feel things differently than anyone else. And the old soul in my five-year-old self told me that everyone has that capacity — to imagine, to make things, to see qualities beyond the obvious in everyday objects.

These happy early years gave me a storehouse of hope, belief, love, and wonderment that sustain me still.

Spirit of Freedom, 1988
copper wire woven on loom,
sculpted, electroplated, oxidized
28 × 23 × 23 cm

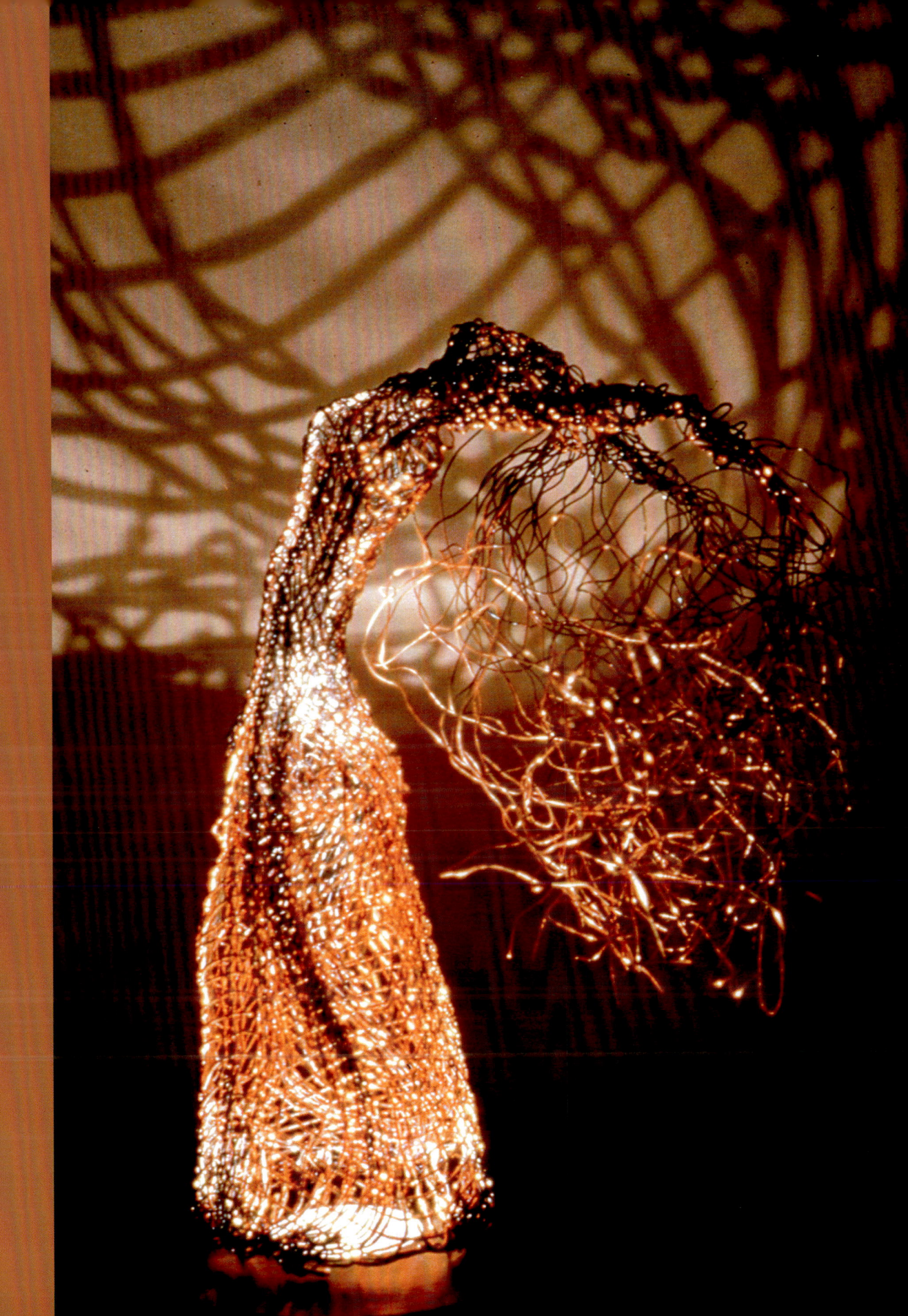

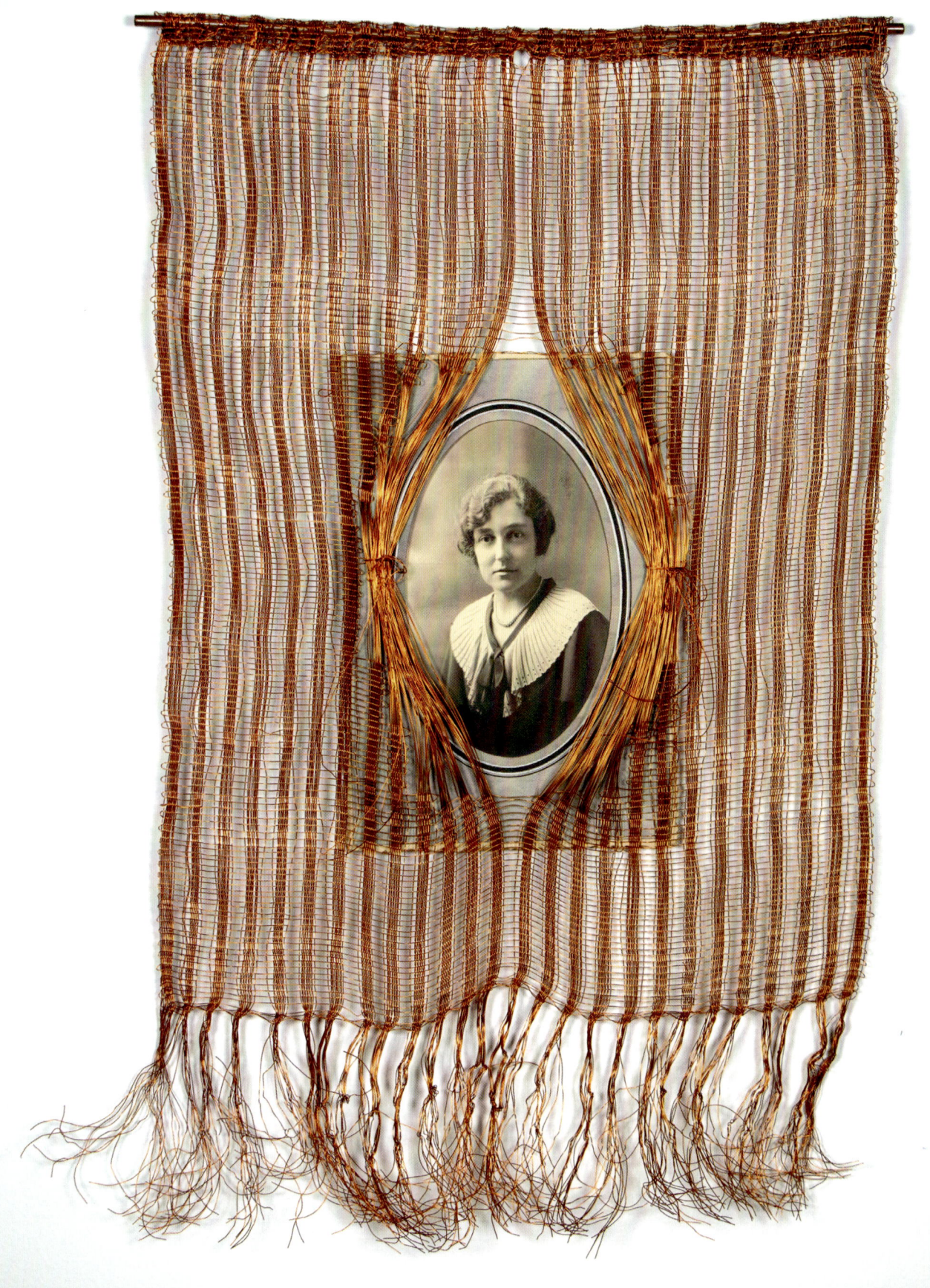

Fortunate Adversity

I was eight years old when we moved to Victory Heights in Pictou in 1945, and my father worked as a welder at the busy war-driven shipyards. Shortly thereafter, my mother contracted diphtheria, a disease that had been all but wiped out by the availability of new vaccines. We were quarantined, with a large sign on the door of our wartime prefab house warning people to stay away.

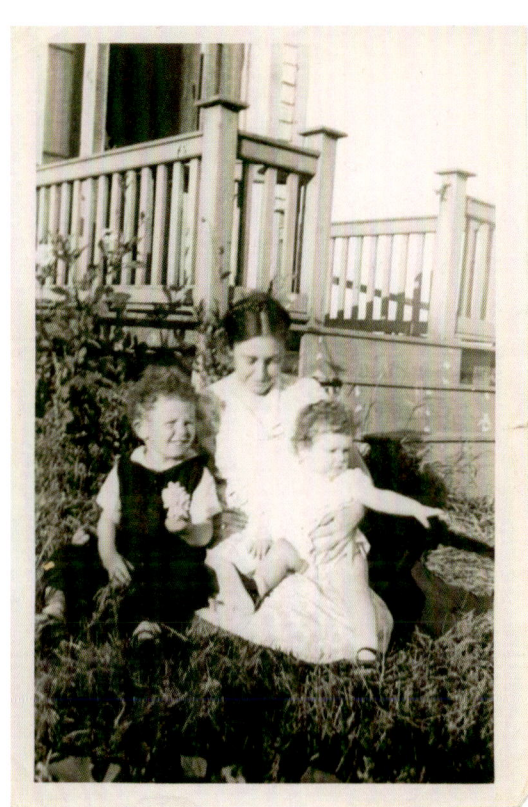

Mom, Robbie and Dawn, 1938
Image courtesy of the Artist

opposite: *Anna Reid's Daughter*, 1982
copper wire double-woven on loom with embedded photograph
51 x 12 cm

Once the quarantine ended, a beautiful young nurse named Marie started coming to care for my mother, my older brother, and me. Marie lived in Little Harbour with her husband and daughter, and my father drove her back and forth to Pictou each day, about an hour each way. After my mother's physical health improved, Marie stopped working in our home, but as it turned out, the relationship between her and my father had escalated. He began leaving at night to go see her.

My mother was twelve years older than my dad and had always been very gentle and quite "proper." The aftermath of her illness combined with this new emotional agony now sent her into a soul-shattering depression, transforming this robust, pretty woman into a despondent and wizened shell of herself.

She began to wail. Into the middle of the night she would cry as she watched out the front window for cars coming up the hill. She studied each one, relentlessly looking for the lights of my father's green 1937 Plymouth. My brother Robbie, two years older than me, was unable to bear the sound of her despair and would leave the room. But I felt a need to comfort this sobbing, boney creature I hardly recognized. I would hold her, try to reassure her, and wonder how one woman's tears could make my pajamas so wet. I was overcome by soggy tissues and her eyes swollen in pain. I longed for relief, for both of us.

When my father returned after driving Marie home each night, my mother's grief turned to rage. Her wracked body exploded into wild, frenzied screaming — pounding, throwing, out of control. I was eight years old and terrified. A new pattern emerged, in which she constantly begged for her husband's love, and he continued to deny what was happening. I thought she would be impossible to love, but I also resented my father for not loving her enough to "fix" her. I wanted my mother back.

The new and shameful family secret was that my mother was mentally ill. On several occasions, she was taken away for treatment. She resisted medications and electroshock therapy, which were both somewhat primitive back then. She once recalled for me the horror of the shock being applied while she was still conscious. Her short-term memory was affected by the procedure, so on returning home, she was convinced that the dishes were different, the cupboards rearranged, the walls all painted.

She was a strange and pitiful sight. In efforts to recover, she tried bright red lipstick and powder for the first time in her forty-four years. Her shaky hand missed the perimeter of her lips. The ribbon in her lank, thin hair was awkwardly arranged like a hastily wrapped Christmas package. Her glasses magnified her swollen eyes. I still loved her soul, sensed her goodness, and knew my mom was hidden somewhere deep inside. But for several years, she ceased to be my mother, and I felt like hers. My father ran away to Montréal with Marie, who he eventually married and also divorced.

These difficult years caused anguish in my own soul that I mitigated by spending time outside the house: I learned to be sociable. I had an overwhelming urge to reveal the "family secret," which we all tried to hide from the world. One day, I finally, unintentionally, confided in my friend Gail's mother. To this day, I'm grateful she didn't "turn me in" or reject me. She instead met my purging with kindness, and my burden of guilt was eased into healing.

The other balm to my young soul was art. My greatest joy when I was thirteen was private art lessons that I paid for by selling Christmas cards door to door. I studied first with Ina McAskill, who had strict rules on line and perspective. Later,

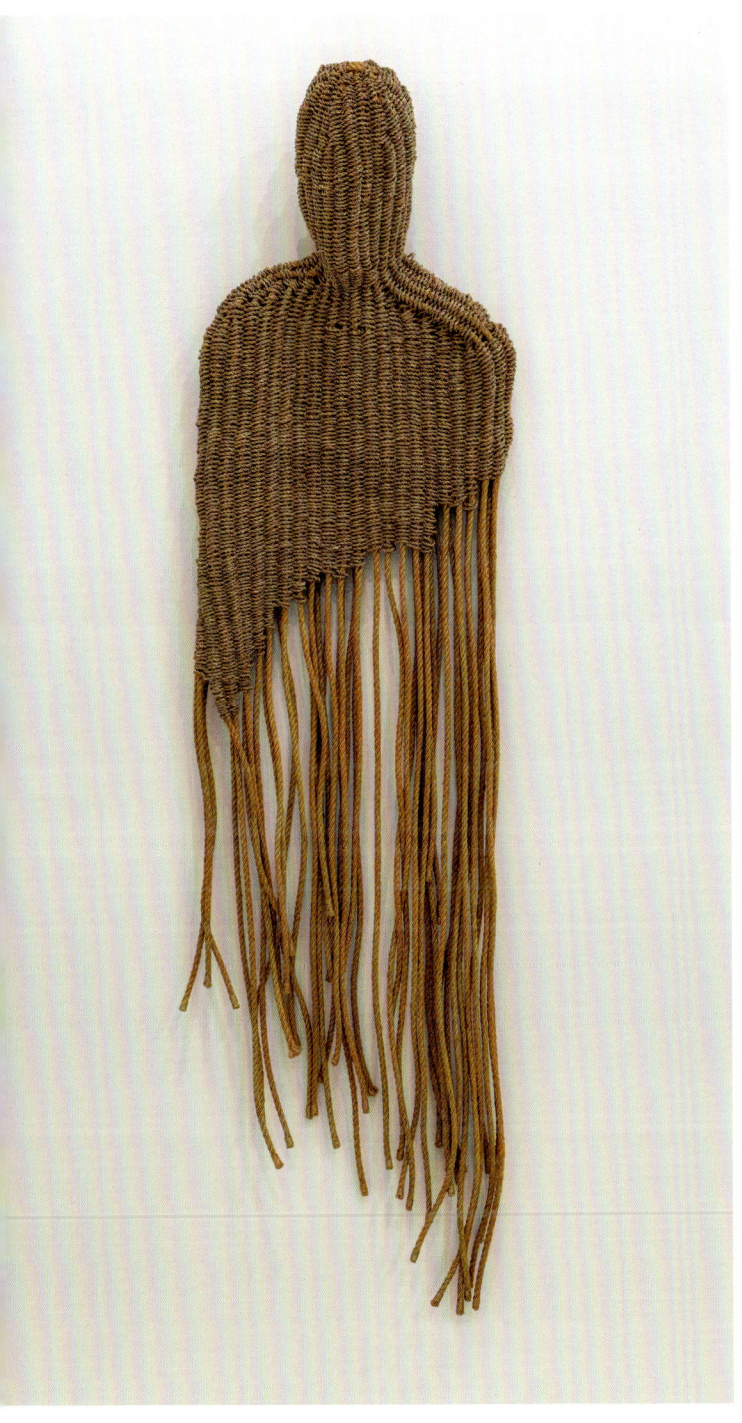

and even better, were my lessons with the vivacious and free-spirited Cherie Smith, whose liberating instructions were, "Generously wet the watercolour paper and allow the colour to flow."

My mother slowly recovered and returned to work, teaching grade 1 until she retired in 1965. As her wholeness returned, so too did my love and my respect for her courage, her lack of bitterness, and her humility. Her transcending of the dark years and coming into the light was such a gift to us both. While my early years instilled in me the ability to dream and gave me the desire to create, these complicated years tempered my musings and creative urges with forgiveness, empathy, and a belief in redemption.

Presence, 1981 (p. 25)
twined seagrass over hemp rope
243 × 76 × 10 cm

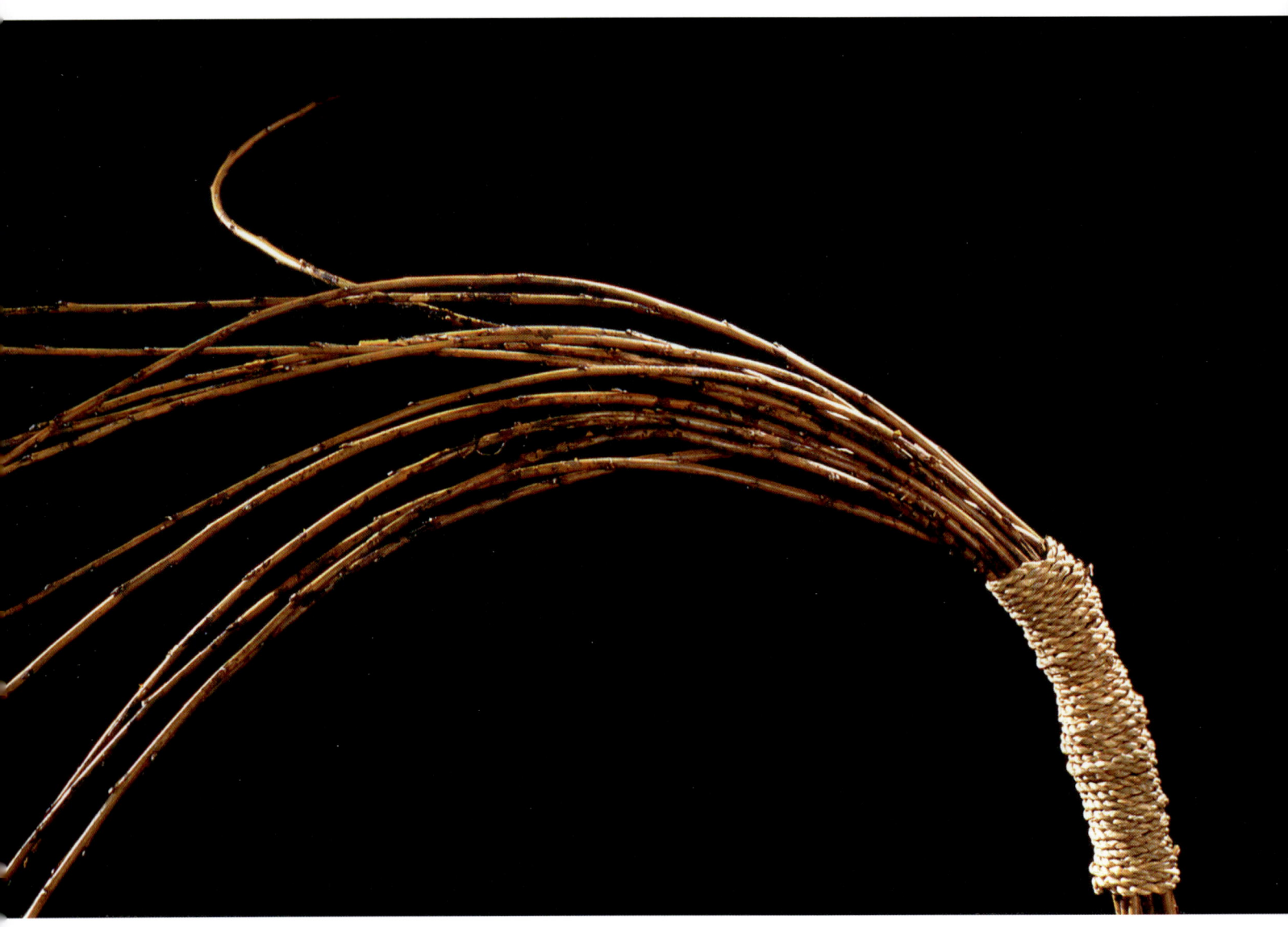

Recovery, 2004
twined and wrapped English
willow and seagrass
120 × 74 × 50 cm

opposite: *Recovery* (detail), 2004

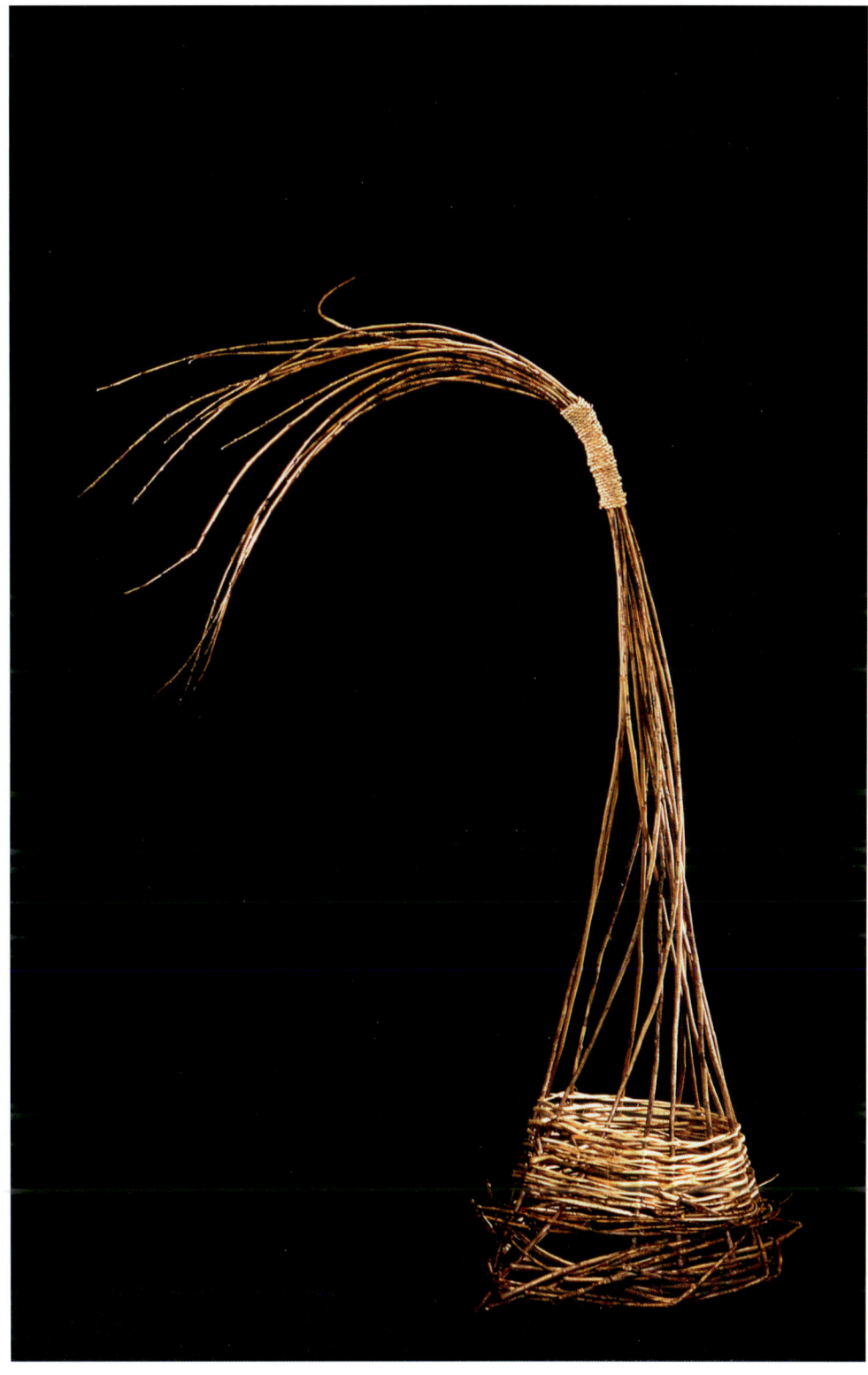

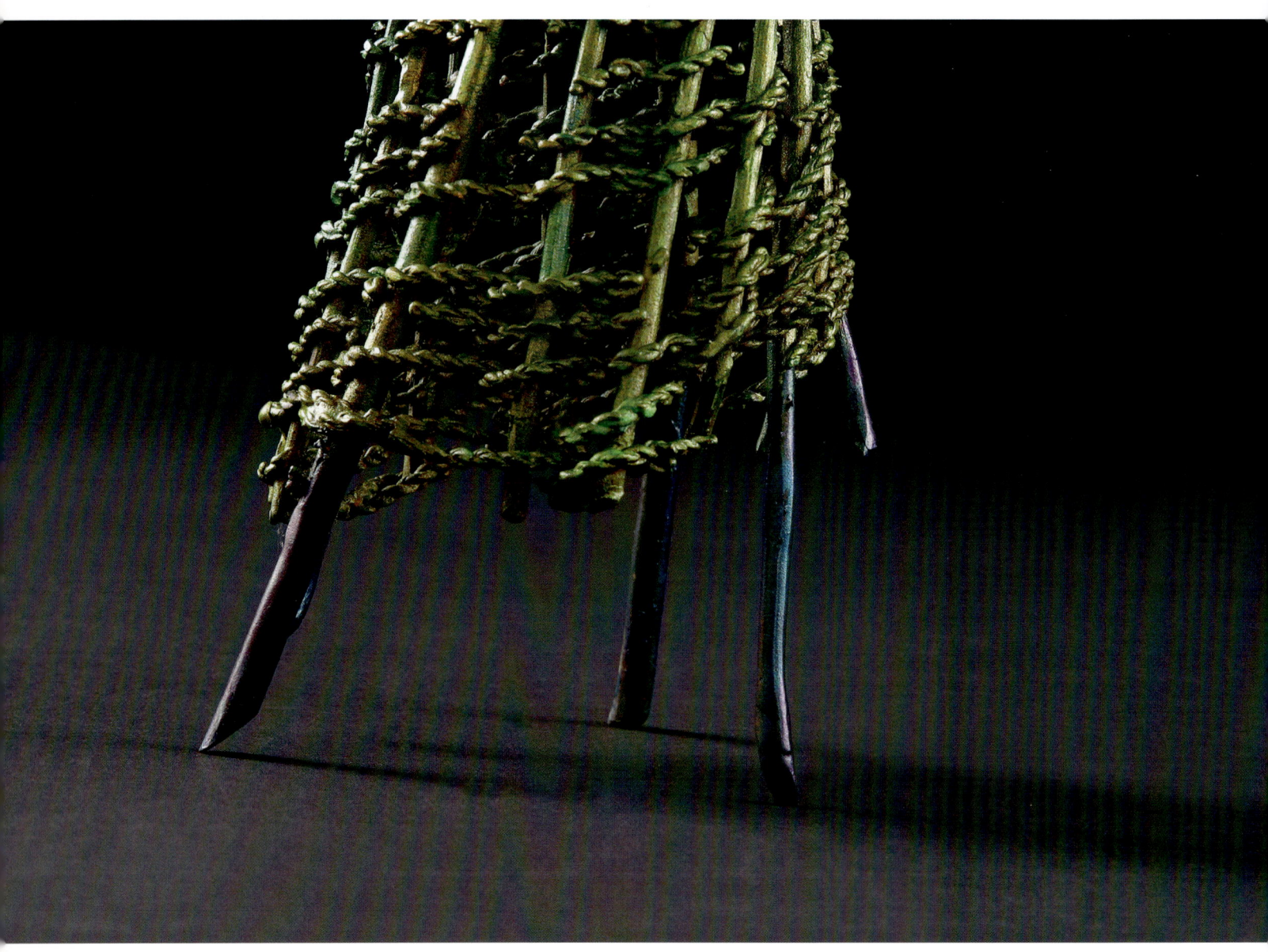

Echoes of the Past, 2018
bronze, cast from twined willow
and seagrass
69 × 38 × 13 cm

opposite: *Echoes of the Past*
(detail), 2018

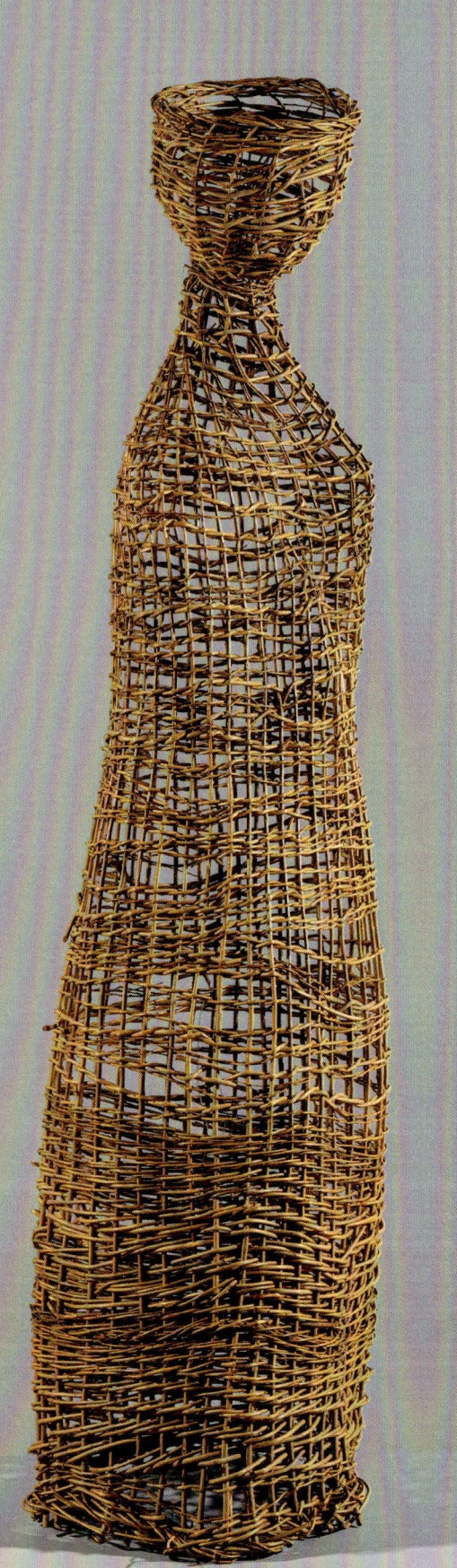

The Mount Allison Years

In the fall of 1954, I arrived on the Mount Allison University campus, where I majored in psychology. I was a caregiver by nature, and social work seemed a natural career path. But the two major gifts of those years were the deep friendships that developed and my experiences with art.

Visits to my friends' homes gave me hope that happy family life was possible, and when I shared parts of my tattered, imperfect childhood with close friends and meaningful boyfriends, their acceptance affirmed my deep-rooted shame was unnecessary. That trusting and truth-telling allowed me to develop lifelong relationships. Lorna, Jessie, and Joan became my soul sisters, and our intimate group widened to embrace nine beloved women we affectionately called "Scraggs." We still giggle about the origin of the nickname, as "scraggy" means "scrawny, bony, lanky," which none of us could claim to be. These friendships remain strong to this day and even extend to the next generation.

My true passion was to create. I just couldn't imagine it as a livelihood. The fine arts minor, being offered for the first time at Mount A, was a wonderful compromise. The generous amount of time I spent in the Owens Art Gallery and in the weaving studio downstairs formed the foundation for a career change decades later.

The 1950s were heady years for the Fine Arts Department at Mount Allison, and for the Owens Art Gallery, which housed the department at that time. The program was headed by Lawren P. Harris and had two of its graduates as professors: Ted Pulford, an affable, chain-smoking, talented watercolourist; and Alex Colville, who was just about to burst onto the international art scene. Many of Canada's best-known realist artists emerged from the mentorship and teaching of Colville and his Fine Arts Department colleagues. I loved Colville's courses in art history and, even more so, the two afternoons a week of studio time.

I recall with particular clarity one day in my first year. Colville's personal studio was just off the main studio space (now the Colville Gallery at the current Owens Art Gallery). He'd left his studio door ajar, and a few of us couldn't resist peering in. There, on his easel, was the nearly finished canvas of his iconic *Horse and Train*, now in the collection of the Art Gallery of Hamilton. I was awestruck by its power, and I believed in that moment that Colville's work was destined for international acclaim.

On another evening, as I was working late in the studio, Colville and Pulford approached me. I assumed they were anxious to leave for the night; instead, they asked me why I wasn't a fine arts major. I blushed from the attention and stammered a completely inarticulate answer. I didn't change course, but that moment of recognition from my painting teachers made me feel, for the first time, that I had the potential to be a *real* artist. It fed my belief in the worth of creating, whether I went on to make a living as an artist or not.

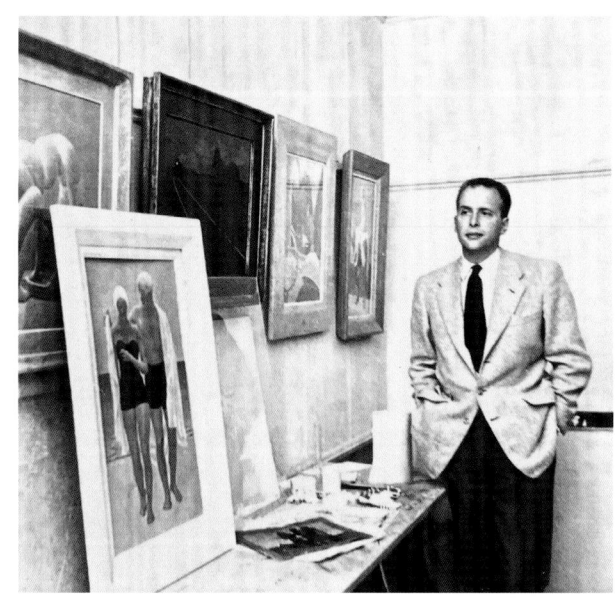

Alex Colville in his office, Owens Art Gallery, Sackville, NB, c. 1955 Image courtesy of A.C. Fine Art Inc. and Mira Goddard Gallery

Encouragement is the spine of true mentoring. And those first words of support from Colville started a mentorship that lasted until his death in 2013. Colville was a quiet, enigmatic man who exuded dignity. He had experienced World War II as a Canadian war artist and then returned to Sackville, New Brunswick, to teach and raise his family. Both incisive and democratic, he told us more than once, "There is no such thing as a bad painting, if somebody honestly likes it." Those words made a lasting impression on me. Even now, when I see works that I dislike or don't understand, Colville's words ring in my head.

As our paths crossed over time, Colville's encouragement continued — occasionally on beautifully hand-scripted notes. Having supported his family by teaching during his increasingly renowned artmaking years, he was sympathetic to my own path, working as a social worker while growing as a weaver/sculptor.

One day, many years later, while visiting the Owens Art Gallery, I remarked to then-director Gemey Kelly, that it would be interesting to organize an exhibition of Colville's students who were still working as professional artists. Gemey invited me to organize the show with her, and in the summer of 2007 *A Tribute to Alex Colville: Then and Now* opened. Colville included a couple early paintings alongside more current work, and the ten other artists in the show did the same. These included Glenn Adams, D.P. Brown, Hugh Mackenzie, Roger Savage, Ken Tolmie, and myself, as well as my good friends and former classmates Tom Forrestall, Christopher Pratt, Mary Pratt, and Nancy Steven. Each of us penned a statement to present to Colville at the opening, and these were also printed in the exhibition brochure.

Unfortunately, our beloved teacher, then age eighty-seven, fell off his bicycle a few days before the opening. He broke his pelvis and was unable to attend. I visited him in Wolfville a month later to present him with a handsome book of handwritten tributes from his former students.

Moving Forward (2), 2018
twined willow, acrylic paint
20 × 42 × 8.7 cm

His personal encouragement, then and now, gave me
"permission" and confidence to pursue the making
of art, against all odds. I am indebted to Alex Colville,
the artist and the philosopher-teacher.

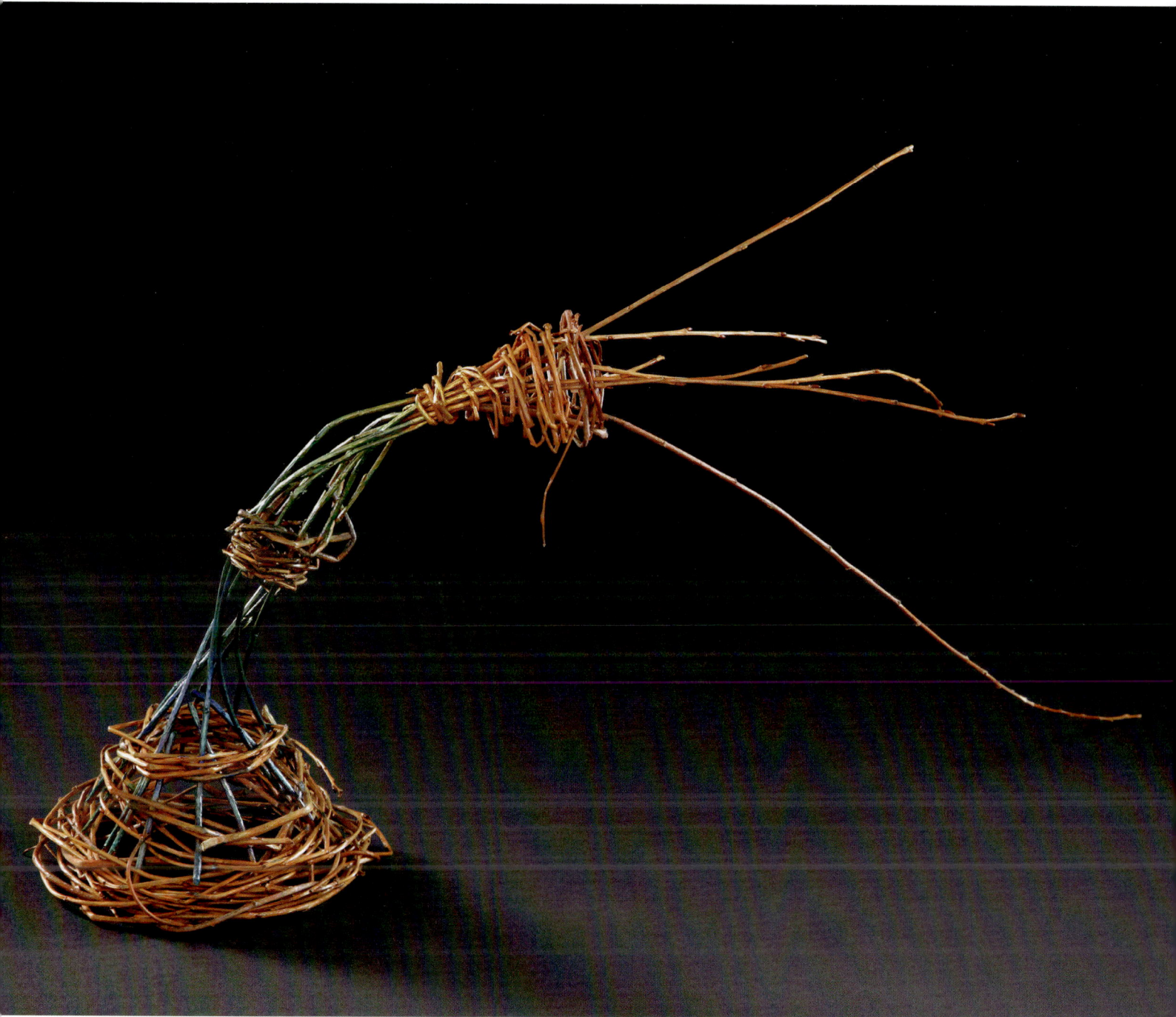

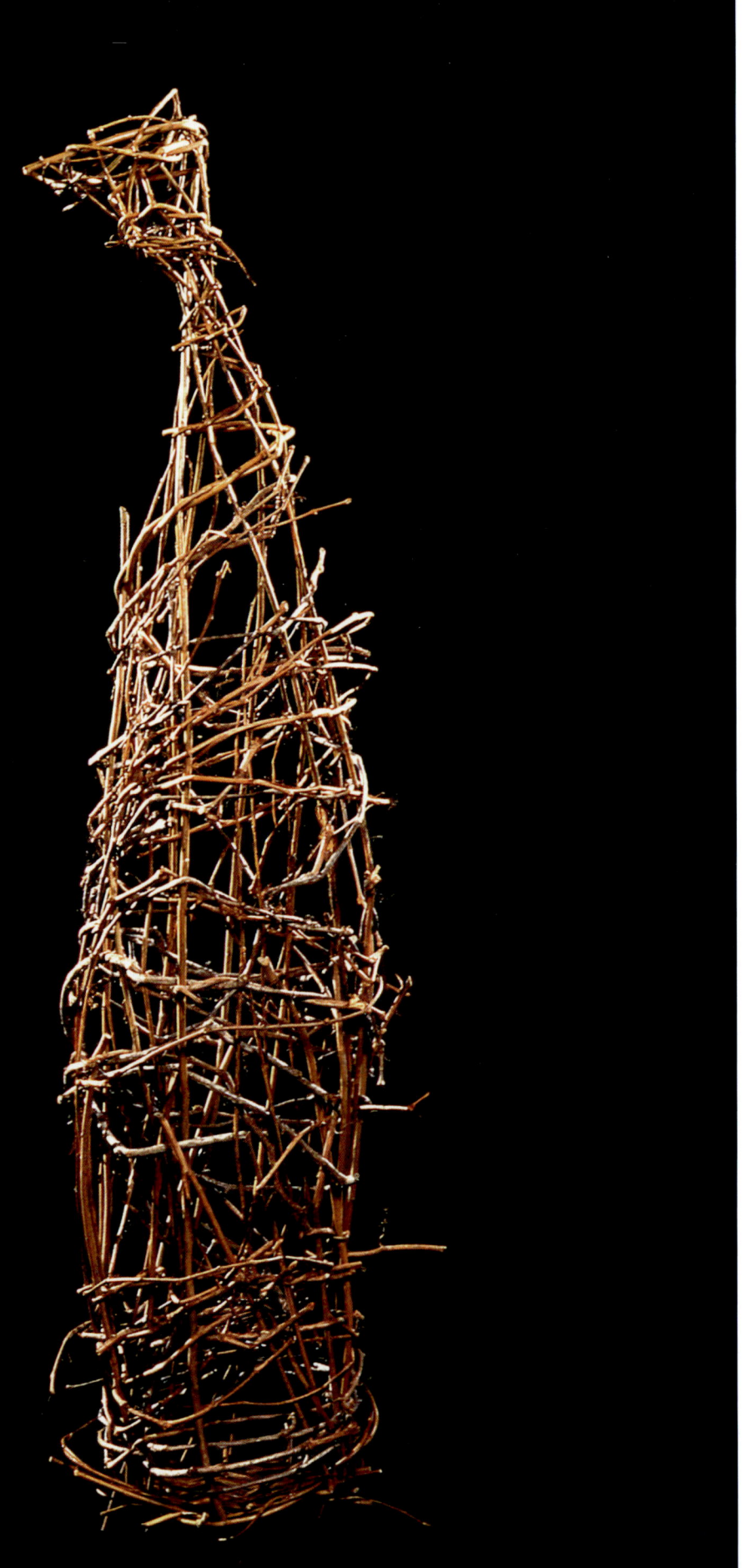

Motherhood in Willow, 2005
twined willow and grapevine
106 × 31 × 31 cm

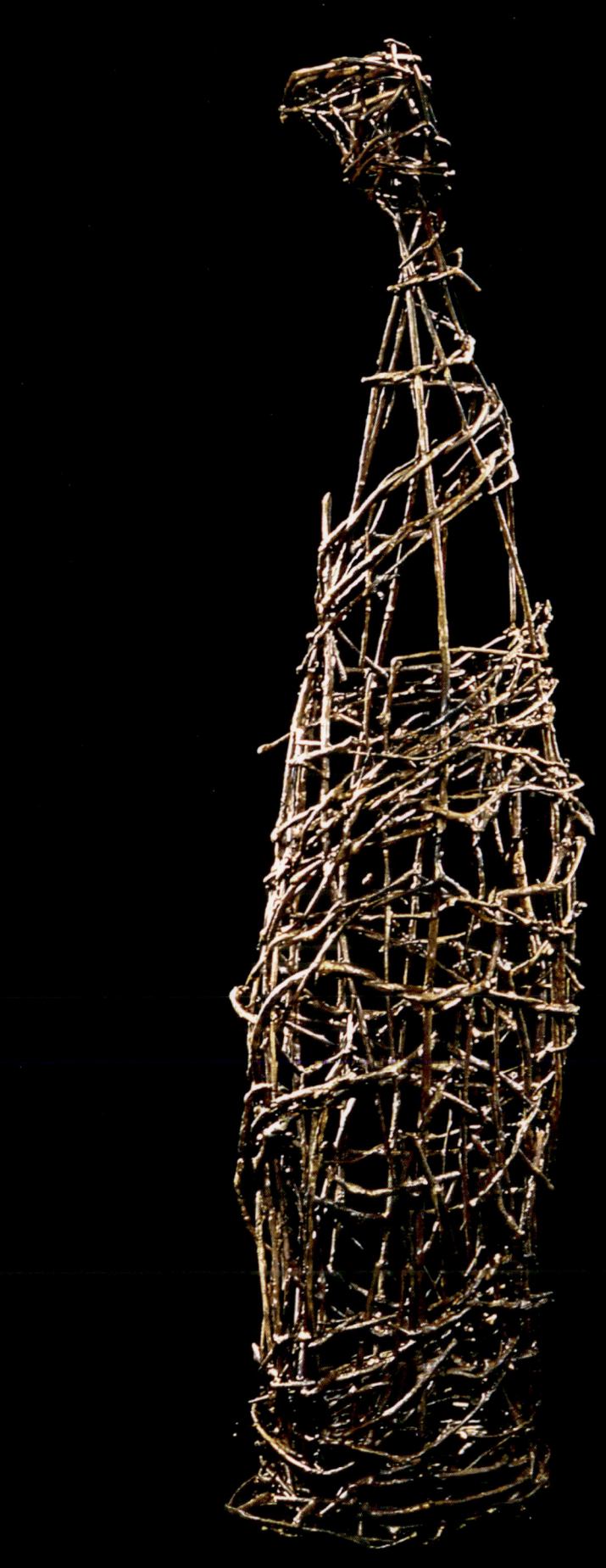

Motherhood in Bronze, 2009
patinated bronze
106 × 31 × 31 cm

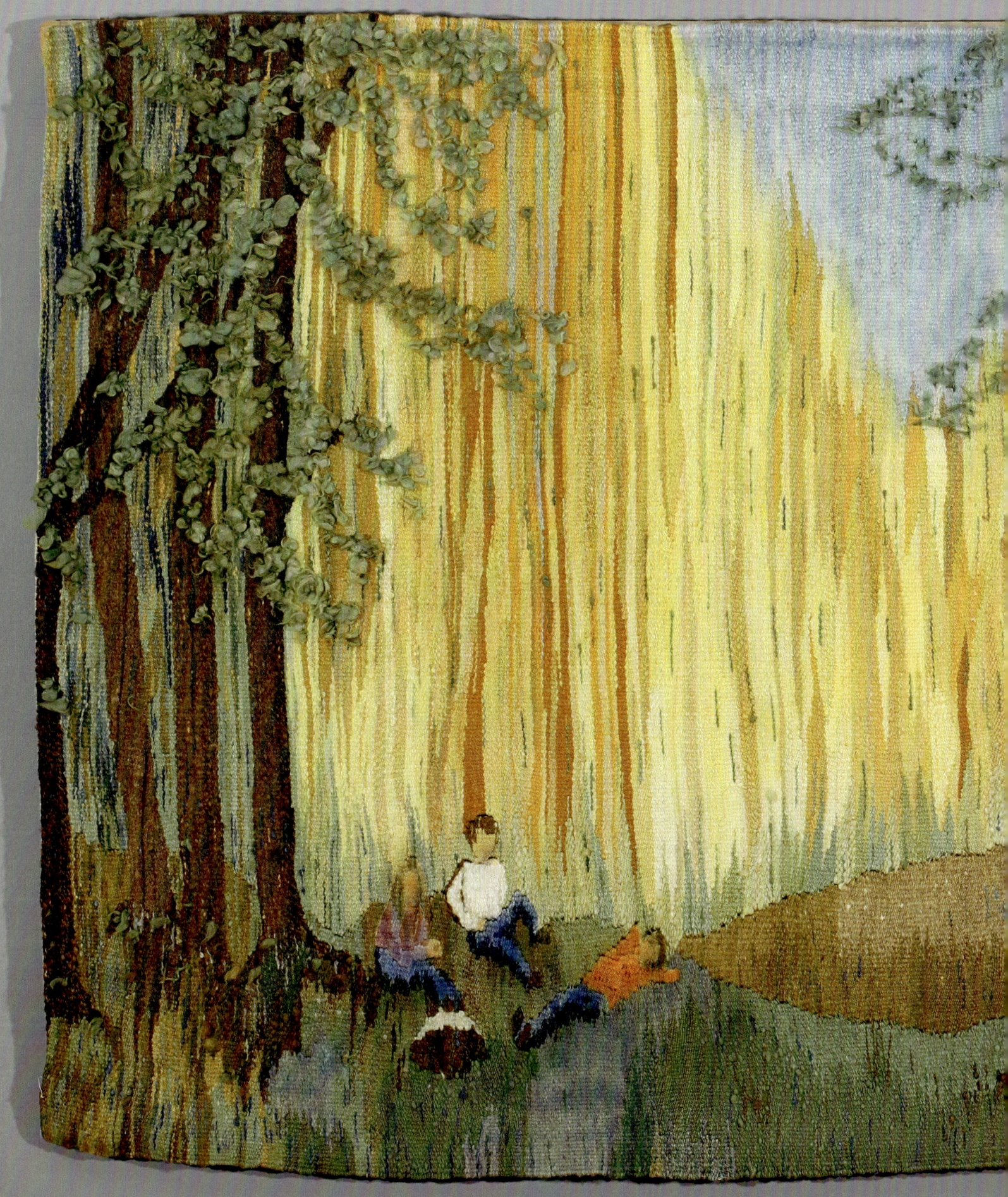

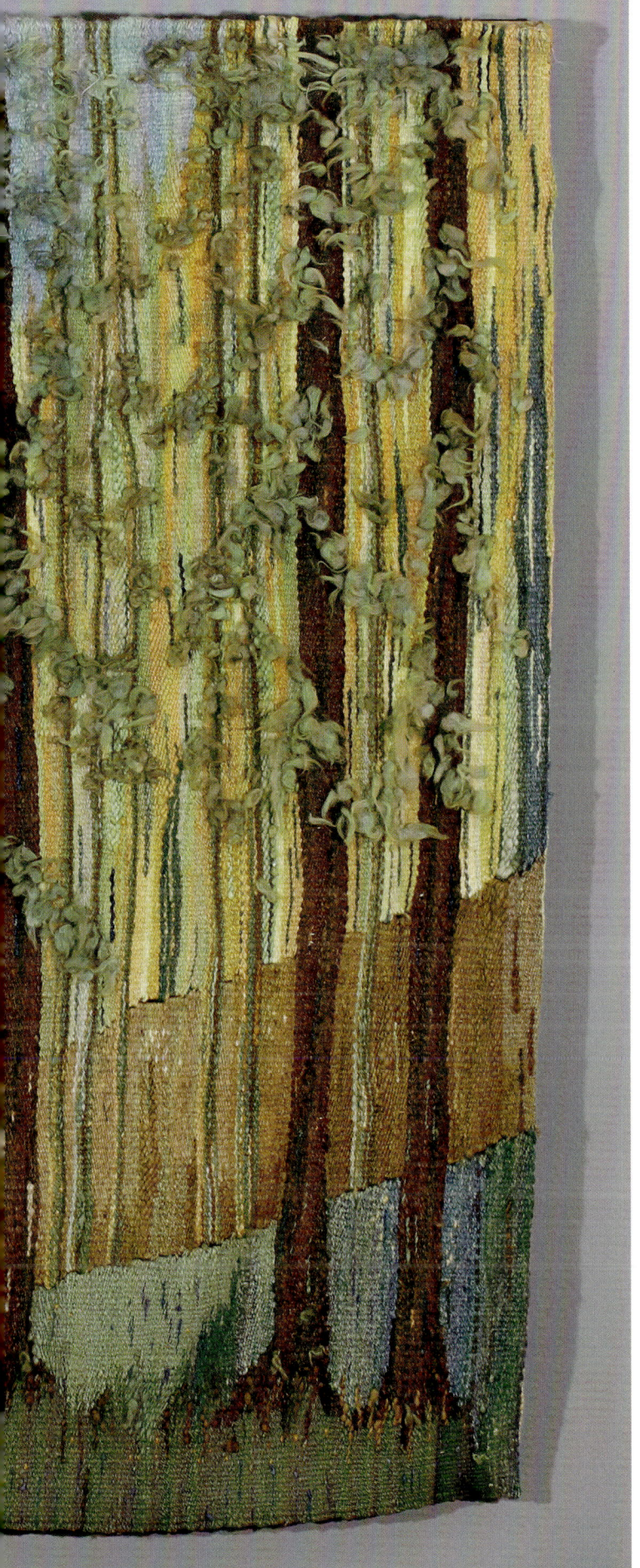

This tapestry was inspired by the Impressionist painters, the great Polish tapestry weavers, and most importantly by my children, sitting in a wooded spot behind our house under sunlit trees. It was my first major commission, and I was learning as I went.... It was truly a labour of love.

Once Upon a Time, 1975
hand-spun, naturally dyed wool on linen warp
122 × 152 cm

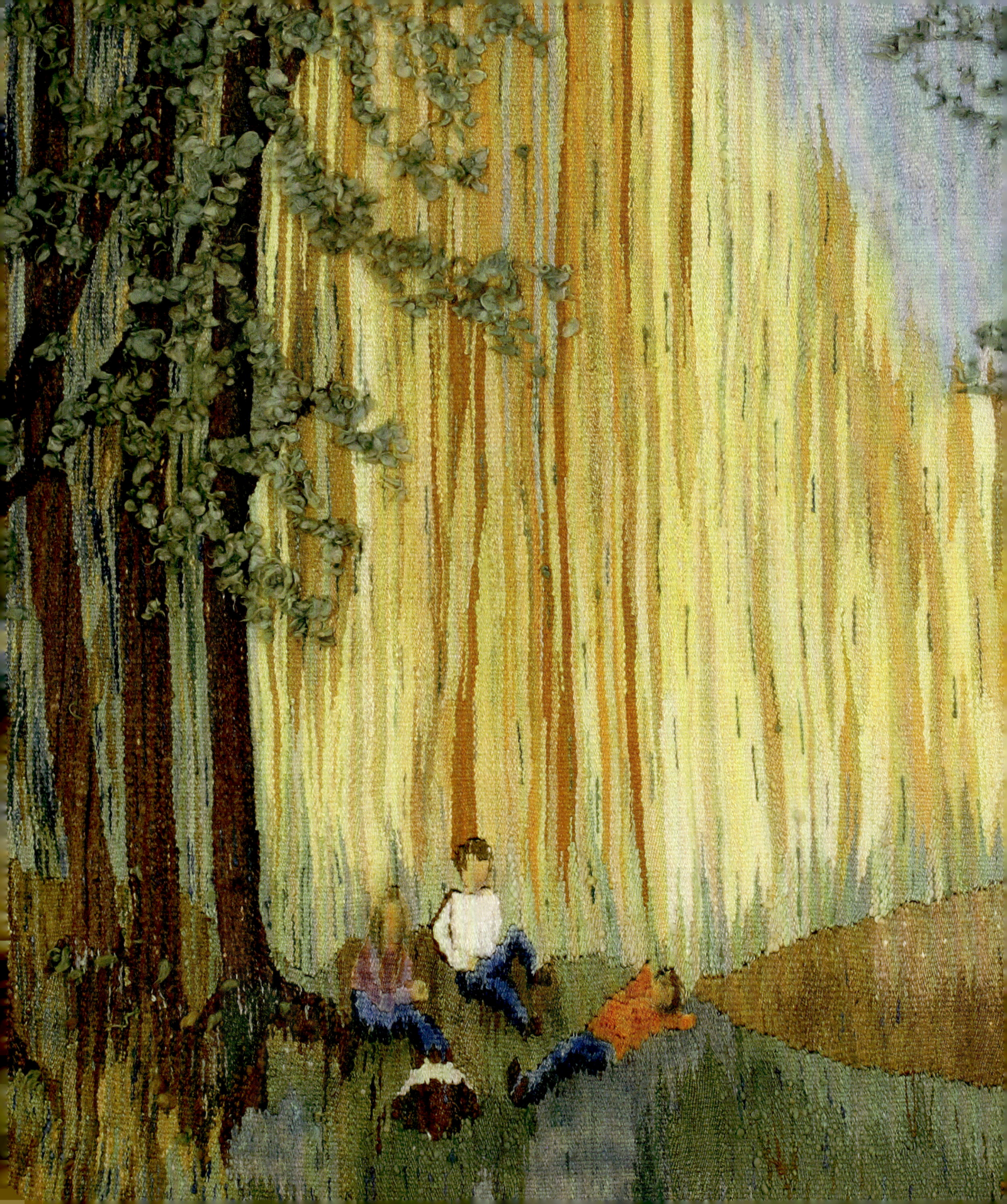

Once Upon a Time

While studying social work at Dalhousie University in 1961, I met Scott MacNutt. I answered "yes" to his proposal ten days later, and we married eleven days after that. In rapid succession, one, two, and three years later, we had Jamie, Laura, and Clive. Motherhood and social work eclipsed my pursuits in weaving and sculpture. When my children were babies, the only creative activity that seemed possible was the occasional painting, drawing, or needlepoint depicting them.

But the muse never left me. The creative urge resurfaced, ready to flourish, in the mid-1970s, when my father gave me an old spinning wheel from Pictou County. After teaching myself (and others!) to spin every conceivable kind of yarn, I explored natural dyeing — and then, with encouragement from my trusted friend Patty (Patricia Pollett McClelland), who was teaching weaving at the Nova Scotia College of Art and Design, I returned to the creative activity I had longed for since I'd left Mount A — and in truth, since I'd pulled apart that piece of silk when I was a child: weaving.

By that time, my husband Scott had been appointed Nova Scotia's minister of health, and the province was building a new hospital in Dartmouth. The hospital administrator suggested I create something to adorn the new building when it opened. I accepted the challenge.

The resulting 122 × 152 centimetre pastoral tapestry *Once Upon a Time* is basically a love poem to my children. This tapestry was inspired by the Impressionist painters, the great Polish tapestry weavers, and most importantly by my children, sitting in a wooded spot behind our house under sunlit trees.

It was my first major commission, and I was learning as I went. I wove it with hand-spun, naturally dyed wool from Nova Scotia sheep. The one exception is the wool in the little girl's shoes, which I spun from dog hair harvested from Laura's pet poodle, Charlie.

Once Upon a Time (detail), 1975
hand-spun, naturally dyed wool
on linen warp
122 × 152 cm

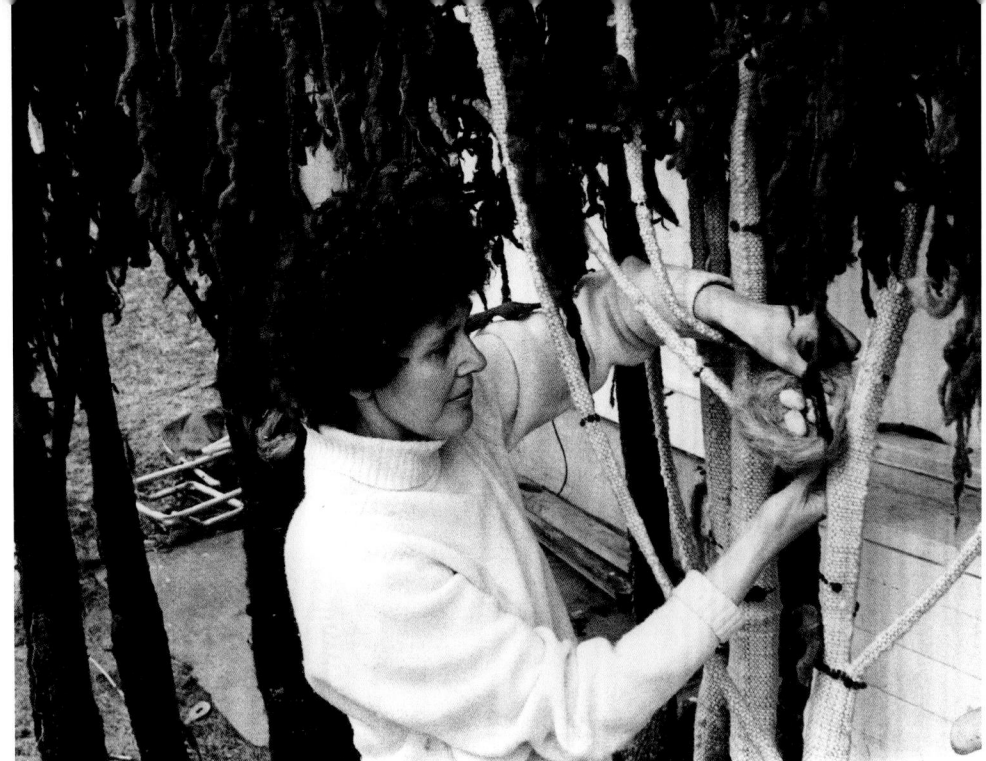

Birch Trees in progress, 1978
naturally dyed white and
coloured wool double-woven
on loom, with dyed felted fleece
sculpted foliage hung from yarn-
wrapped welded steel armature
335 cm high

After being spun and plied, the skeins were dipped in pots of colour brewed from local plants: lilacs and lupines, buttercups and clover, hollyhocks and goldenrod, dahlias and marigolds, cockscomb and coreopsis, smartweed and beach pea, and some sweet fern and bracken from the back road behind our house. The colour range was broadened by onion skins, rhubarb leaves, sumac, privet berries, spruce needles, and branches. The red shades came from *Umbilicaria*, a lichen from seacoast rocks. A soft green came from adapting a Navajo recipe I found in Oliver Wells's book *Salish Weaving, Primitive and Modern*, and experimenting with copper pennies and ammonia. The cobalt came from precious blue indigo.

It took two years to create this tapestry on a loom set up behind the furnace in the basement of our home on Lyngby Avenue. It was truly a labour of love. My children still tease me about the pungent and sometimes peaty smells that had continually wafted through the house from the dye pots on the stove. They most certainly would have preferred apple pie with a touch of cinnamon!

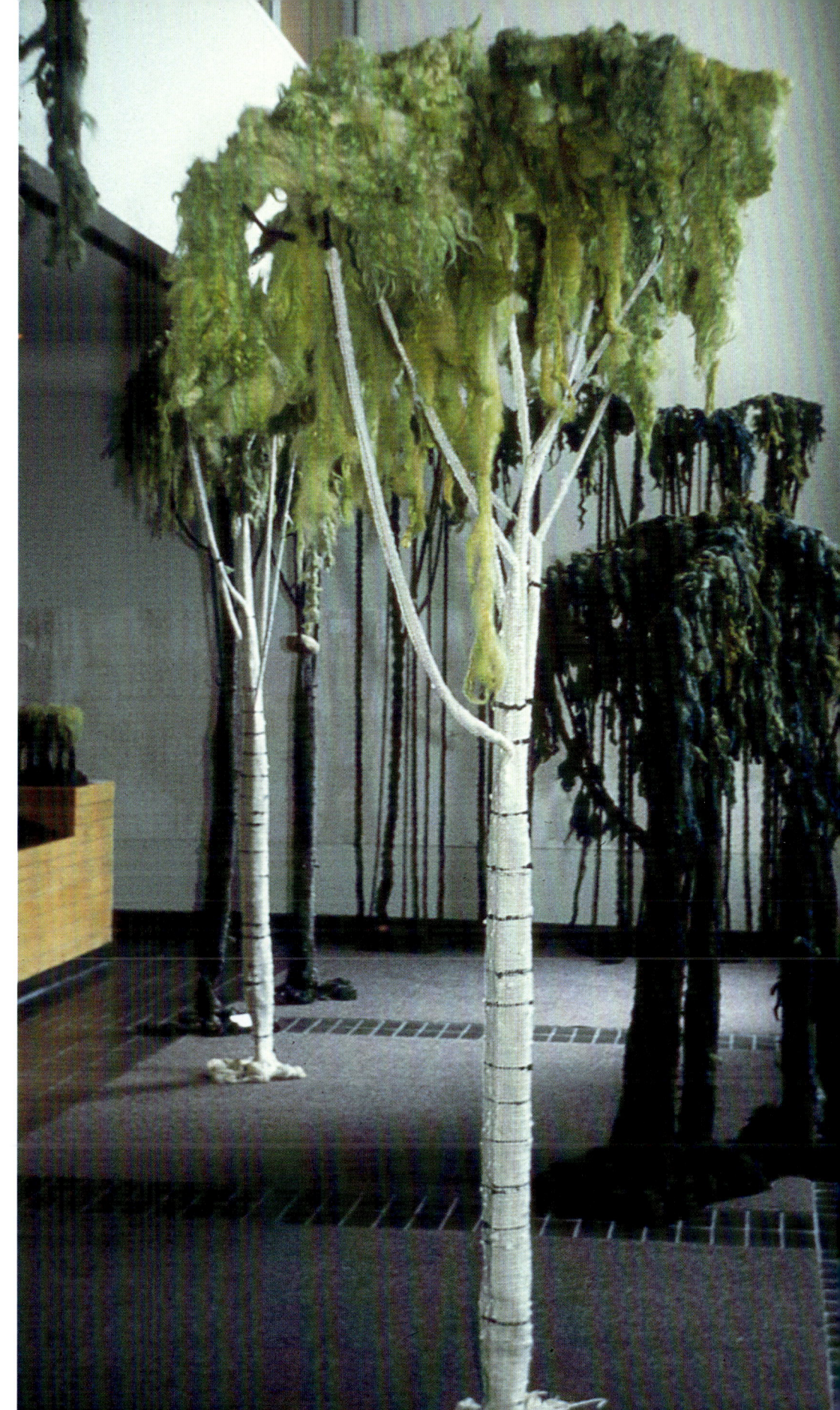

Trees and Other Things, 1978
hand-spun, naturally dyed wool, woven
on loom; fleece sculpted and hung from
a yarn-wrapped, welded steel armature
214 cm high

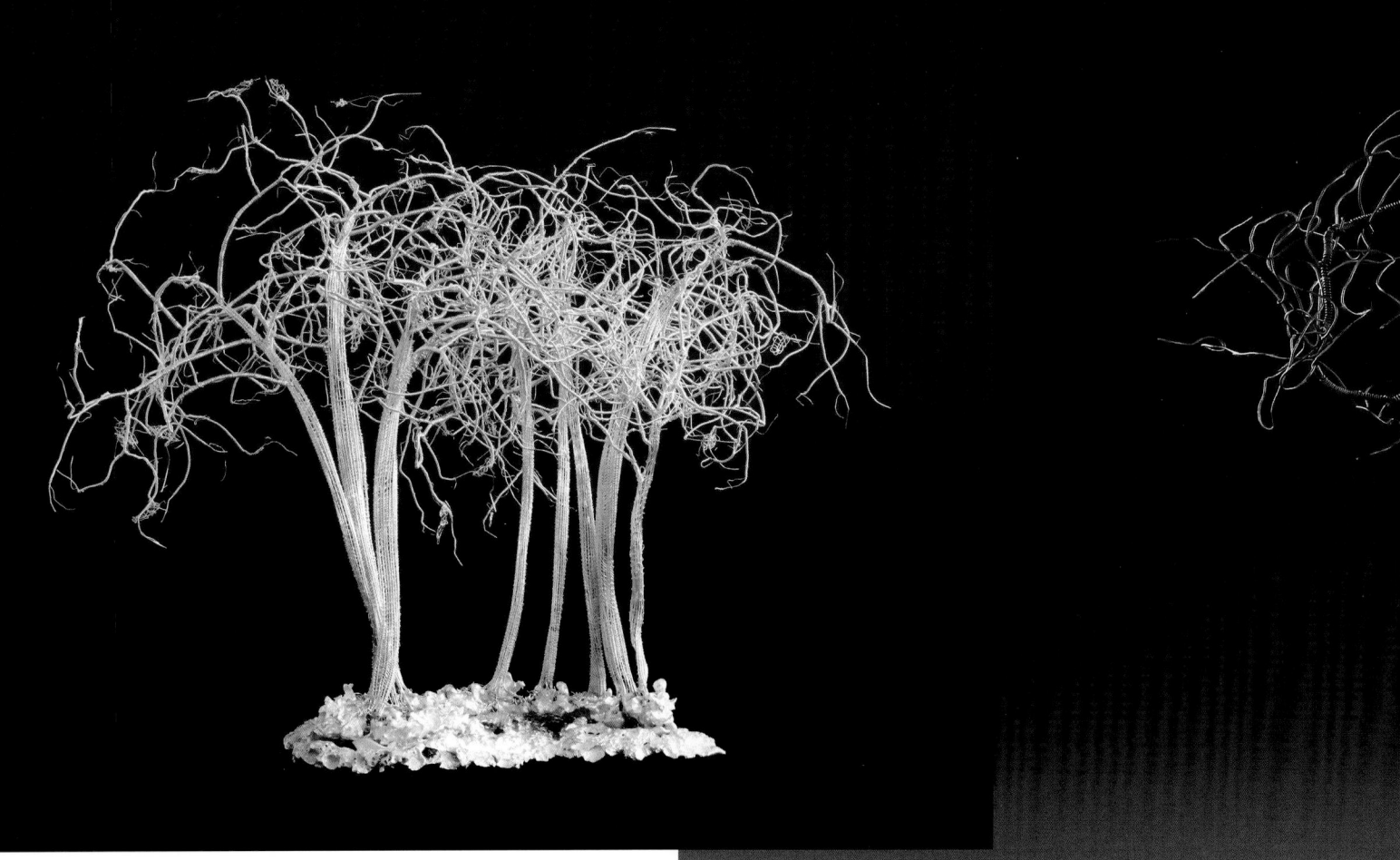

above: *Silver Thaw (3)*, 1987
fine silver woven on loom, cast silver base
20 cm high

Thicket, 1982
copper wire woven on loom, sculpted, wrapped
branches electroplated, patinated
56 × 33 × 48 cm

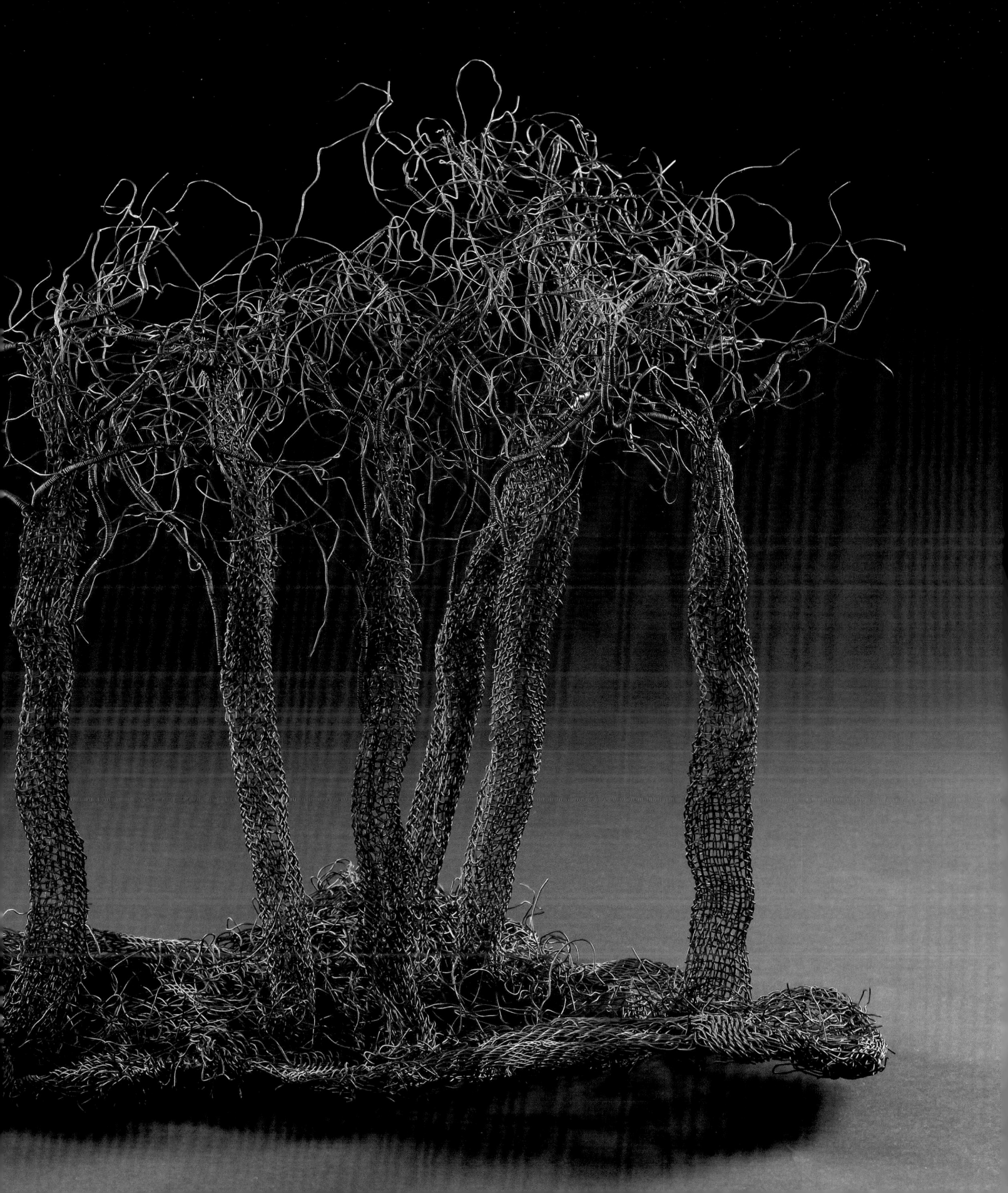

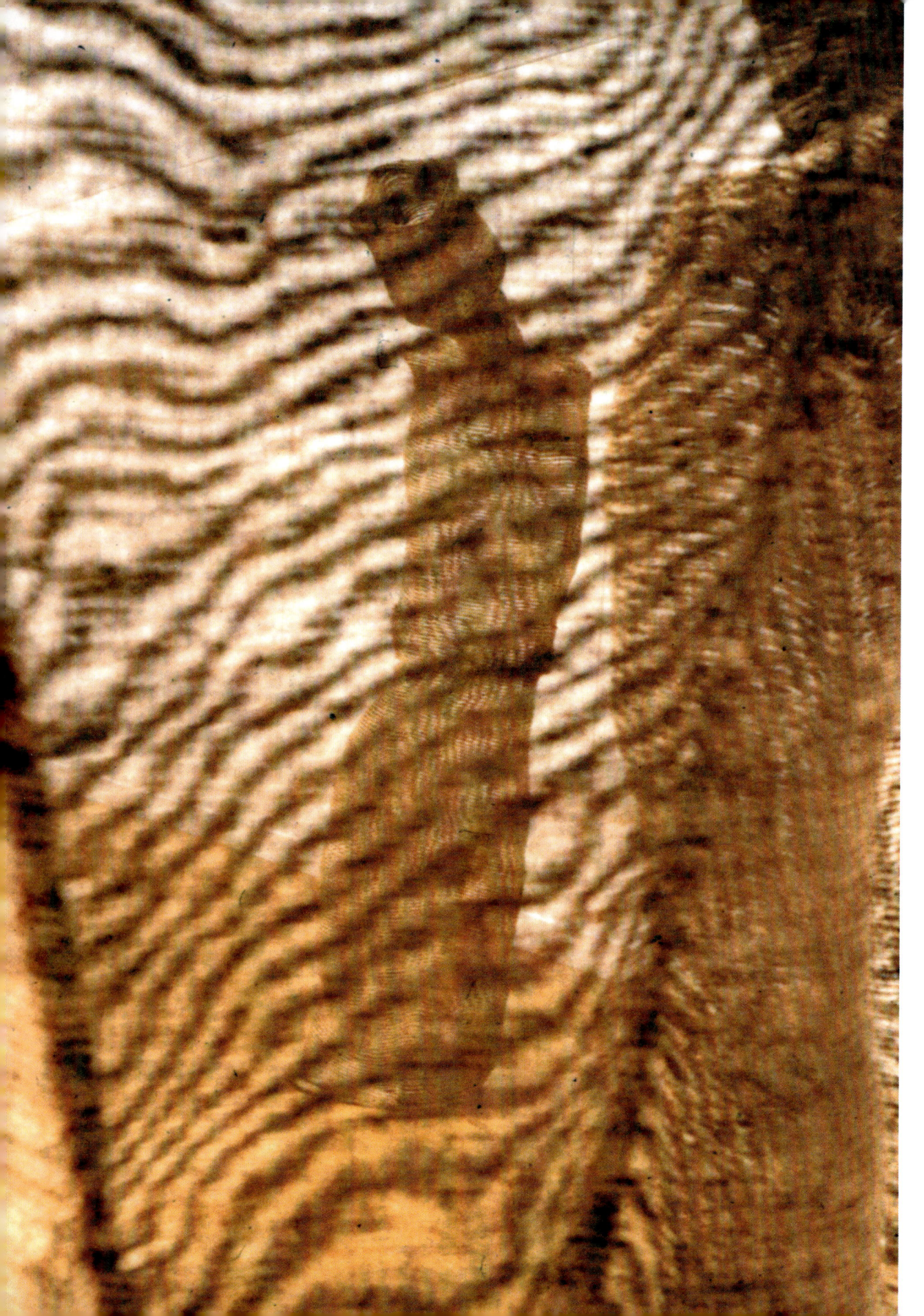

Kindred Spirits

Opening the book *Beyond Craft: The Art Fabric* by Mildred Constantine and Jack Lenor Larsen was a transformative experience. The in-depth profiles of international weavers and sumptuous pictures of works that were both dramatic and inspiring literally took my breath away. Weaving that functioned simply to feed the soul. I hungrily digested it, savouring each chapter. Lenore Tawney, Magdalena Abakanowicz, Helena Hernmarck, and Barbara Falkowska — all four featured artists were inspired by the human spirit, capturing the expression of human emotion in a way that resonated with me. (Little did I know that one day I would get to know all these artists — and exhibit alongside them.)

Jack Larsen was an icon. His influence as an internationally renowned textile designer and author helped establish the ancient craft of weaving as an art, and its modern pioneers as artists whose works were suddenly being exhibited and collected by major galleries and museums. When Larsen agreed to come to the Fifth Annual Nova Scotia Weavers' Conference in October 1979, there was enormous excitement among weavers across the region. Nearly two hundred of us gathered for the opening reception. Given his importance to the field and his reputation as somewhat aloof, I was feeling a little intimidated. Sadly, Jack was a no-show for the reception. He missed two planes and ended up in Montréal. When he finally arrived a day later, I smiled and shook his hand enthusiastically. He was apologetic and seemed relieved at the warm welcome, which dispelled my anxiety and put me in the happy position of making him feel comfortable.

He did not disappoint! Despite losing a day, he covered every session and topic promised and then some. He spoke about weaving as a business, both professional and amateur, and as an art. And on the topic of quality he delivered this unforgettable line: "Some weavers are craftsmen, some are artists. Some are neither — and rarely they are both!"

As I helped him take his collection of fabrics to the presentation room, he asked what I did. I answered simply, "Some large works, some small." However, when I took him to the airport in a taxi, I hesitantly showed him my primitive portfolio, which was basically a binder of pictures. He looked through it thoughtfully, saying little. When he handed it back at the airport, he told me in his inimitable voice, "You are an artist. You must come to New York." I was incredulous — and quietly thrilled.

The following summer, Jack arranged for me to teach Design Based on Spinning at the Haystack Mountain School of Craft in Deer Isle, Maine. Subsequently, he invited me to New York City. My exposure to Jack's world was underway, and so began a friendship that became a mentorship.

For four decades, I frequently visited Jack's city loft, his Round House, and later, his six-hectare LongHouse Reserve in East Hampton. My visits were filled with museum tours and gallery openings, opera, Broadway shows, and intimate dinner parties that Jack and his partner Peter hosted for international artists of all kinds. Jack introduced me to the world of textile arts and the North American Arts and Crafts movement. He also came to Nova Scotia on numerous occasions and became part of our art/craft community — jurying exhibitions, lecturing at the Nova Scotia College of Art and Design, and even opening my show *All the Ancients Walk Inside Us* at the Art Gallery of Nova Scotia in 1997.

But most significant to me was our close personal relationship. I felt a warm connection that belied his austere — even superior — facade. His stature in the world of textile and art dwarfed my own, but he trusted my confidence in personal matters. Most importantly, he respected my judgment — or rather, non-judgment — in matters of the heart. I was honoured when, a few years into our relationship, he identified me as one of his five adopted "sisters," women who were all important to him in different ways.

Jack would often read and write in the evening. He'd sit at his desk, wearing a kimono and handwriting personal correspondence in his puzzling hybrid of cursive and block print. This was Jack at his most relaxed, and it was the subject of my sketch *Man in a Kimono*. For me, it's the essence of Jack.

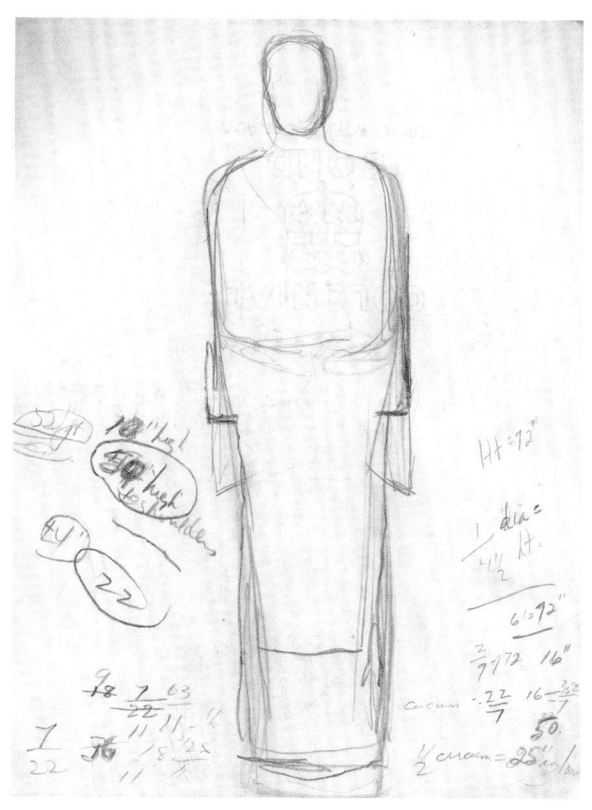

Man in a Kimono, 1980
graphite on paper
28 × 21 cm

That tiny notebook sketch became my essential *Kindred Spirit* form, one of my most recognizable figures, which inspired my work for decades. The woven *Kindred Spirits* that evolved from that sketch were central to my first major solo exhibition at the MSVU Art Gallery in 1984, *Woven Forms: Sculptural Figures*. I was thirty-seven years old. It would be a decade more before I felt secure enough to withdraw from my counselling career and become a full-time sculptor.

When Jack died in 2020 at the age of ninety-three, I felt a great personal loss. His honest critiques could sometimes sting: "Tiffany trees, Woolworth base," he said of one piece. But his advice and encouragement were invaluable in empowering me for over forty years. And his last handwritten note before he died was reservedly reassuring: "Dawn: <u>Big</u> Apology. We lunched outdoors on a table with your bronze now without paint and pleasantly tarnished. Without my paint taboo, I finally saw that it <u>is</u> interlaced with vines, charmingly organic, and in a sense <u>un</u>masked and beautiful. Thank <u>you</u>, Jack."

With his constant refrain, "The best way to get what you want is to ask for it" ringing in my ears, I contacted the board of LongHouse, offering to donate a major sculpture honouring my dear friend and mentor. *Jack, Larger than Life*, which I had made in homage to him a few years earlier, is woven from willow and stands 324 centimetres tall. It is now part of the permanent collection at LongHouse Reserve, an expansive integrated environment Jack created in East Hampton, New York. The sculpture debuted at a special exhibition celebrating his life, which LongHouse also called *Jack, Larger than Life*. The gift was unconditional, though I hope it will someday be cast in bronze, so that *Jack, Larger than Life* can live outdoors, where he himself was happiest.

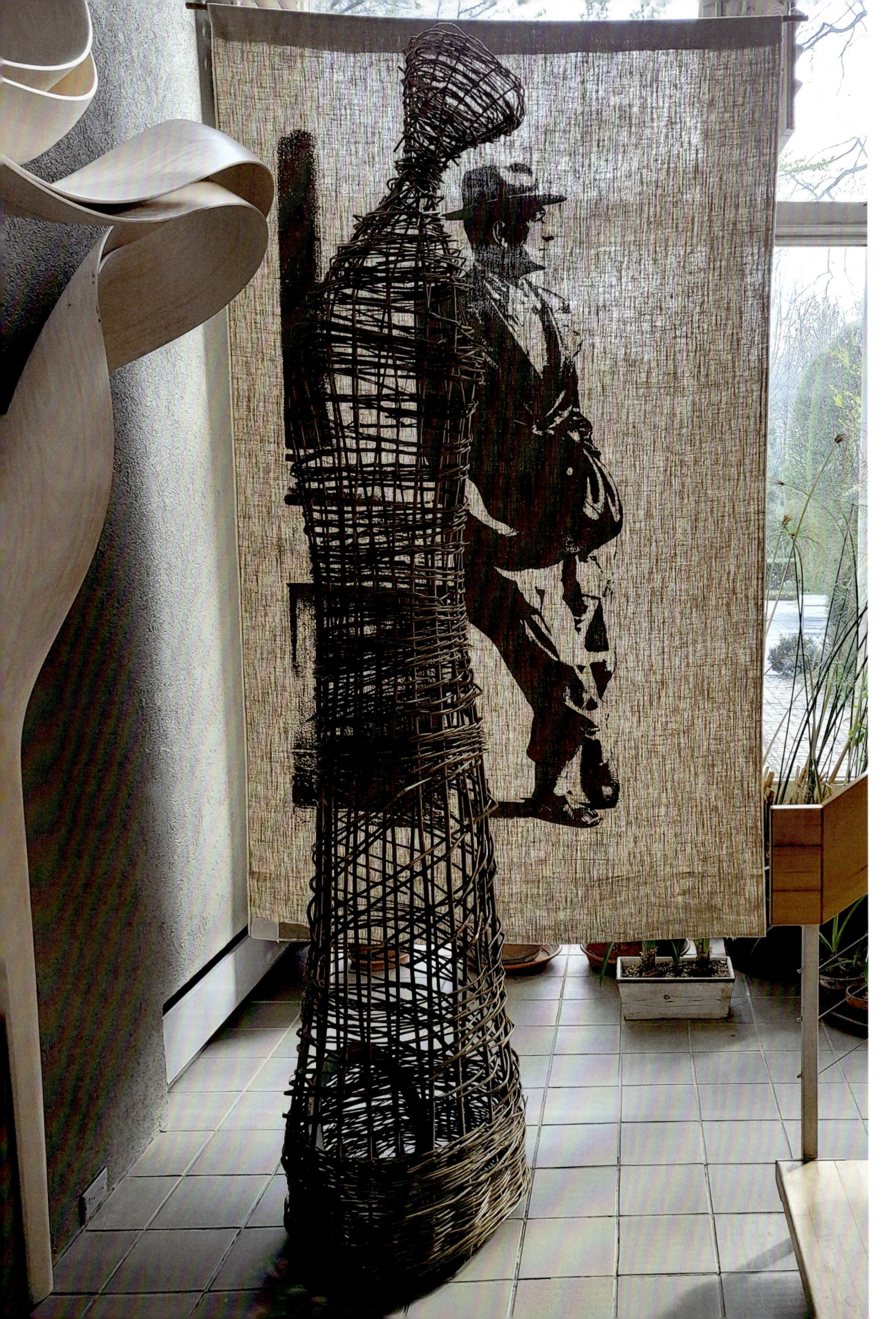

Jack, Larger than Life, 2020
twined willow
324 × 51 × 51 cm

opposite (foreground): *Jack, Larger than Life*, 2021; (background) silkscreen exhibition banner

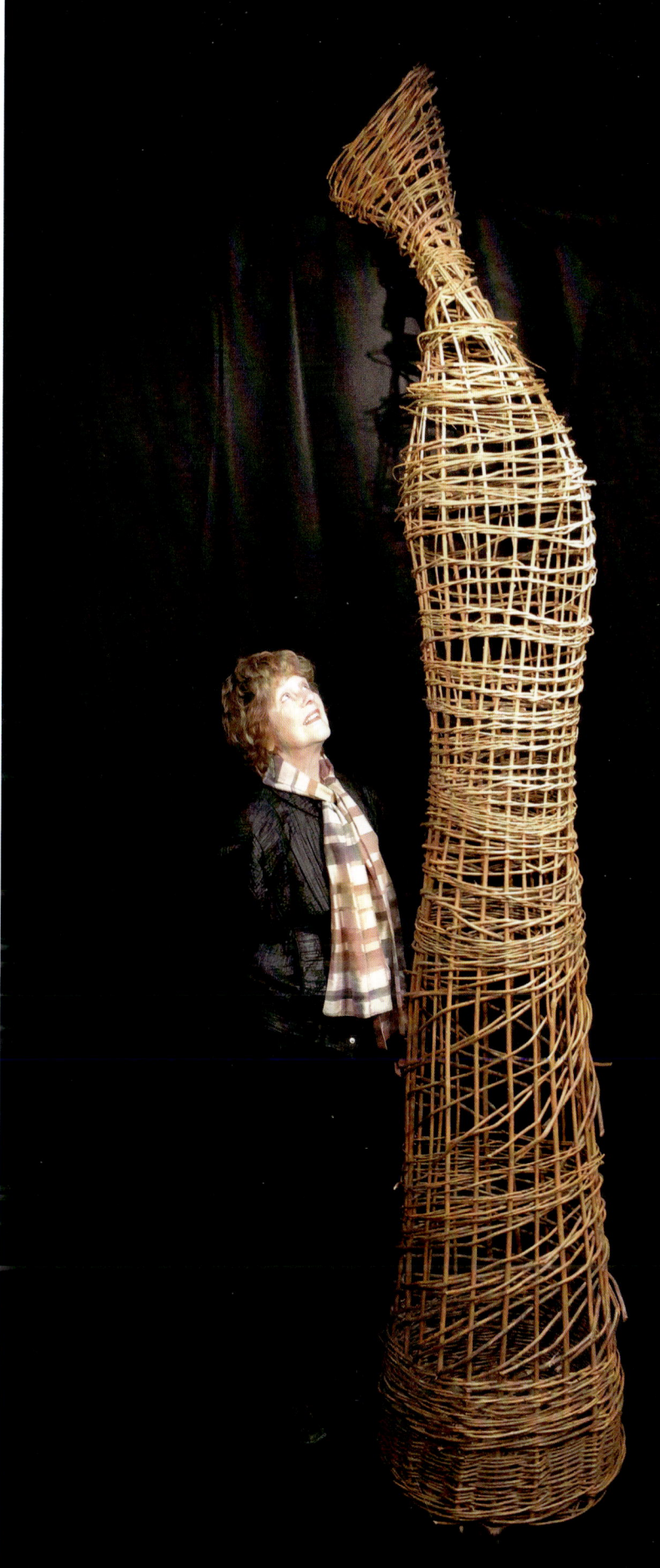

Kindred Spirits, 1984
seagrass woven on copper wire
warp loom, sculpted, welded
metal armature
dimensions variable
Installation at Crystal Crescent
Beach, NS

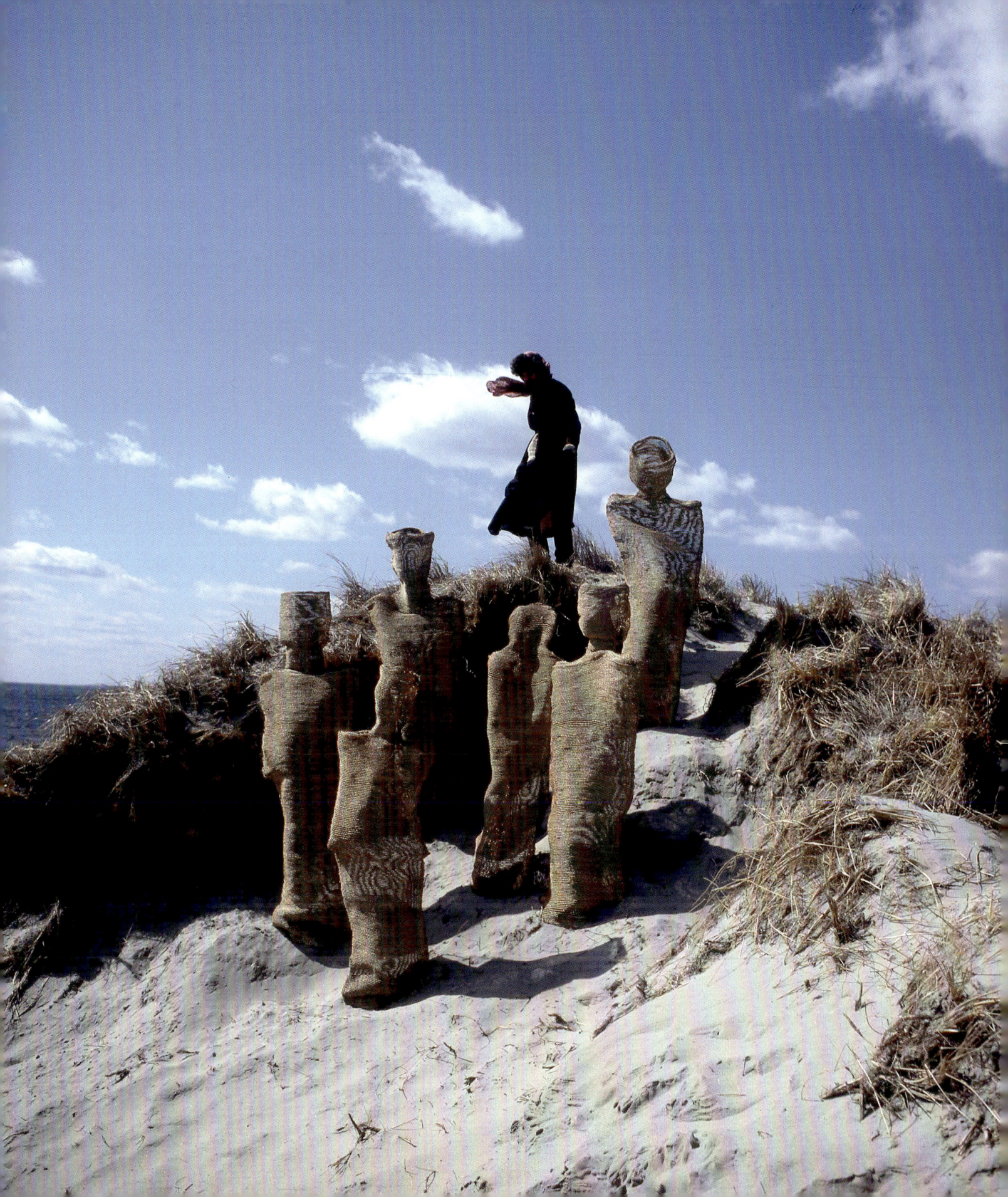

*Kindred Spirit*s, 1984
seagrass woven on copper wire warp
loom, sculpted, welded metal armature
dimensions variable

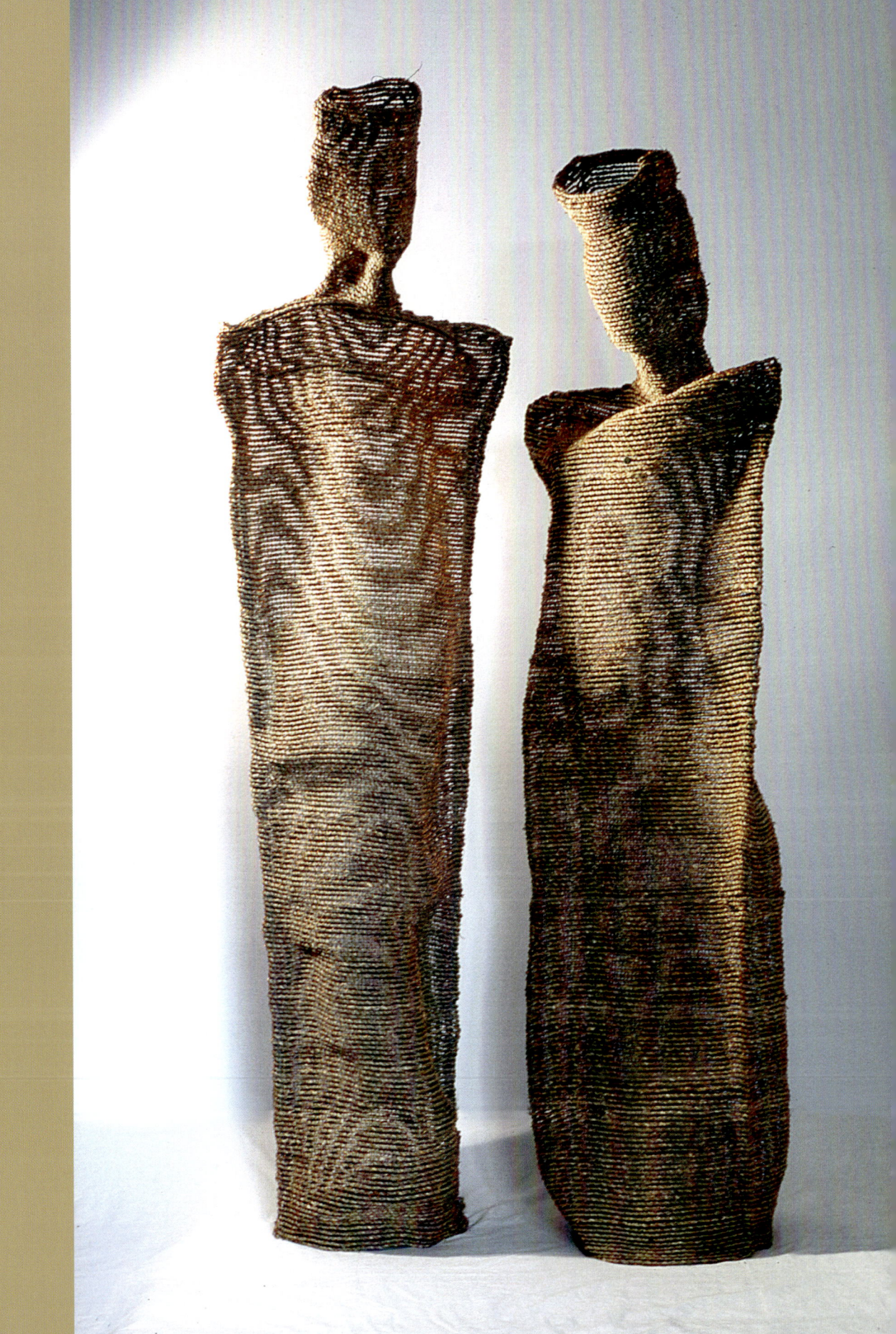

Giacometti, A Kindred Spirit, 1984
seagrass and copper wire, welded
metal armature
174 × 60 cm

overleaf: *Kindred Spirits*, 1990
patinated bronze, cast from woven
fisherman's ropes
dimensions variable
Alderney Gate Plaza, Halifax, NS

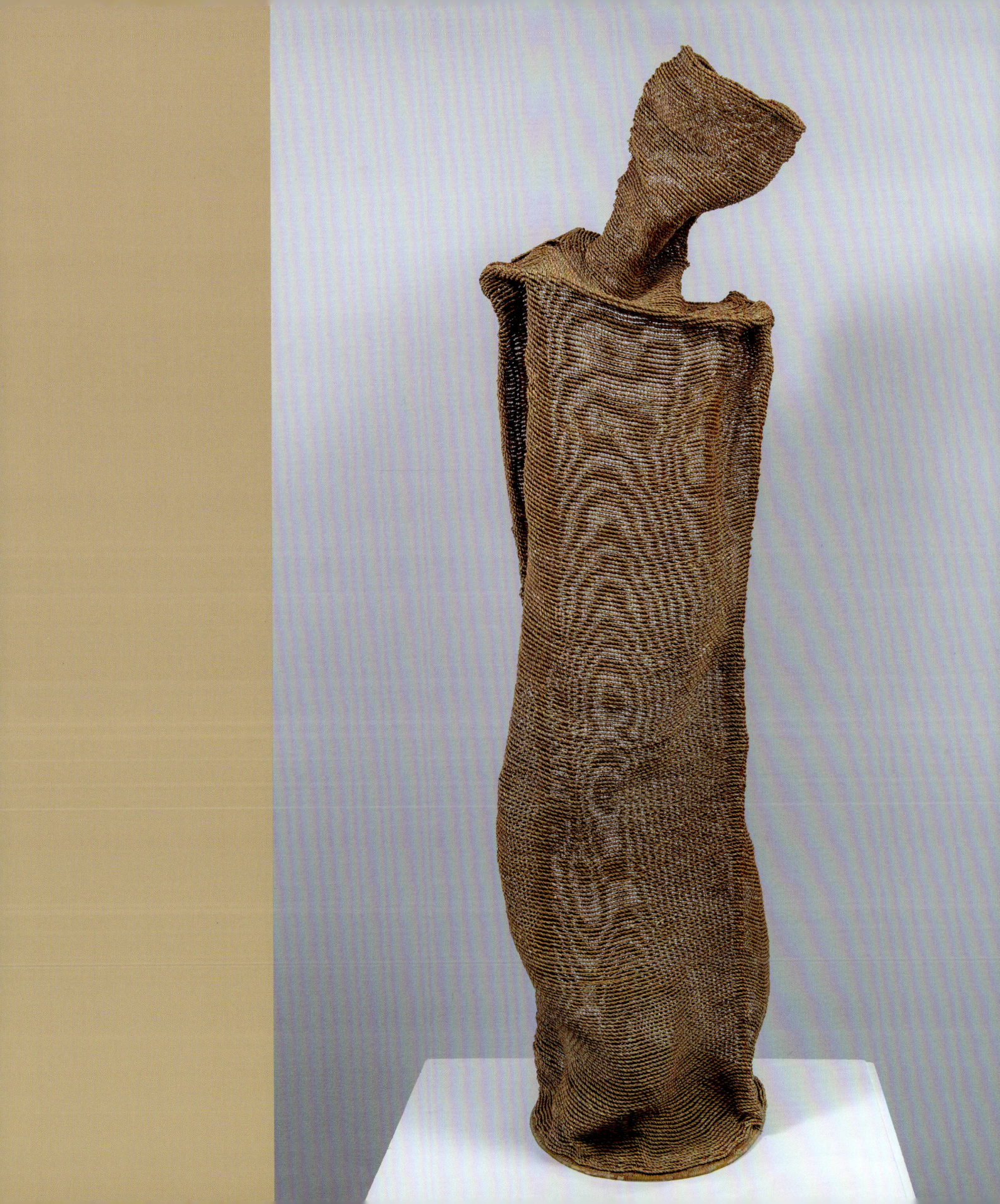

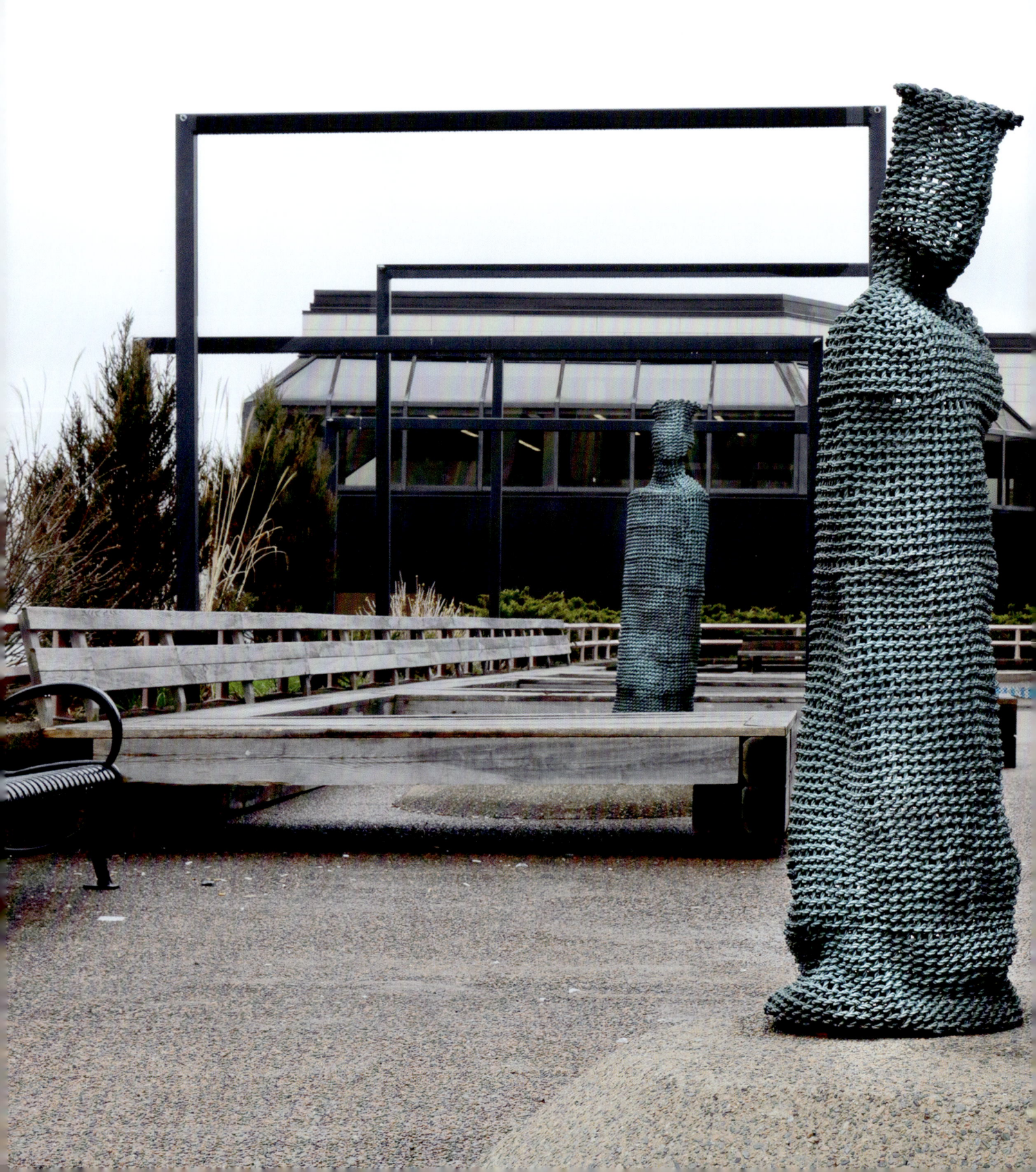

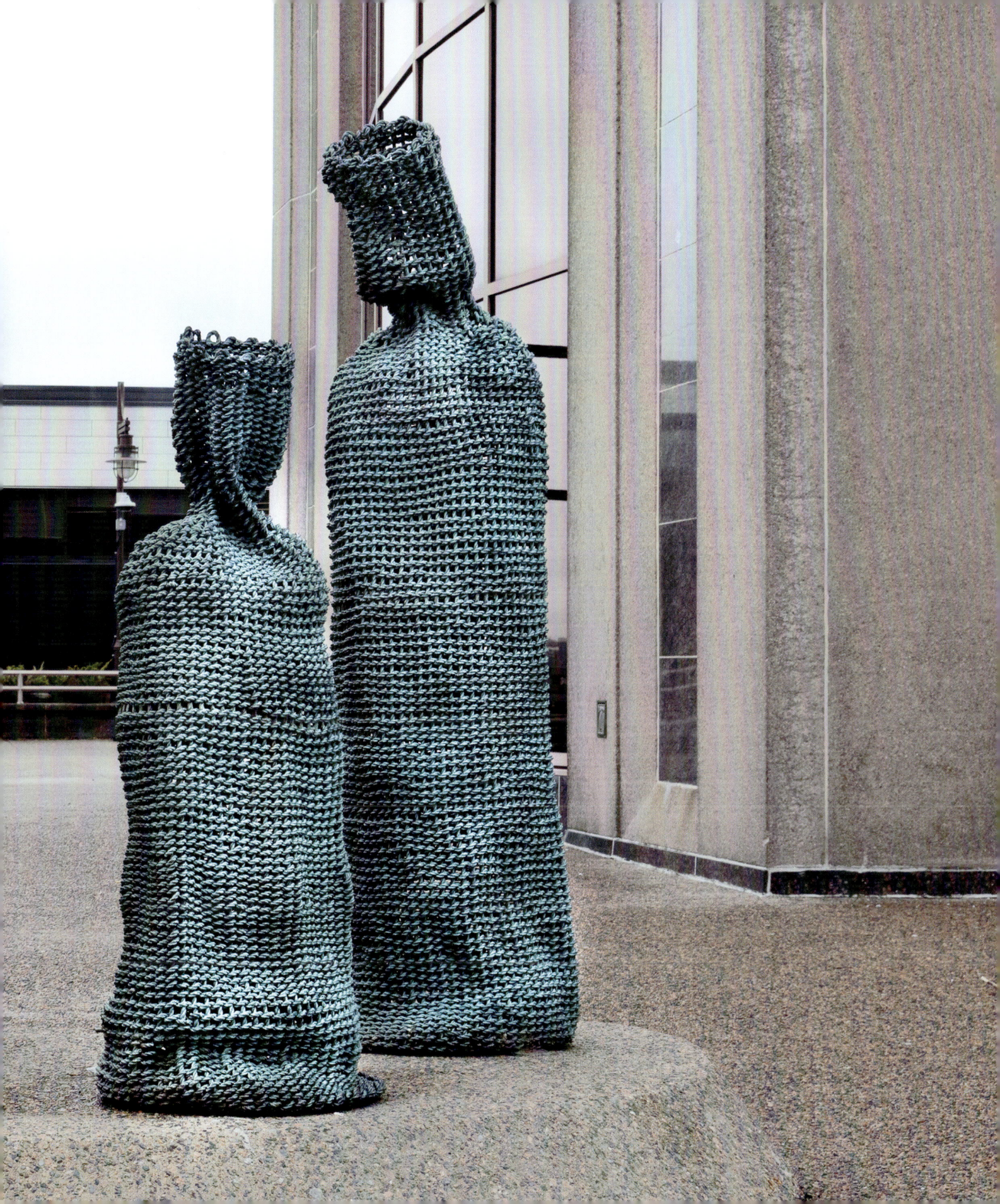

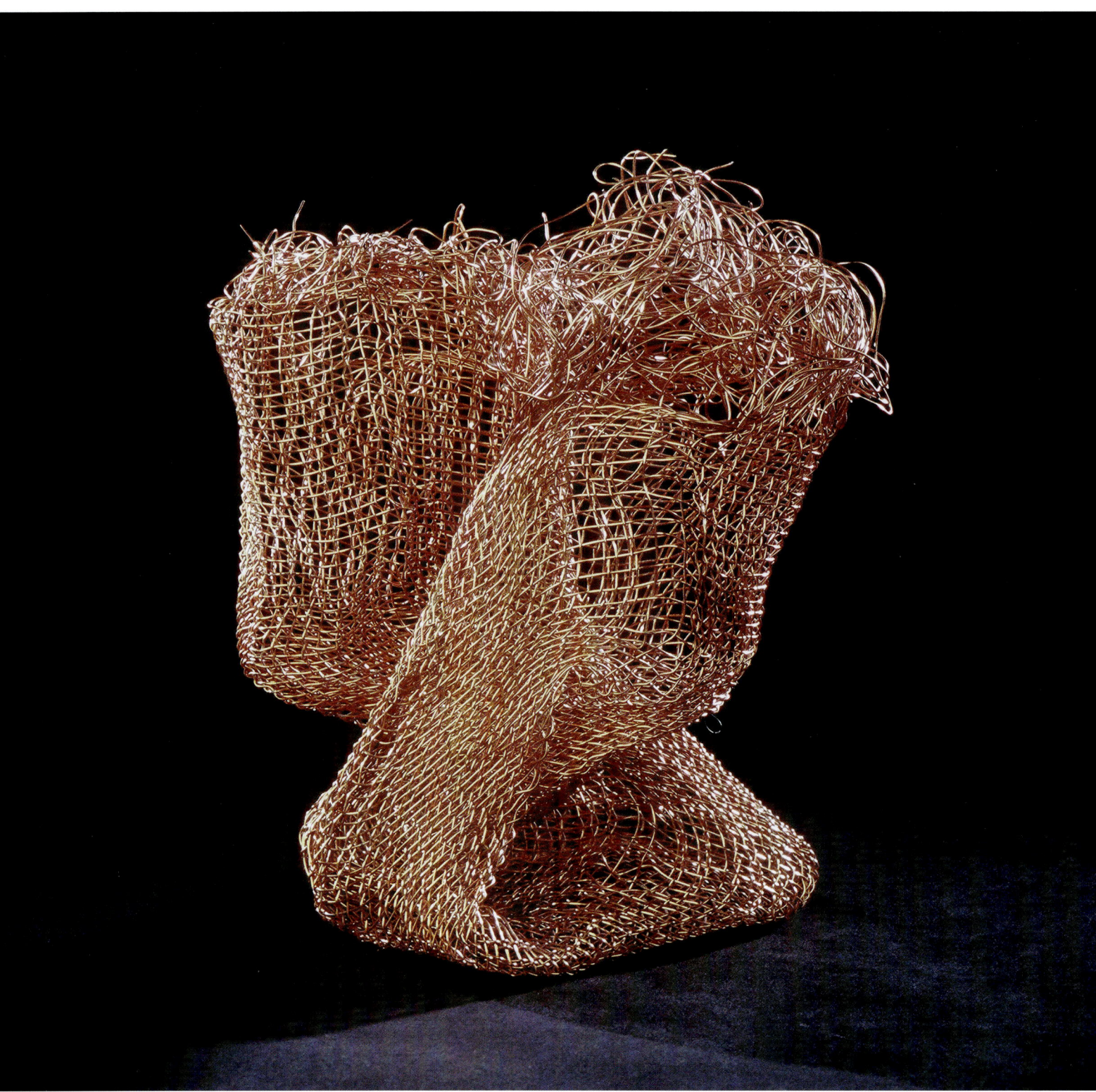

Love

Full disclosure: I use the word *love* a lot. I don't save it only for the "unconditional" circumstance, or the passionate affair of the heart, or for profound maternal love. I use it liberally in all its facets.

When I am creating, my love of people is my richest collaborator. I am fascinated by posture, gait, and nuances of facial expressions. In public or in crowds, I'm often drawn to observe an individual's movement and manner — so much so that my daughter frequently chides me, "Mom! You're staring!"

It's easy to focus on joyful, heart-bursting love, and many of my pieces do that. Silver figures exuding joy and the lightness of love. Women dancing with wild abandon. A mother tenderly embracing her child. Semi-figurative sculptures with wings, celebrating and elevating body and mood.

But love isn't always easy. Or simple. When I met my first husband Scott, he'd said, "Life with me will never be dull," and he was right. There was much laughter, much joy. Three beautiful children. Also much worry, much pain, and many surprises. Betrayal. Aggression. More than once, he broke my heart.

Finally, twenty-two years later, I broke his heart: I left.

Vulnerability and grief are the price of love — and also what draws us to care for people. We admire perfection in people and their accomplishments, but when someone exposes their flaws and limitations to us, rather than turning away, we are moved to compassion. I am deeply drawn to the beauty of this human frailty. It has created some of my most unflinching pieces, the ones that elicit the strongest responses.

On reflection, a few of my smaller works feel more important, or important in a different way, than the major commissions, the works in museum collections or the outdoor public installations. They are very personal pieces that emerged without intention when I was witness to the pain and grief of others.

Embrace, 1988
copper wire woven on loom, sculpted
18 × 15 × 8 cm

Vulnerability, 1986–1994
seagrass woven on copper wire warp
loom, sculpted, welded metal armature,
intentionally left outside to deteriorate
over several years
183 × 186 cm

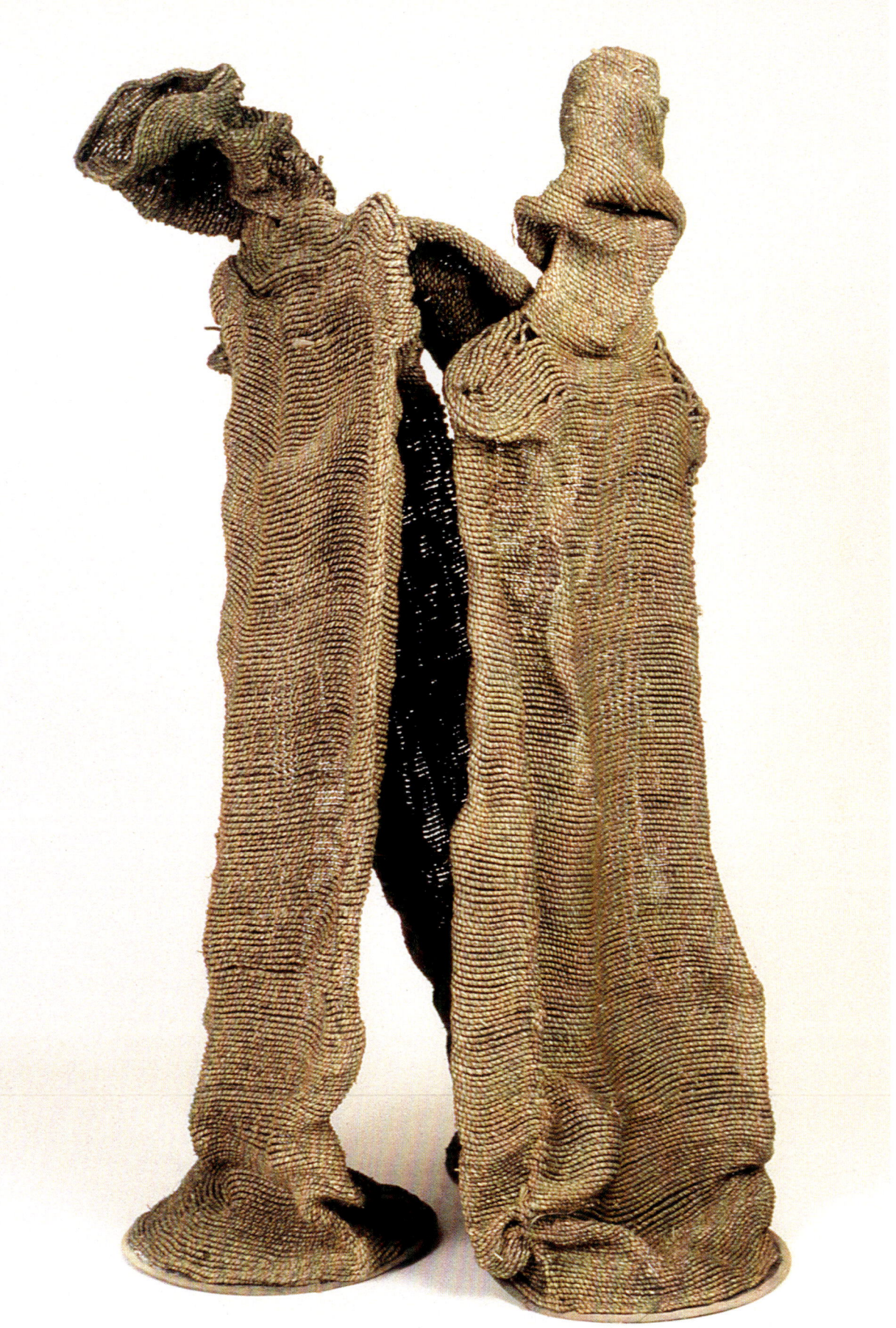

Invincible Summer, 2019
copper woven wire cloth, sculpted,
electroplated, and patinated
68 × 20 × 36 cm

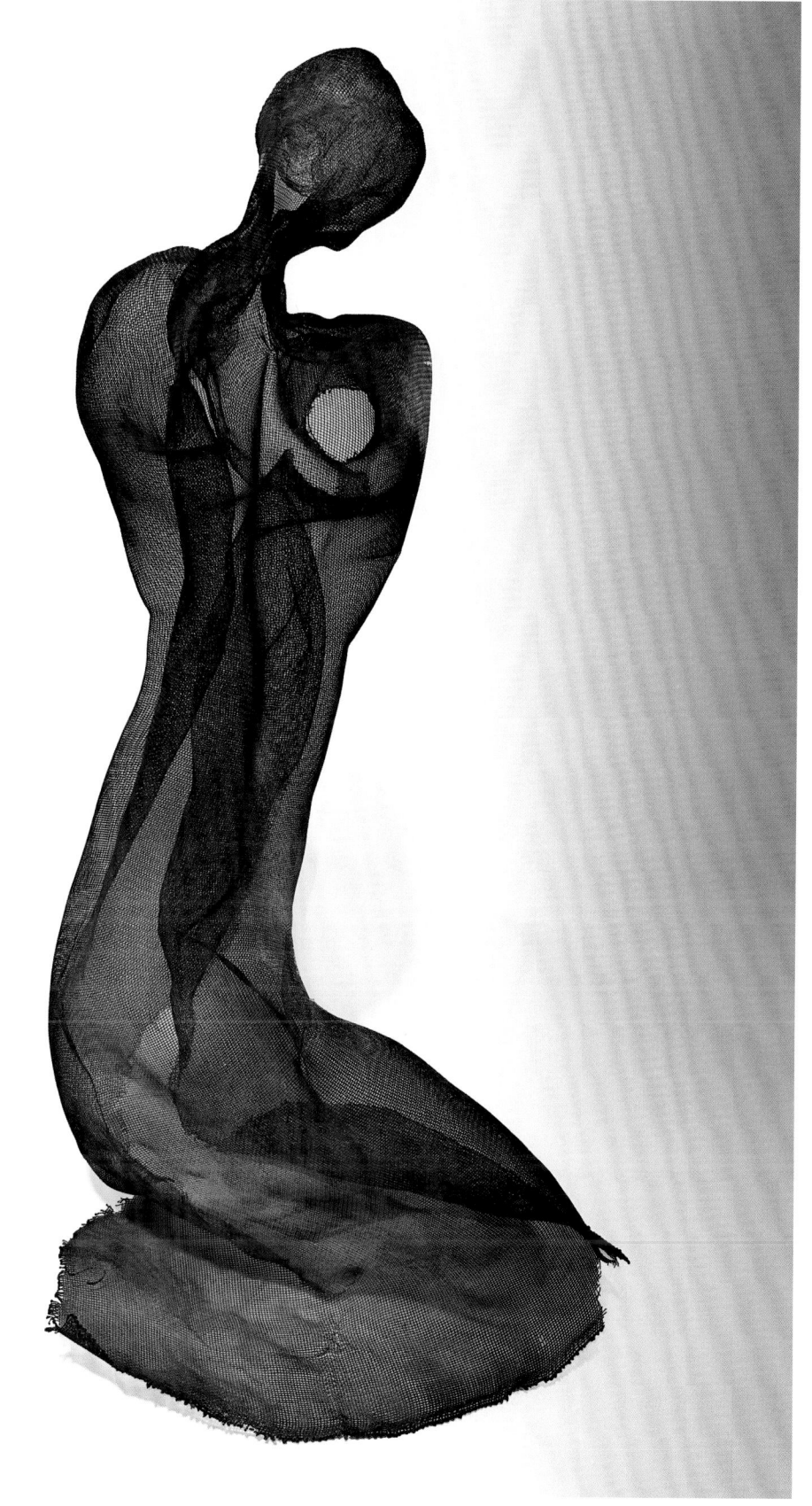

The Craig Gallery once asked me to submit a work based on a love poem for a February exhibition. I immediately thought of my young cousin Maggie, whose world had been shattered when she lost her beloved to a sudden death and then, in quick succession, her grandmother and mother to terminal cancer. Witnessing her experience such extreme grief with a fragile grace evoked for me this quote from Albert Camus: "In the depth of winter, I finally learned that within me there lay an invincible summer." My sculpture *Invincible Summer* now sits in Maggie's home, where I hope the bent-but-not-broken figure is a constant reminder of her strength.

Man in Black Coat was created after spending time with someone dear to me who was facing judgment and shame. Seeing a loved one cowering, downcast, shutting himself off, affected me deeply. I could do nothing but be there for him, so I created this small work in honour of my love for him.

Anguish is another work that is most important to me. Three young girls were on a carefree getaway to Prince Edward Island. My daughter Laura was driving along notoriously difficult country roads while they sang and laughed. As they went through an intersection, there was a tragic accident. Only dear Catherine, who was sitting in the back seat, was injured. She was not buckled up and catapulted sideways through the window.

All three girls were rushed by ambulance to the hospital, and Catherine was taken upstairs to neurosurgery. Laura and her friend Elizabeth were not as seriously injured. They were both in shock, and waited in a room downstairs where I joined them. They were in no shape to ask the difficult questions, so I went upstairs to inquire about Catherine's condition. The doctors were still working on her, but

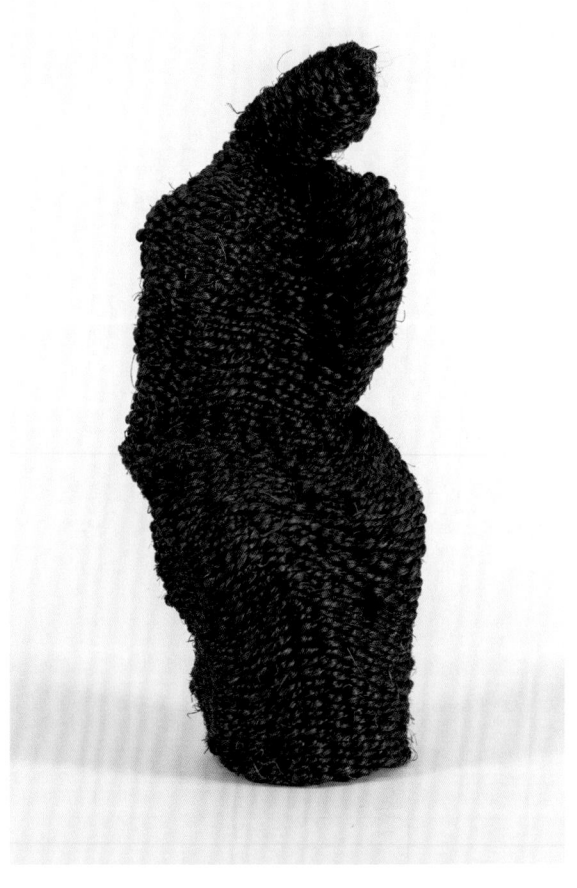

Man in Black Coat, 1984
twined dyed sisal and copper wire
24 × 11 × 10 cm

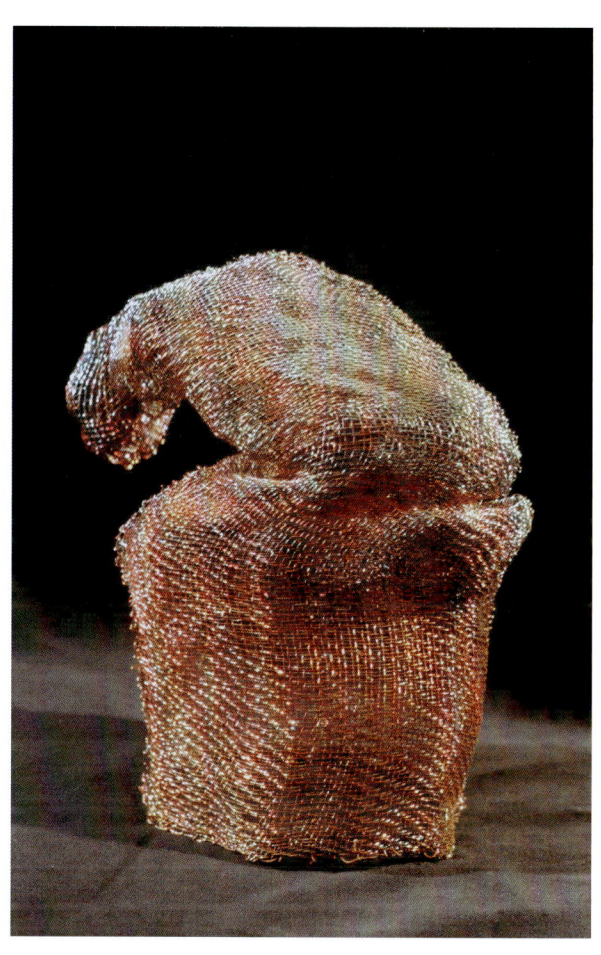

Anguish, 1988
copper wire, woven on loom,
sculpted, electroplated, oxidized
23 × 10 × 10 cm

a nurse told me that the swelling in her brain was irreversible. Death was imminent, she said. Catherine's mother in Toronto should be notified. I went downstairs to deliver this news and watched as it triggered anguish beyond grief. No denial, no blackout, no oblivion to mask the pain. I thought Laura would implode from her angst. She let out a haunting, visceral moan. Her body doubled over into a fetal curl. Inconsolable, she fled the room, propelled herself to the nearest exit, and ran. She told me later she'd wished for her own heart to stop. A furrow formed in her brow, never to disappear.

The energy that survives such a grief can, at its best, fuel goodness. Out of the shadow of her anguish, Laura poured her heart and soul into acts of kindness and bravery and brilliant achievements as an artist. Trained as an architect, she has been a high-school art teacher and an art director in film. As a social advocate, she has channelled her drive to do for others. *Anguish* is a testament to Laura's resilience and my deep love for her.

Requiem, 1992
bronze, cast from twined paper
50 × 48 × 49 cm

While my brother was dying of throat cancer, and the sculpture was still woven paper, I unconsciously created its broken parts. The significance of that only registered when it came back from the foundry in bronze.

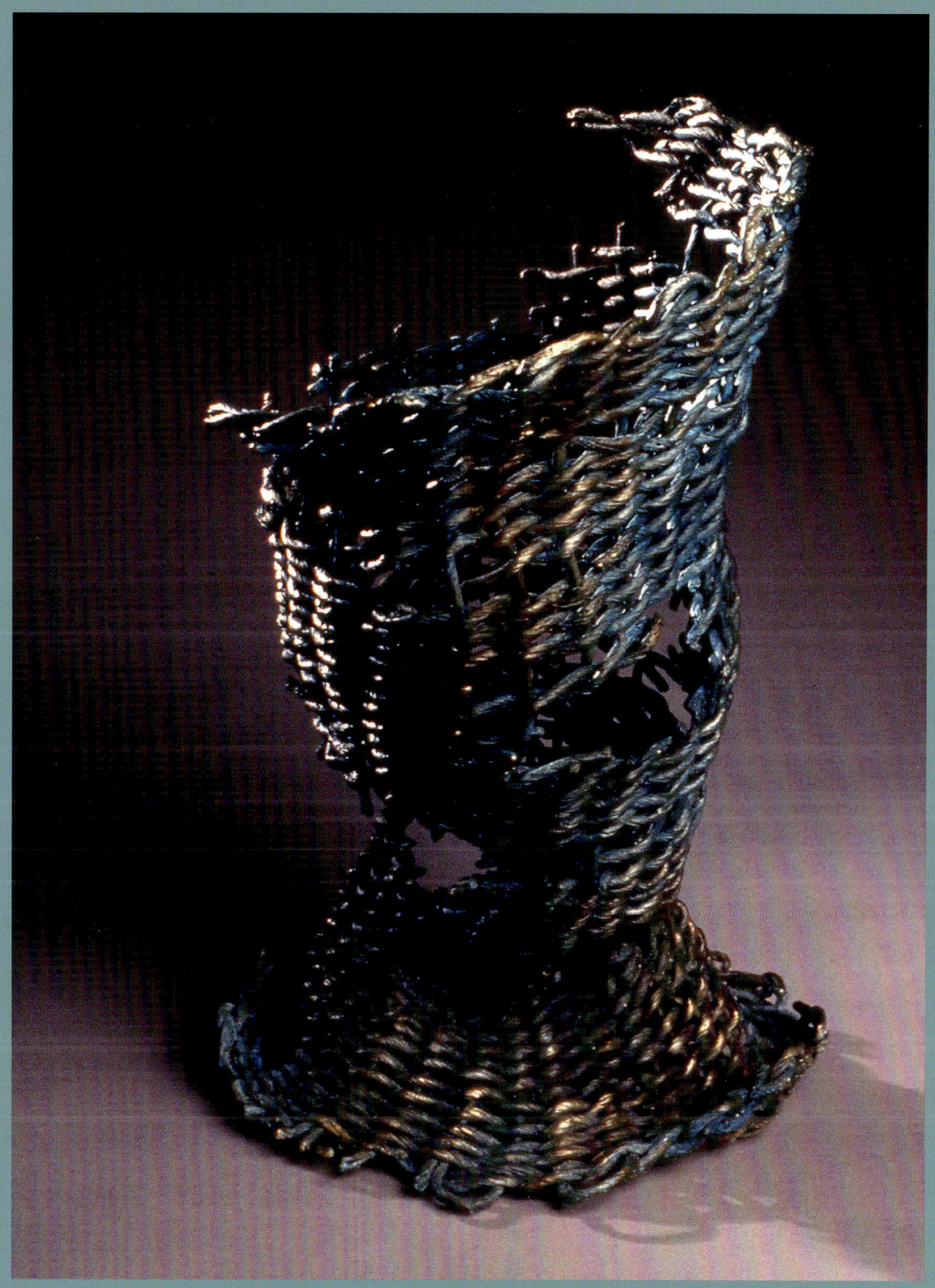

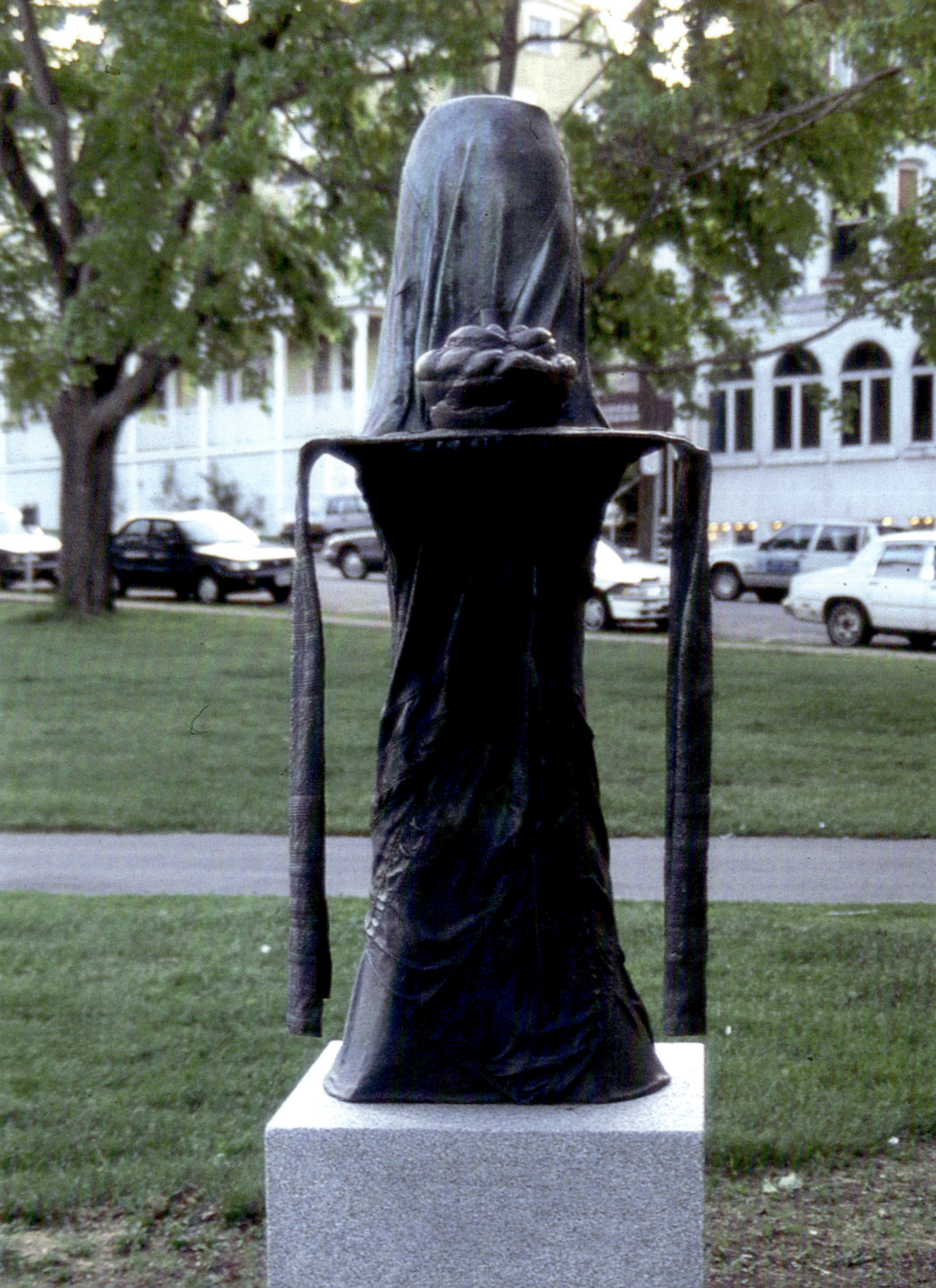

Vytaiemo

Early in 1991, Thomas Stefanyk, a young Ukrainian living in Halifax, contacted me to discuss his concept for a sculpture. He and the Ukrainian Canadian Congress knew of *Kindred Spirits*, my sculpture at the Alderney Gate ferry terminal in Dartmouth, Nova Scotia. They wanted to commission me to create a piece to mark the one-hundredth anniversary of the first wave of Ukrainian immigration into Canada through Halifax.

Thomas brought drawings to our meeting and explained his idea in detail: an abstracted figurative work draped in the original Canadian Red Ensign (our unofficial flag in 1891) and the "new" Canadian flag we fly today. Holding a ceremonial Ukrainian bread called *korovai*, topped with a salt cellar and presented on a special embroidered cloth called a *rushnyk*, the figure would welcome immigrants to Canada. Throughout the creation process, I tried to use truly Ukrainian materials: Thomas provided an embroidered *rushnyk* made in Ukraine as well as an actual *korovai*, baked by a Ukrainian, all for me to use in the sculpture. This project was truly a collaboration between Thomas and me.

Artcast, an outstanding art foundry in Georgetown, Ontario, has helped me cast my work for decades. In this work, the flags and the ceremonial *rushnyk* had been dipped in diluted glue and draped around a carved Styrofoam core. The folks at Artcast recommended casting techniques that allowed for the authentic representation of the original fabrics and of the bread and salt. The textures that came through in the bronze are remarkable. Thomas Stefanyk chose the title *Vytaiemo*, which he told me is the traditional Ukrainian word for "welcome."

The Ukrainian community donated *Vytaiemo* to the City of Halifax for display in a public place, and in 1992, it was placed near Pier 21, on the edge of the now-named Peace and Friendship Park. Overshadowed by the infamous monumental statue of Edward Cornwallis (since removed due to outrage for his brutal treatment of the M'ikmaq), *Vytaiemo*

Vytaeimo, 1991
bronze, cast from bread and fabric
142 × 61 × 61 cm

remained a little-known curiosity in the eyes of the public for thirty years. It was urinated on and vandalized, and late-night marauders bent it out of shape so that the *rushnyk* appeared to be blown by the wind — but in two different directions! At the time of writing, phone calls to the City of Halifax had not yet resulted in repairs.

When Russia invaded Ukraine on February 24, 2022, *Vytaiemo* suddenly gained significance and profile. As we mourn the desecration of Ukraine and embrace the arrival of a new wave of Ukrainian nationals, the sculpture has drawn small gatherings and had flowers and notes placed at its base. I tracked down my collaborator Thomas Stefanyk in Edmonton to apprise him of this, and he seemed happy for the renewed recognition of our work. Sadly, he died in August 2022. I like to think Thomas would be proud that *Vytaiemo* has become a beacon of hope and welcome for Canadian Ukrainians.

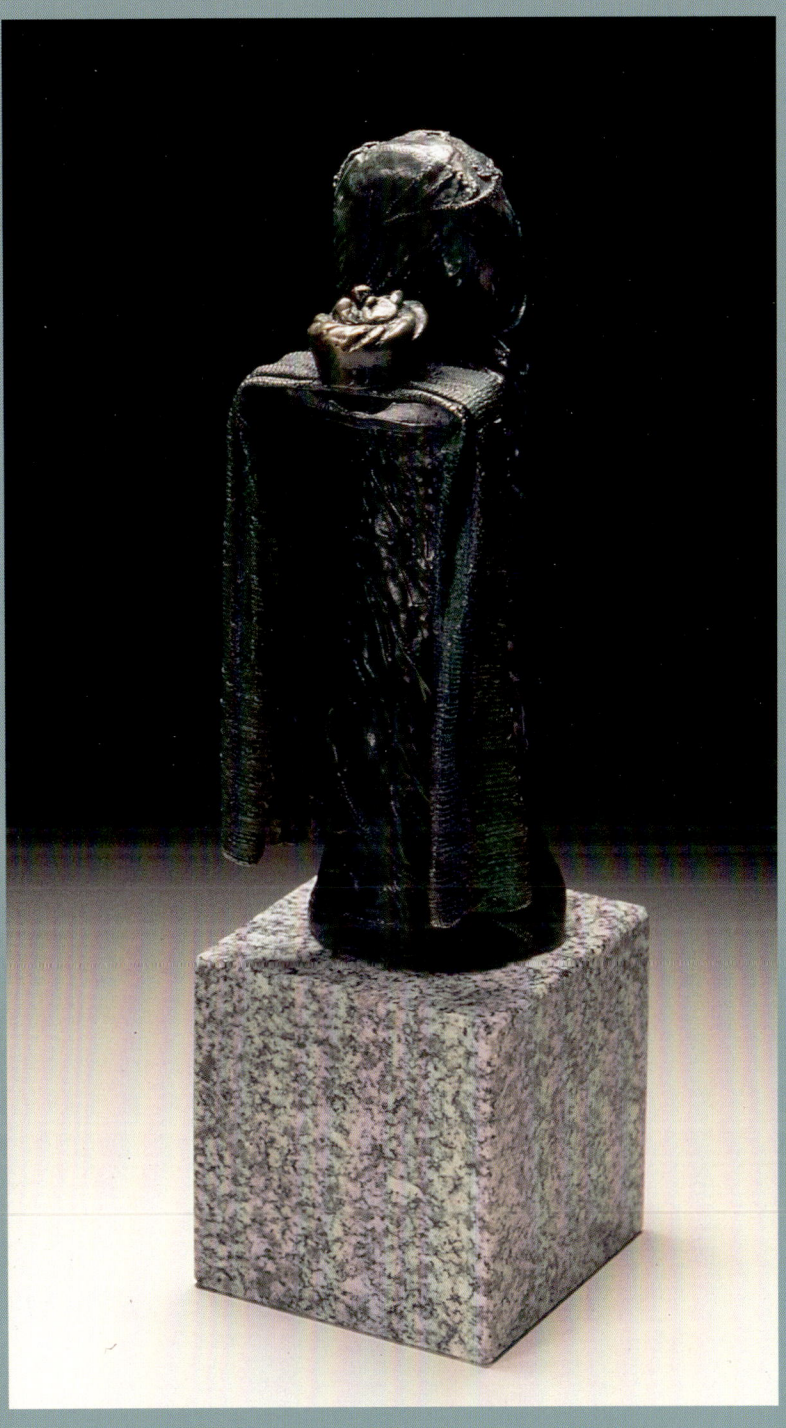

Vytaeimo, maquette, 1991
bronze cast from bread and fabric
19 cm high

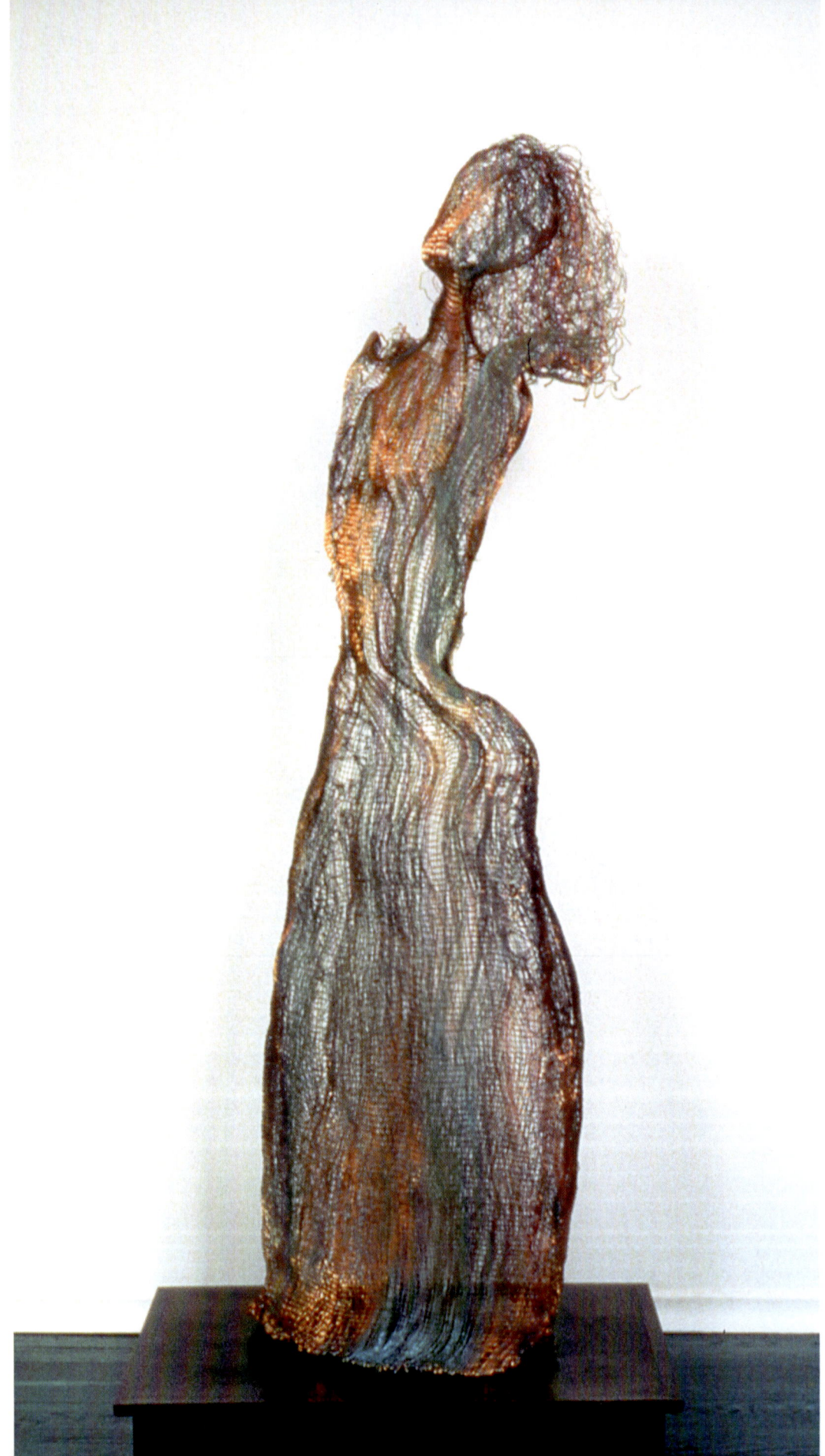

Courage

My college roommate and dear friend Lorna McMahon (Gillis) underwent breast cancer surgery, chemotherapy, and radiation in the mid-1990s. To me, she became even more beautiful in summoning the courage to endure treatment. Although she went on to survive her cancer for more than twenty-five years, Lorna transcended her moments of rage, fear, and grief with such determination that she inspired my deeply personal piece *Transcendence*.

Transcendence was woven on a loom from copper wire, then sculpted to become a free-standing, triumphant woman, with wild copper hair flowing in defiance. Her one severed breast only strengthened her appearance. Metaphorically, the electroplating, where the sculpture was zapped by ions of copper in an electrolytic bath, and the patination, where chemicals were applied to alter the figure's colour, mimicked the cancer treatment processes of radiation and chemotherapy.

I made this work when I was chosen as one of twenty Canadian women artists commissioned by the Chalmers Foundation to create artworks commemorating the stories of breast cancer survivors for an exhibition called *Survivors, in Search of a Voice: The Art of Courage* (1995–1998). Spearheaded by Joan Chalmers, a fierce advocate of art in craft media, and curated and managed by Joan's life partner Barbra Amesbury, it opened at the Royal Ontario Museum in Toronto and then toured Canada and the US for more than two years. The Chalmers Foundation afterwards purchased *Transcendence* and donated it to the art collection at the Mayo Clinic in Rochester, Minnesota. Such support enabled my retirement from social work.

When the exhibition came to the Beaverbrook Art Gallery in Fredericton in 1996, I attended the opening, along with my friend Joan Carlisle-Irving who came up from Saint Andrews. The event was presided over by the Honourable Margaret Norrie McCain, New Brunswick's first female lieutenant-governor. Joan and Margaret had

Transcendence, 1995
copper wire woven on loom,
sculpted, electroplated,
patinated
165 × 61 × 56 cm

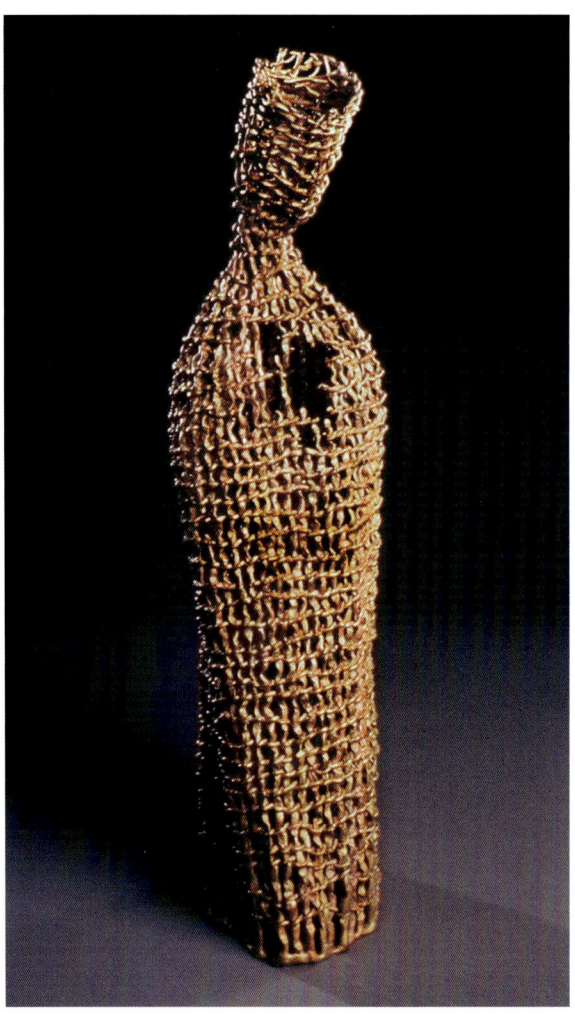

Courage, 1992
bronze, cast from twined
inflorescence and twined paper
48 × 12 × 12 cm

been friends since their crib days, and when Margaret invited Joan to overnight at her official residence, she graciously included me.

Early the next morning I woke to breakfast sounds and went downstairs to find the lieutenant-governor having a bowl of cereal in the kitchen. She invited me to drop the formality and call her Margie. Although her life experience was in sharp contrast to mine, we both had connections to Joan and to our alma mater, Mount Allison University. We also discovered we were both trained social workers, and we bonded over our passion for helping others. I had just retired after forty years in the field, while her long-time service to others was benevolent and ongoing. I knew she had established the Muriel McQueen Fergusson Foundation for the elimination of family violence. She worked tirelessly in the fields of human rights and women's rights and to promote universal early childhood education.

Our conversation wandered to my sculptures. *Transcendence* had been her introduction to my art. I gave her some cards of my current work that I had with me. She was drawn in particular to one called *Courage*, a forty-eight-centimetre-high willow sculpture cast in bronze by burning out the original woven material. Her reaction was strong and immediate.

"Is it for sale?" she asked.

"Yes," I replied.

"I want to buy it," she said.

I was reluctant to accept her offer until she had a chance to examine the piece in person. I wanted her to at least view the program *Kindred Spirits: The Art of Dawn MacNutt* that CBC TV had produced a year earlier, where *Courage* was featured. But she was sure she wanted it and insisted on full payment right away. I offered to send it to her, but she wanted me to keep it until her home in Nova Scotia was completed. Almost two years later, she came to my studio to collect *Courage* and purchased two more pieces while she was there.

And so began a remarkable period of thoughtful, heartfelt collecting of my work. Several members of her family also bought pieces. Having such strong support enabled me to continue to develop as an artist and persist with the extremely expensive process of casting my woven work in bronze. Why does bronze matter? Because it allows my woven sculpture to endure outdoors. Margie McCain's patronage has allowed me to thrive in the medium I feel passionate about.

While I had sold her the work by that name, her purchases gave *me* courage as I navigated those early years of working as a full-time artist.

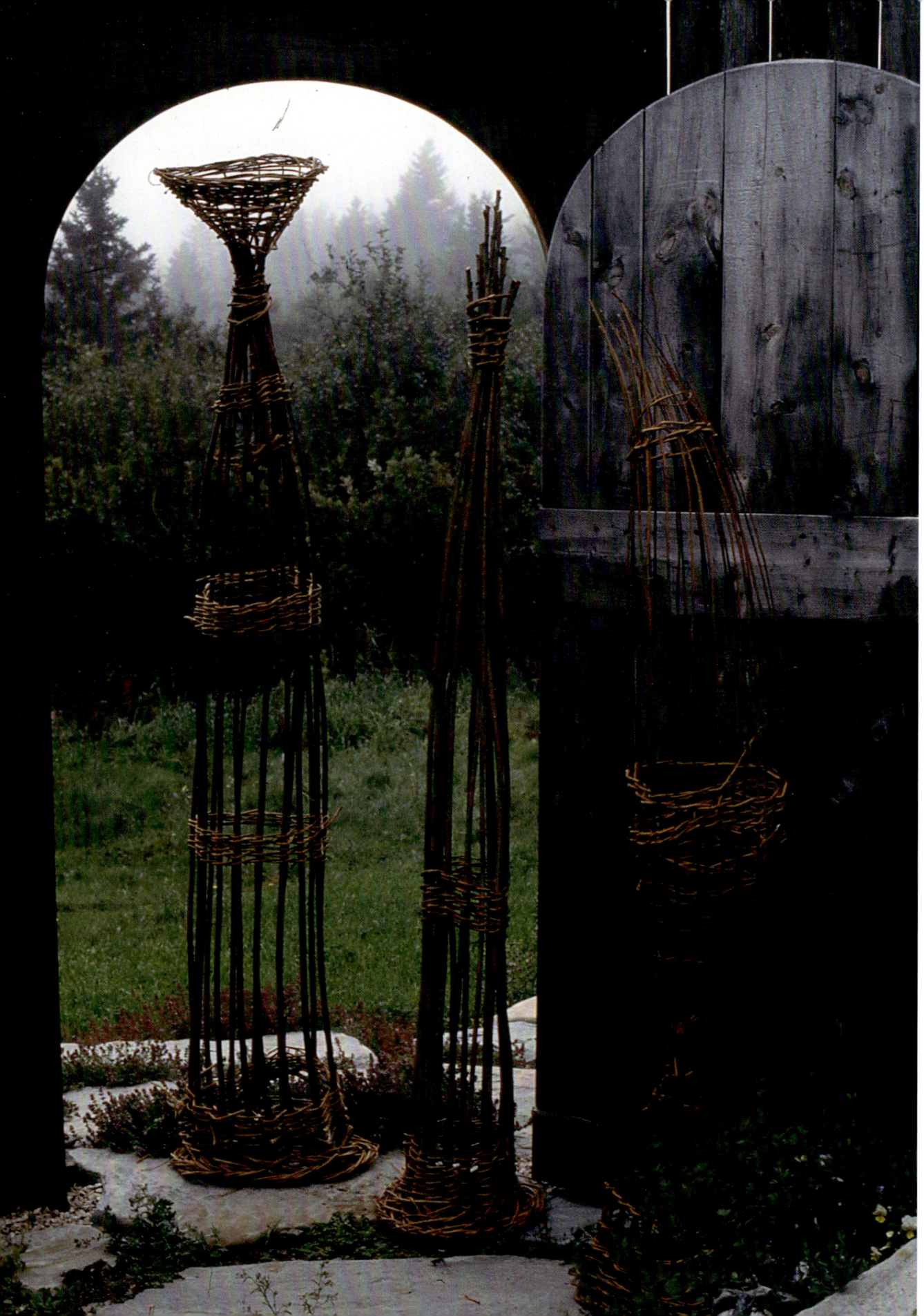

All the Ancients Walk Inside Us

It was 1995, and I was preparing to travel to Greece for the first time — a lifelong desire of mine — when I received a pleasant shock: an inquiry I'd made to the Art Gallery of Nova Scotia had been successful, and I'd been granted my first solo exhibition there, scheduled for 1997.

I already knew it would be a working trip. I planned to absorb what I saw and felt and record those observations and feelings in a variety of ways as inspiration for new work, so I had packed sketching materials and wire cloth to sculpt tiny maquettes. Taiya Barss, a wonderful artist and friend, accompanied me for part of the trip so she could study the flora and fauna — fodder for her exquisite mixed media paintings. She also kept some beautifully written journals that later became a sidebar to the exhibition catalogue:

> *August 28, 1994.* On our flight to Greece, Dawn talked about ideas for her work, about the thought that humans today hold and reflect the generations that passed before. We feel the same emotions, the joy and pain that people felt a thousand years before.

Once we arrived in Greece, I was utterly mesmerized: I noticed that some people's postures were uncannily mimicking the sculptures they were gazing at. Armed with a tiny Minox camera, I captured eight hundred slides of people in museums, of ancient sculptures, and people looking at sculptures.

At some point I knew the exhibition would be called *All the Ancients Walk Inside Us*. Where did the title come from? I took it from a presentation by sculptor Bill FitzGibbons at an international sculpture

Caryatid and *Timeless Forms*,
1996
twined willow
dimensions variable

79

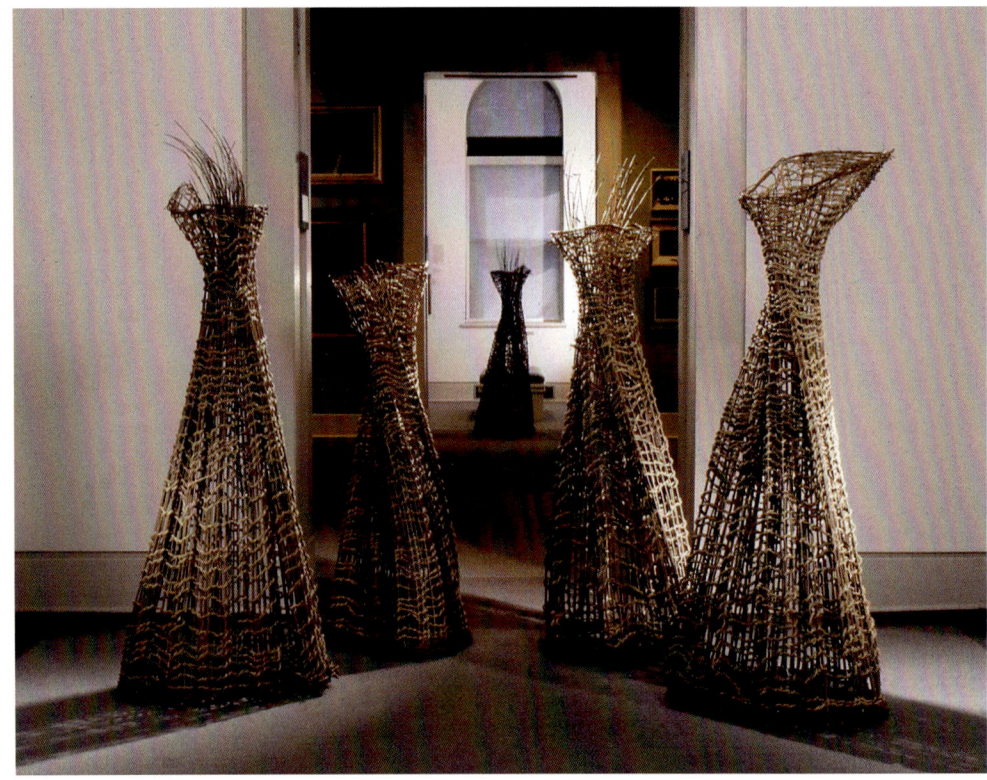

conference in Philadelphia in 1992. He cited Carl Jung as the source, but despite an exhaustive three-year search in library stacks and consultations with Jungian scholars, I could never verify this. I even called FitzGibbons in Texas, but he too was unsure how he came by it.

Nonetheless, the quote aptly described my feelings about the connection between the ancient Greek sculptures I studied in Greece and people today. I created a two-projector slide show for the exhibition in which photographs of life-size marble sculptures dissolved into mirror images of modern-day Greek museum-goers. Large posters also depicted people standing close to sculptures that seemed to mimic their posture and form. And with two years to fully prepare, I was able to amass a gallery full of life-sized willow works reflecting the inspiration from my trip.

> *September 8, 1994.* (Taiya on Athens's National Archaeological Museum)…a group of sculptures rescued from an ancient shipwreck…the power of their human form survived intact.

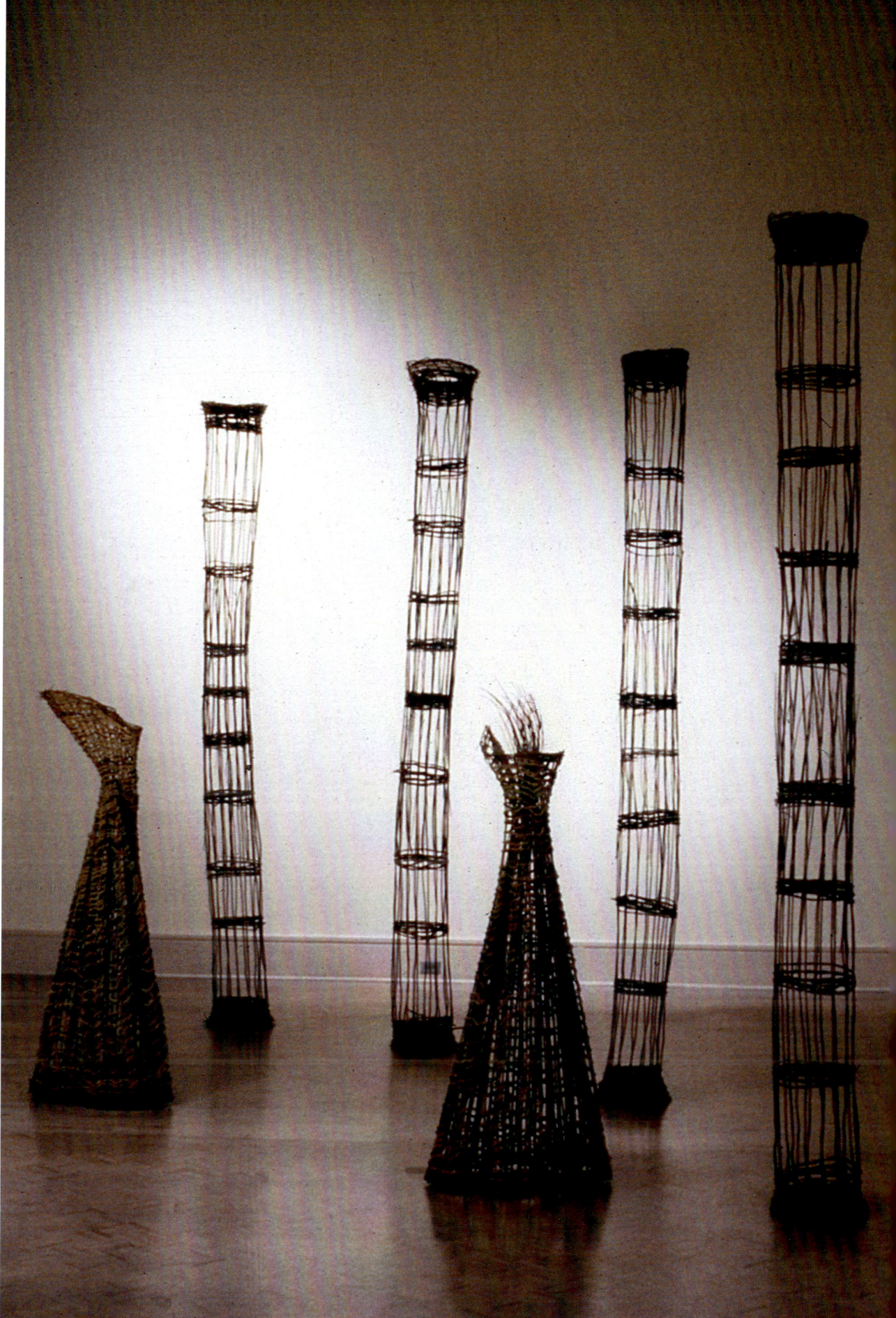

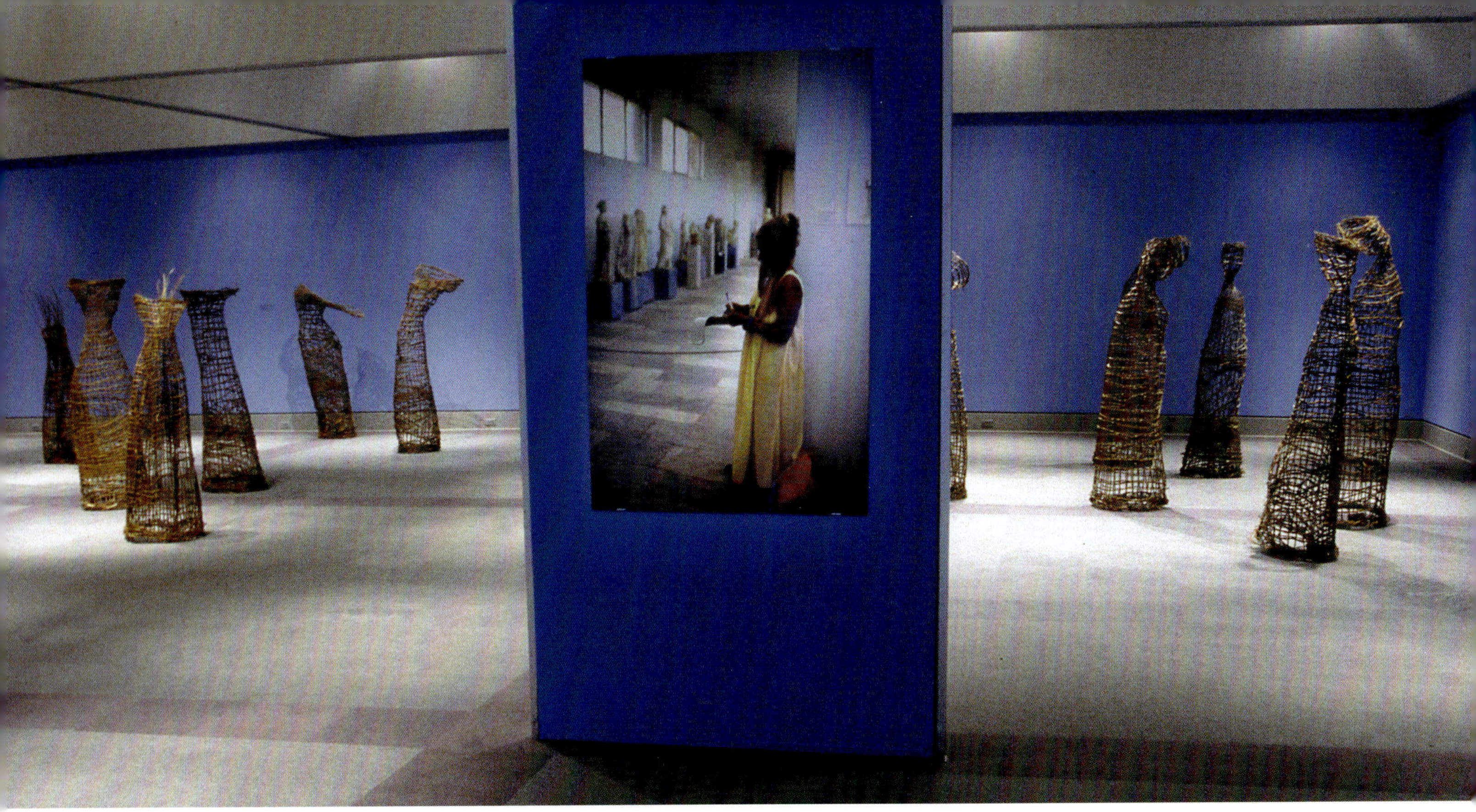

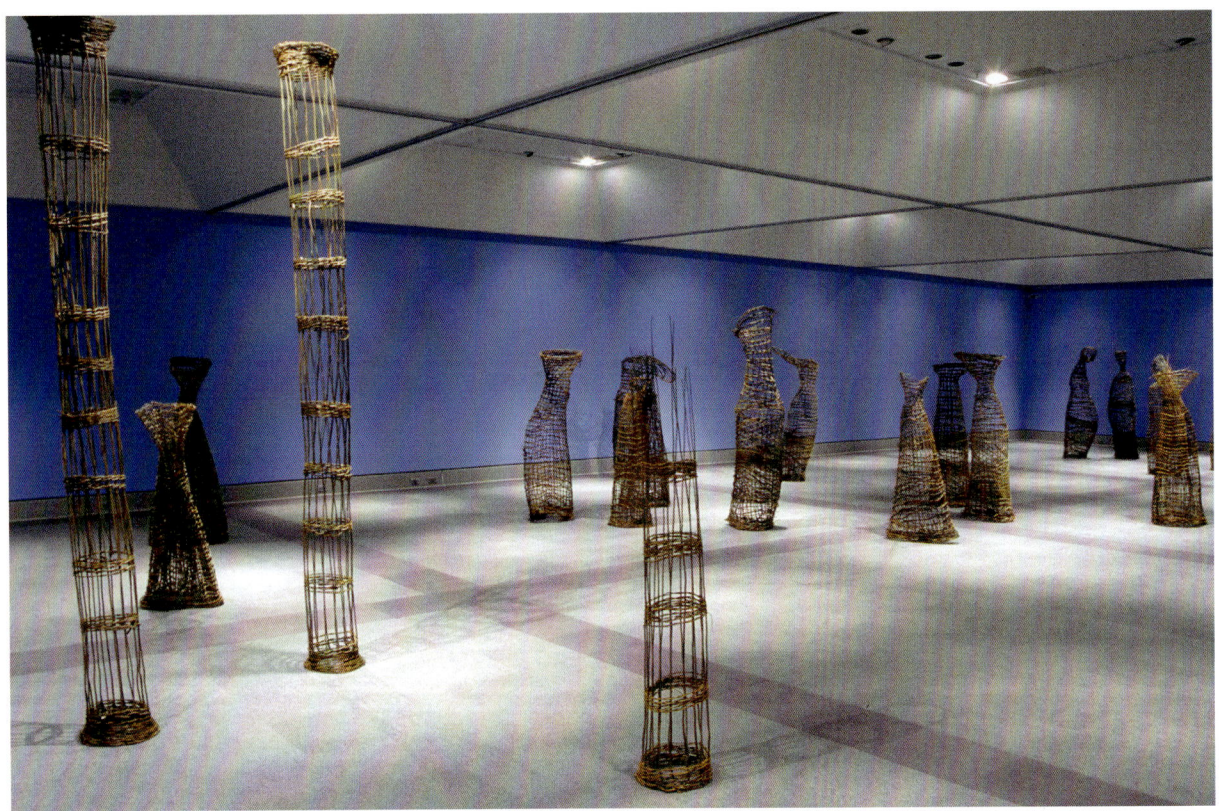

opposite: *All the Ancients Walk Inside Us*, 1997
twined willow
150–305 cm high
Exhibition at the Art Gallery
of Nova Scotia

This connects with Dawn's work, where the imperfections of the human spirit are reflected in fragments missing from the whole, but the flawed form is stronger and more intriguing than if it were perfect.

As the exhibition opening approached in the summer of 1997, I was asked what colour I'd like for the walls of the massive main gallery. Aegean blue, of course!

When the show travelled to other venues, I loved watching the composition of figures and forms change, as though the "crowd" of willow works and sightseers was gathering in renewed configurations. So when Peter Dykhuis curated a version of the show at the Anna Leonowens Gallery in Halifax, I invited him to allow groups of students to actually move the figures around! Since the gallery served the then Nova Scotia College of Art and Design, this provided a fun opportunity to experiment with the composition of sculpture in a gallery installation.

I was able to visit several times during the three months *All the Ancients Walk Inside Us* was installed at the Art Gallery of Nova Scotia. Finally, a few days before the show closed, I sat against a wall and took off my critical lens. Relaxed, I gave myself permission to drink in the body of work as a visitor might. Instead of work I was responsible for, the sculptures became both icons of an ancient time and symbols of a contemporary crowd. It was a rare moment of artistic gratification.

Column, 1997
twined willow
172 × 13 × 13 cm

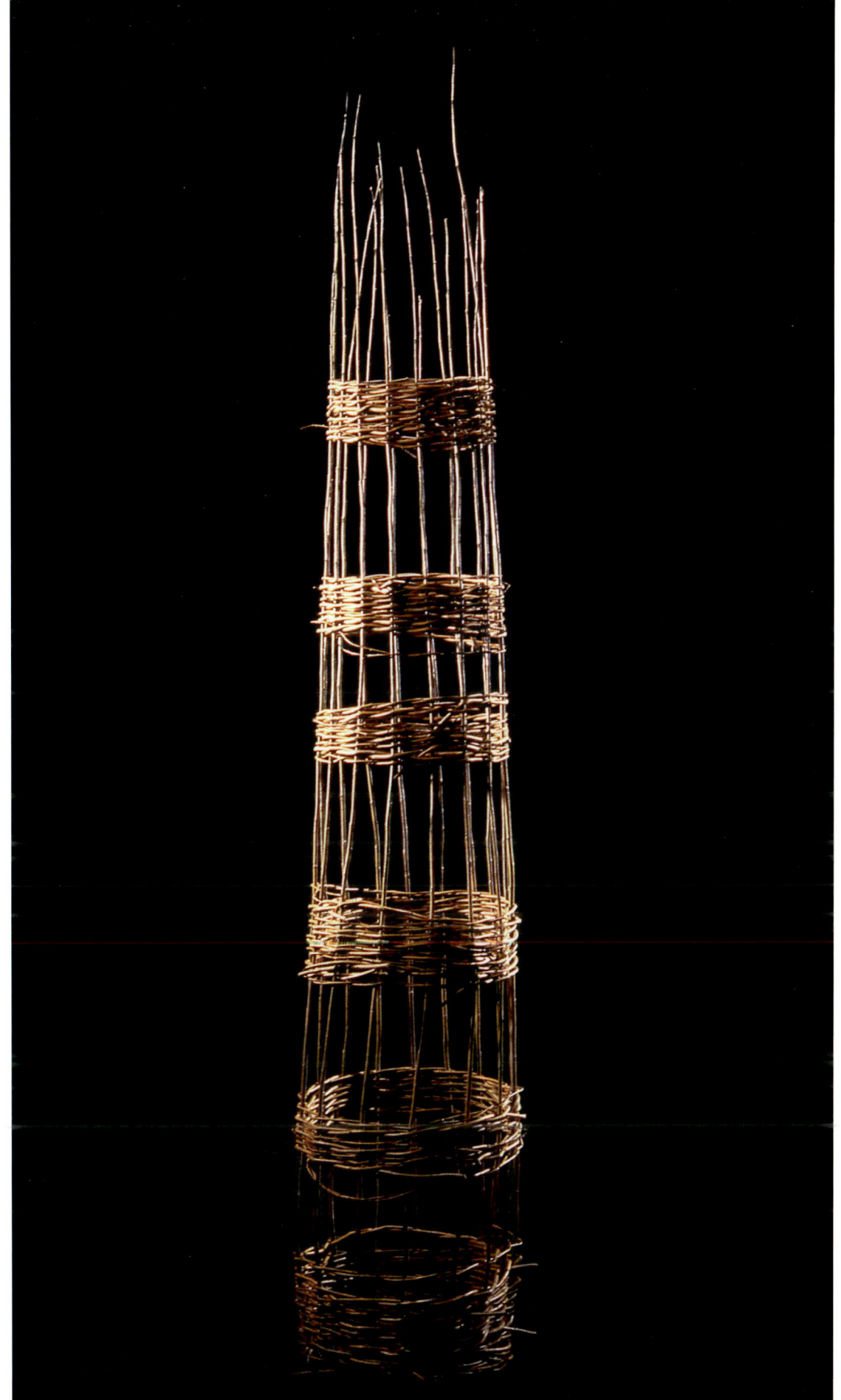

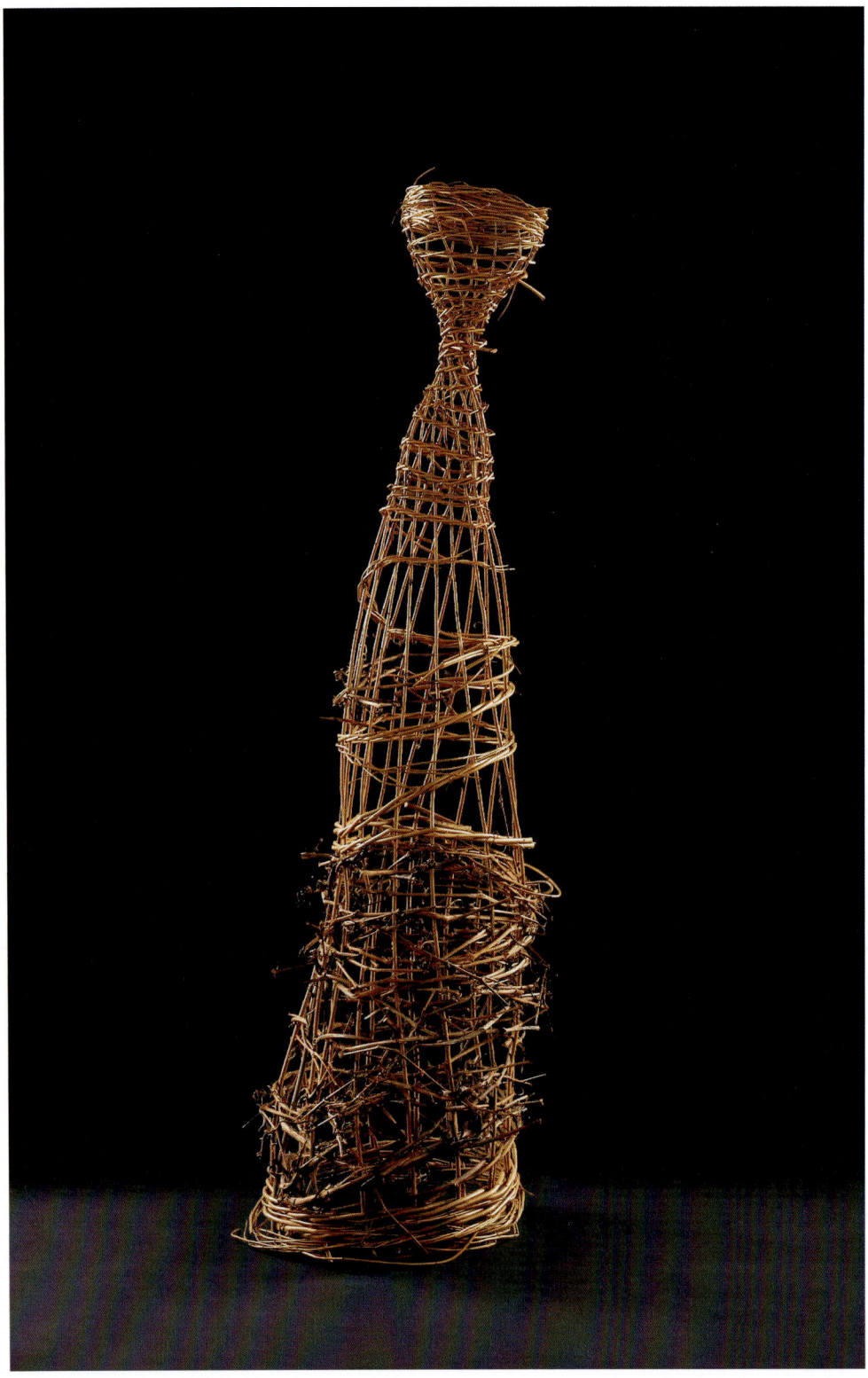

Walk in Peace, 2007 (p. 86)
twined willow and grapevine
147 × 40 cm

opposite: *From the Land*, 2015
twined willow and grapevine
202 × 87 × 52 cm

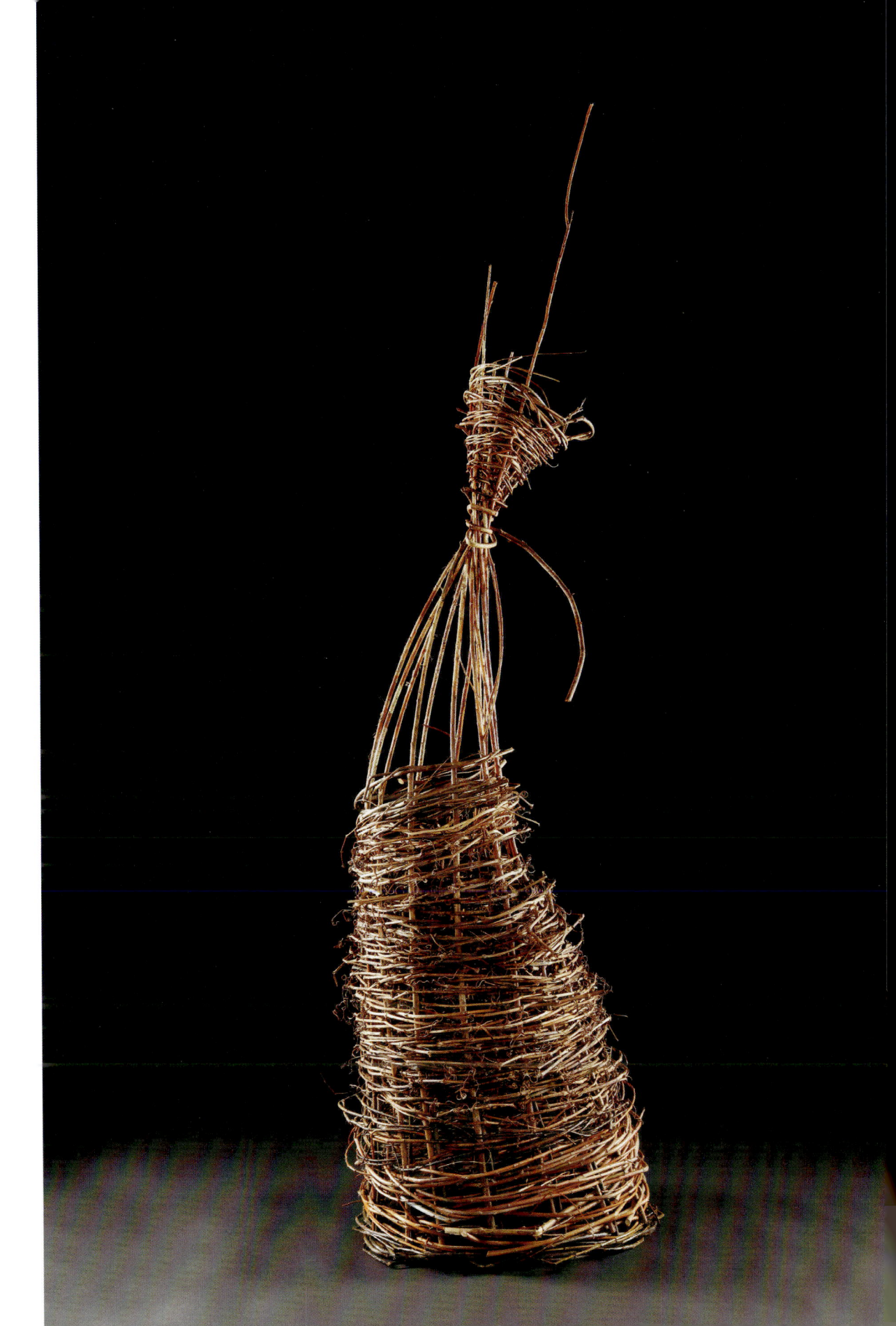

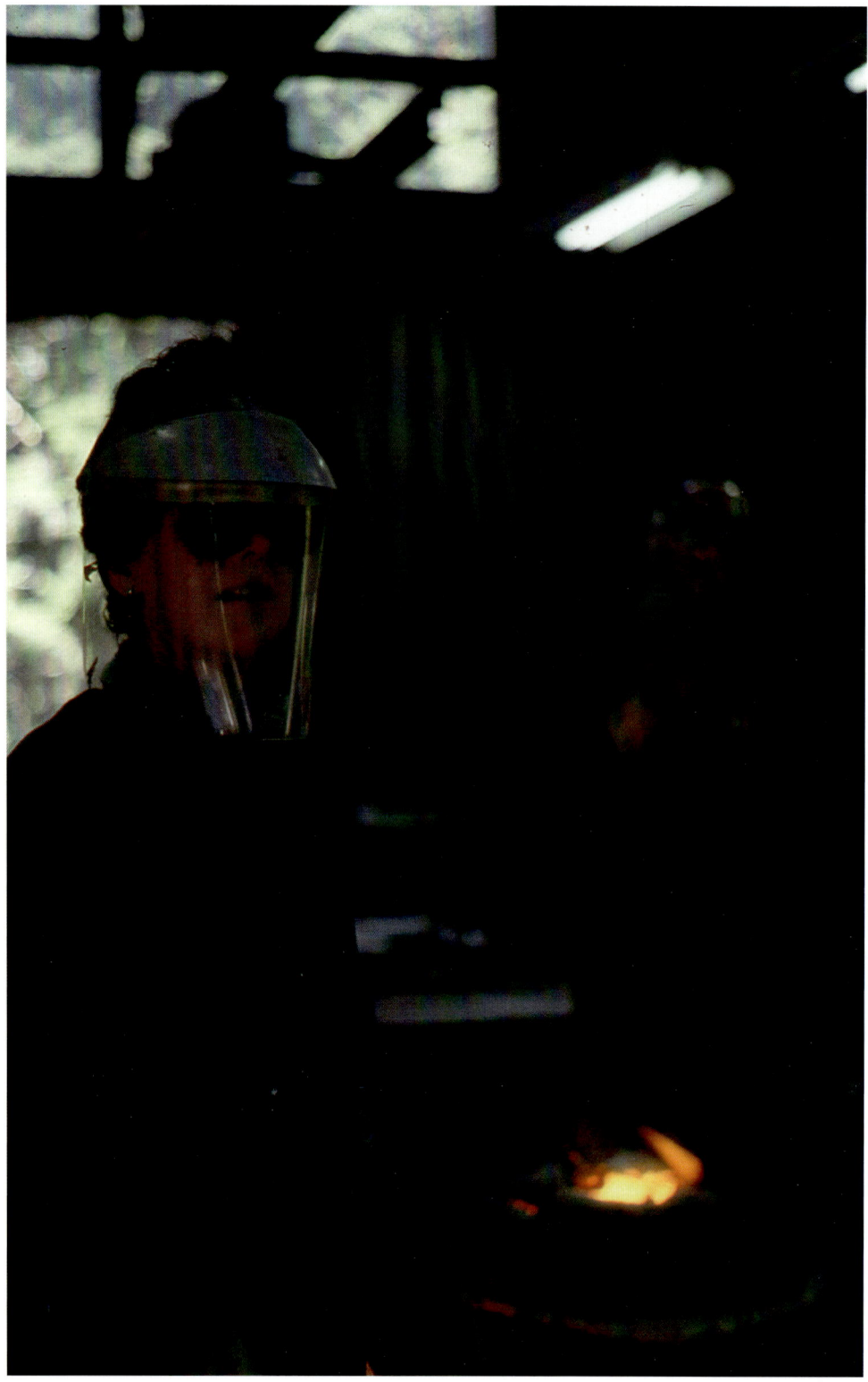

Dawn MacNutt casting bronze at Logy Bay, Newfoundland, 1999.

New Horizons

The large brown manila envelope squeezed through the mail slot and slapped unceremoniously onto the floor of the two-room Dartmouth chalet where I lived and worked. Return address: Canada Council for the Arts. I reckoned the envelope contained slides and materials being returned, so I poured a cup of tea and had lunch, delaying the inevitable rejection. Back in the 1980s and 1990s, Canada Council grants were even scarcer than they are today and much prized. I'd had early success with an Explorations Grant, and it kept me trying for another. I submitted a number of proposals over the years, but time and again the slides were returned with the familiar "We regret…" letter.

Finally, in 1999, I put together a dream proposal for a major grant. This application had no invitation to exhibit and no tightly defined plan. My proposal was this: "I'd like to work at bronze casting small works at the Garden Foundry in Newfoundland, study stone carving at the Dellatolas Marble Sculpture Studio in Tinos, Greece, and explore the use of native materials in Nova Scotia." When I finally ripped open the package and withdrew the slides, the letter read: "We are pleased to…" I'm not one to talk to myself, but that day my involuntary "Whoop!" almost blew the roof off my tiny home. It was incredibly validating, as I'd left social work in 1997 to become a full-time artist. The work created, thanks to this grant, left a lasting mark on my practice.

The Garden Foundry in Logy Bay, Newfoundland, was owned and operated by the talented Bulgarian sculptor Luben Boykov, who fled his native country in 1990 by pretending to go to Cuba on vacation (permitted because it was another communist country). When the plane carrying his family touched down for refuelling, in Gander, Newfoundland, they defected to Canada. In December 1999, Newfoundland's Logy Bay Garden Foundry was in an unheated plastic Quonset hut, bone-chillingly cold. Fierce determination kept me there. That, and buying a heating pad at the local supermarket to place under my feet so my toes wouldn't freeze. Luben and his business sponsor at the foundry, English professor John Evans, frequently squabbled with abandon about the casting process. The affable and gifted sculptor Dennis Gill, who was apprenticing at the foundry at the time, assured me it would all work out. And it did — we cast two of my small willow works into richly textured bronze sculptures, one of which is *Vigil*, only forty centimetres high. While I have worked in foundries before and since, this experience confirmed for me that with ingenuity, unconventional techniques, and solid technical expertise, you can make extraordinary things happen.

My search for sculpture materials that were native to Nova Scotia led me to experiment with wisteria and grapevines from the areas around Digby and Yarmouth. Then, near Bridgewater, I started harvesting wild, unbranched, straight willow elements as used in traditional basket-making. However, the crooked quirks of the unruly branches and vines matched the perfectly imperfect nature of human forms, and the charm of that imperfection crept into my work. The wild resources held an untamed, more organic character than the cultivated materials and were much more interesting to me. It also meant I no longer needed to rely on imported English willow. Following this exploration, I never returned to purchasing "perfect" basketry materials, instead weaving my figures and sculptures from uncultivated boughs. After moving to Pictou County in 2006, I discovered wild willows growing along ditches, on neighbours' properties, and on our own lane to the mailbox. At eighty-seven I am still joyfully exploring and harvesting materials wherever I find them, and wild willow is still my principal working material. The adventure continues!

My human forms have long been inspired by ancient Cycladic figurines. These were sculpted from marble dating back to 2000 BC on the islands that form a circle in the Aegean Sea. In the summer of 2000, the Canada Council grant allowed me to travel to Greece to study stone carving with sculptor Petros Dellatolas on the island of Tinos, which is part of the Cyclades archipelago. I was eager to get to the studio that first day and every day thereafter. As I walked along the shore from my small hotel each morning, the air was a fragrant mix of salt sea and herb grasses. Petros did

Vigil, 1999
bronze, cast from twined willow
40 × 30 × 30 cm

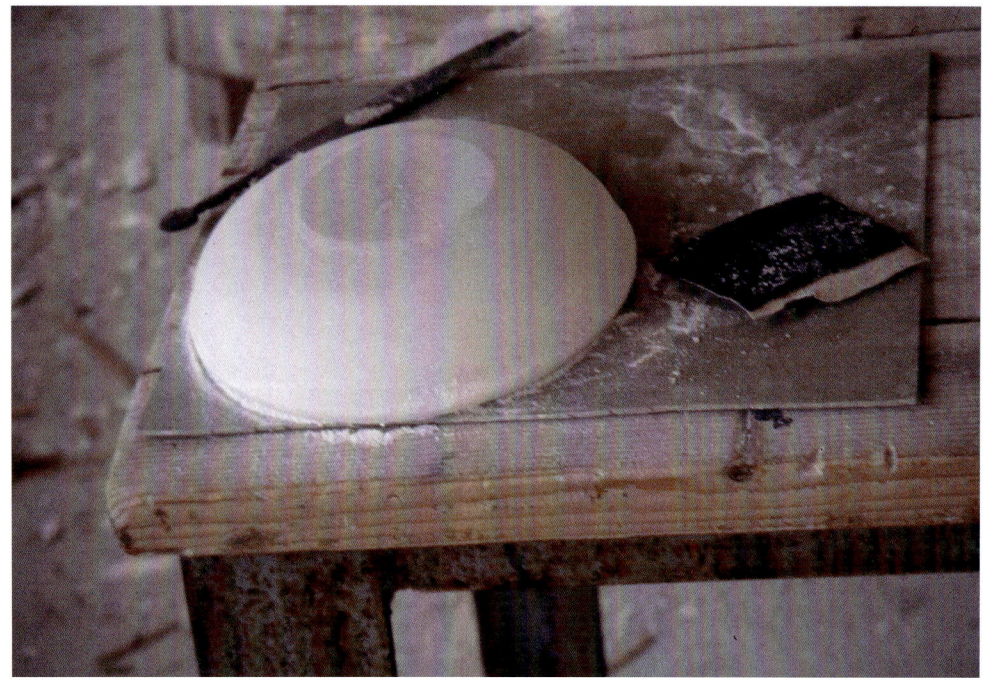

Bowl in progress

below: *Bowl*, 2000
Parian marble
5 × 19 × 19 cm

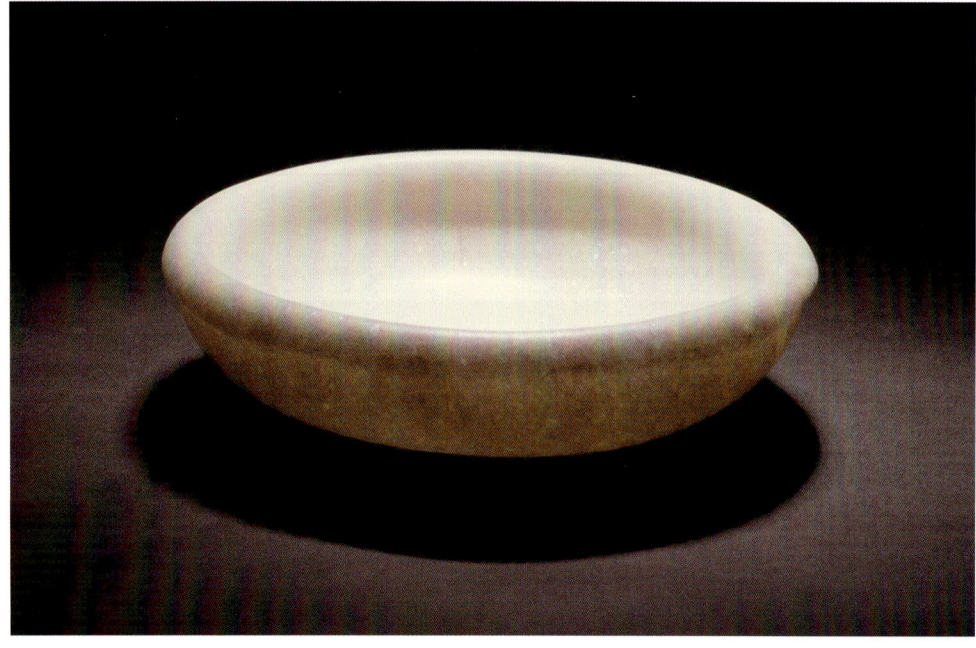

not speak English, but his Chicago-born wife, Anita, discreetly interpreted for him. I told him I wanted to use hand tools exclusively and that I was not there to become a master carver. Instead, I wanted to get inside the mind and soul of those ancient stone carvers who created the iconic Cycladic figurines — to feel transported to the ancient time and place where those bowls and sculptures were created.

After Petros showed me the functions of the various tools he described as *chiselas*, used for hand carving, I chose a block of pure white Parian marble and got started. It was a glorious few weeks working outdoors in the warm wind, under the porch roof at the Dellatolas Marble Sculpture Studio — and as inspirational as I had hoped it would be. I chose to create a simple bowl, similar in shape and scale to some I had seen in collections of Grecian antiquities. I wasn't attempting to produce an original form. Rather, I wanted to make a beautiful, functional bowl.

Petros did not hover over me, but left me to my fledgling attempts to extract bits of stone with these tools that were so new to me. He knew by listening that I had not yet developed a rhythm. He approached me with a gentle "*na, na, na,*" and patiently took the hammer, placed it at the right angle, and starting tapping. He effortlessly put the proper weight behind each rhythmical *k-chnk, k-chnk, k-chnk.* Then it was my turn. We didn't need any other language. I'm as proud of that little bowl as I am of any wild creation before or since. Its satiny finish begs to be touched. When I hold it to the light, I take pleasure in the bowl's evenness and translucence. I came away from the experience even more inspired by the concept of beauty in simplicity.

Sentinel, 2002
bronze, cast from woven willow
and grapevine
431 cm high

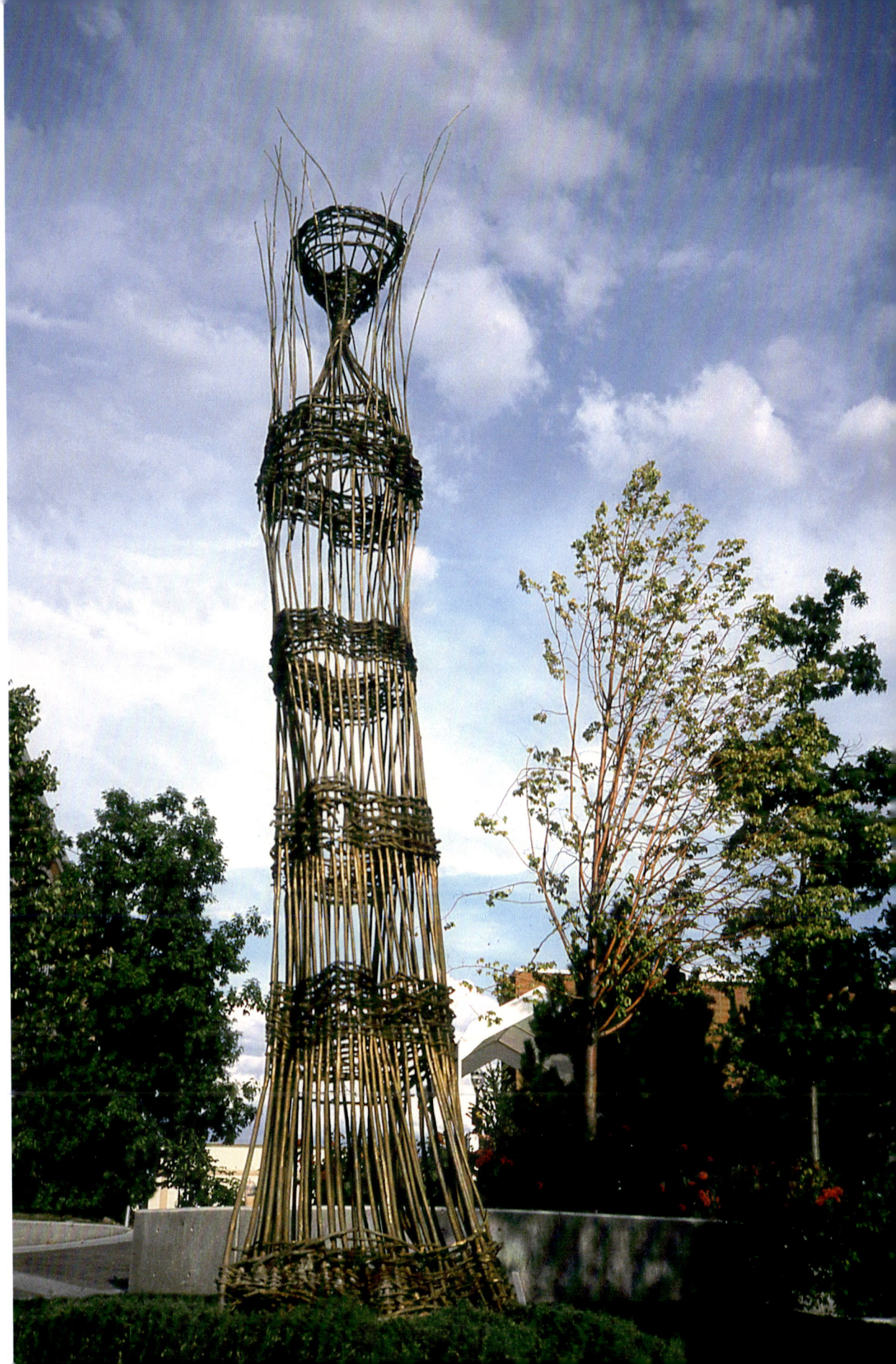

He and She Out Standing in the Field, 2018
living willows
431 cm high

Fresh, two-metre willow elements were planted deep into the soggy soil of our field on a cool day in March 2005. I twined the willow to form two figures. They flourished — in all directions! Several times a season, I climb as far as I dare to reshape them.

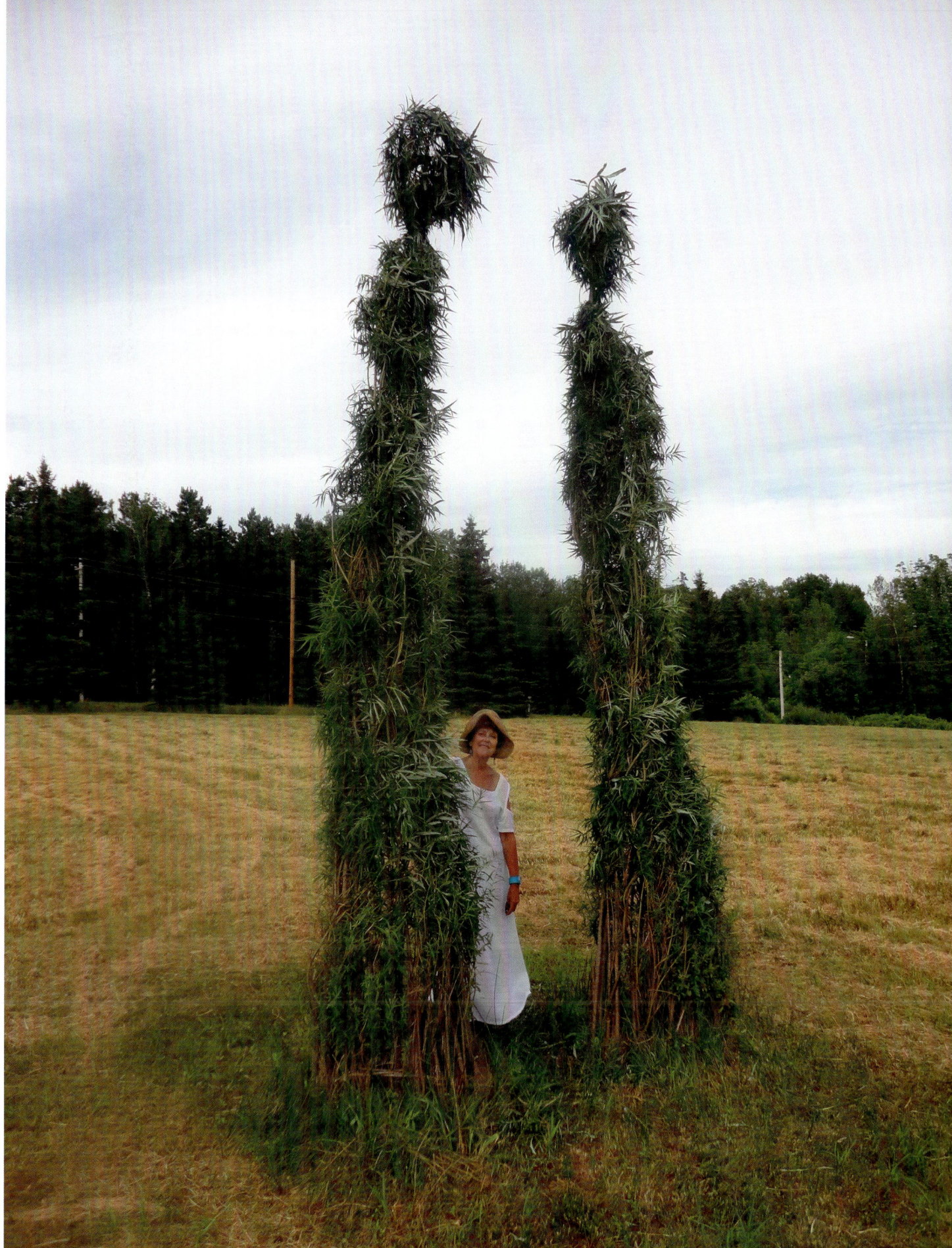

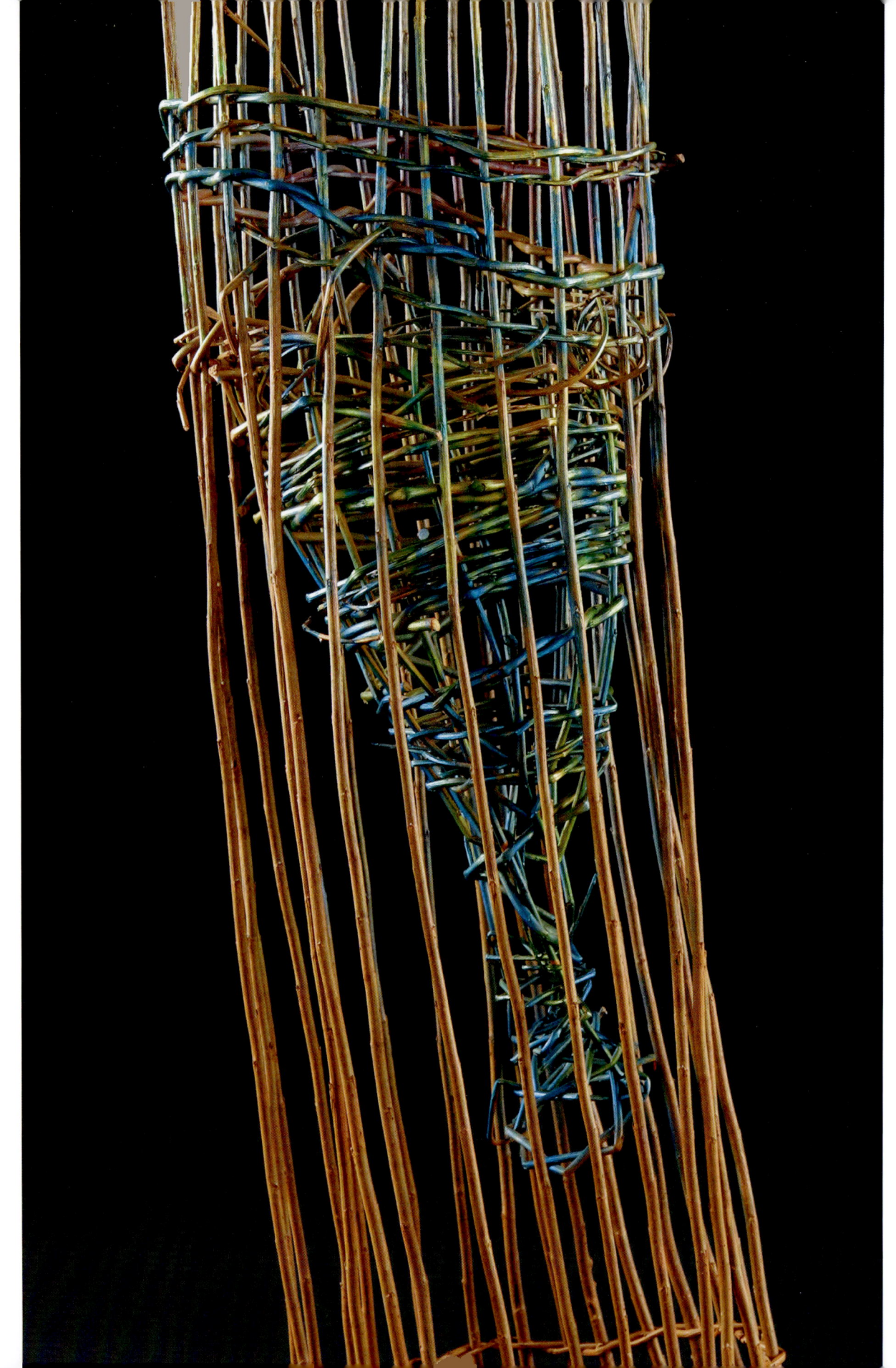

Illumination

It all began with "the gaze." It had been some time since I experienced such direct eye contact. I looked away for a break, and when I glanced back, "the gaze" was still there. We were at the Soho Kitchen in Halifax in 2005, where Mount Allison University alumni gathered frequently for an evening of Chalmers Doane Trio music and a truly inspired menu. Merle Pratt was recently widowed and had come with another Mount A friend. We had been acquainted at university, having arrived on campus on the very same day in the fall of 1954. Now he was tall, bald, and substantial — unrecognizable from the lean, dark-haired Merle I recalled from fifty years previously.

Merle wrote to me a few weeks after the evening of "the gaze." He wondered, if he came to the city, would I like to attend the Multicultural Festival with him? A date with a good man was always a pleasure, but it soon became clear to me he was looking for a soulmate. I had been single for twenty-two years, had a full life, and I was not keen to give up my independence. But after many months of going back and forth, I left Dartmouth to move into Merle's home in Little Harbour. And in 2007, when I was seventy, we were married.

I was already aware of Merle's fondness for bright colour. He had identified one of his spare bedrooms as "the painting room," and many of his own colourful paintings hung on his walls. Merle's style showed joy and enthusiasm. Folk art was not my favourite style of painting, but as I observed his liberty in using bright colours, I came to appreciate it. Often his hostess gifts were rocks he painted with pictures of fantastical animals or whimsical houses. Attached to a spruce tree in the yard, there was a homemade weathervane with a different colourful fish painted on each side, swimming in the wind.

In those early days, Merle accompanied me to SOFA (Sculptural Objects Functional Art and Design) in Chicago where I was presenting and exhibiting. He was so impressed by the massive explosion of art in

Spirit Within (detail), 2004
twined willow, acrylic paint
158 × 33 × 28 cm

craft media that he came home bursting with creative energy. He cut down several birch saplings, wrapped them in stripes of varicoloured electrical tape, tied on a spray of gaudy artificial flowers with ribbons, and speared the poles along the edge of the roadway between the house and the main road. Neighbours who had heard that Merle's new wife was an artist presumed the "whimsy poles" were my doing!

When COVID-19 disrupted so many lives for several years, I felt deeply blessed to be with someone so congenial, creative, and funny. And it didn't hurt that he is also an adventurous chef. When thoughts turned to the forbidden pleasure of eating in restaurants, we coped by developing our own menus. French cuisine at a Parisian café set up in the dining room. Dinner theatre in the TV room. Tapas Mediterraneo in the sunroom. Sequestering at home became a joy because we were together.

Merle was an engineer and worked in management. So, when I was working in the studio, his natural inclination was to make "helpful" suggestions. I would push back, and eventually he understood that his advice was unwelcome. The one admonishment he found irresistible, however, was to repeatedly say he thought my work would be even better with added colour. It got me thinking, and when I was in a Halifax art store one day, I found a translucent water-based auto paint in semi-transparent, pearlized, and iridescent colours. I began to apply a bit of colour to willow, then to woven wire cloth, and finally to bronze. Rejecting the recommended airbrush technique, I used only a paint brush, freely mixing on the palette as I went. Because of the sheerness of the paint, the original colour and texture of the sculpture remained dominant. I was hooked on the effect.

The added dimension of colour has unlocked a whole new domain of possibilities, and during this happy phase of my life it is a constant consideration in my work. I feel enriched by it and grateful for the nudge from Merle. Not every work cries out for colour, or for the same amount of colour. That choice emerges during the process, and the mystery of the decision is part of the pleasure. Merle's encouragement has illuminated both my work and my life.

Spirit Within, 2004
twined willow, acrylic paint
158 × 33 × 28 cm

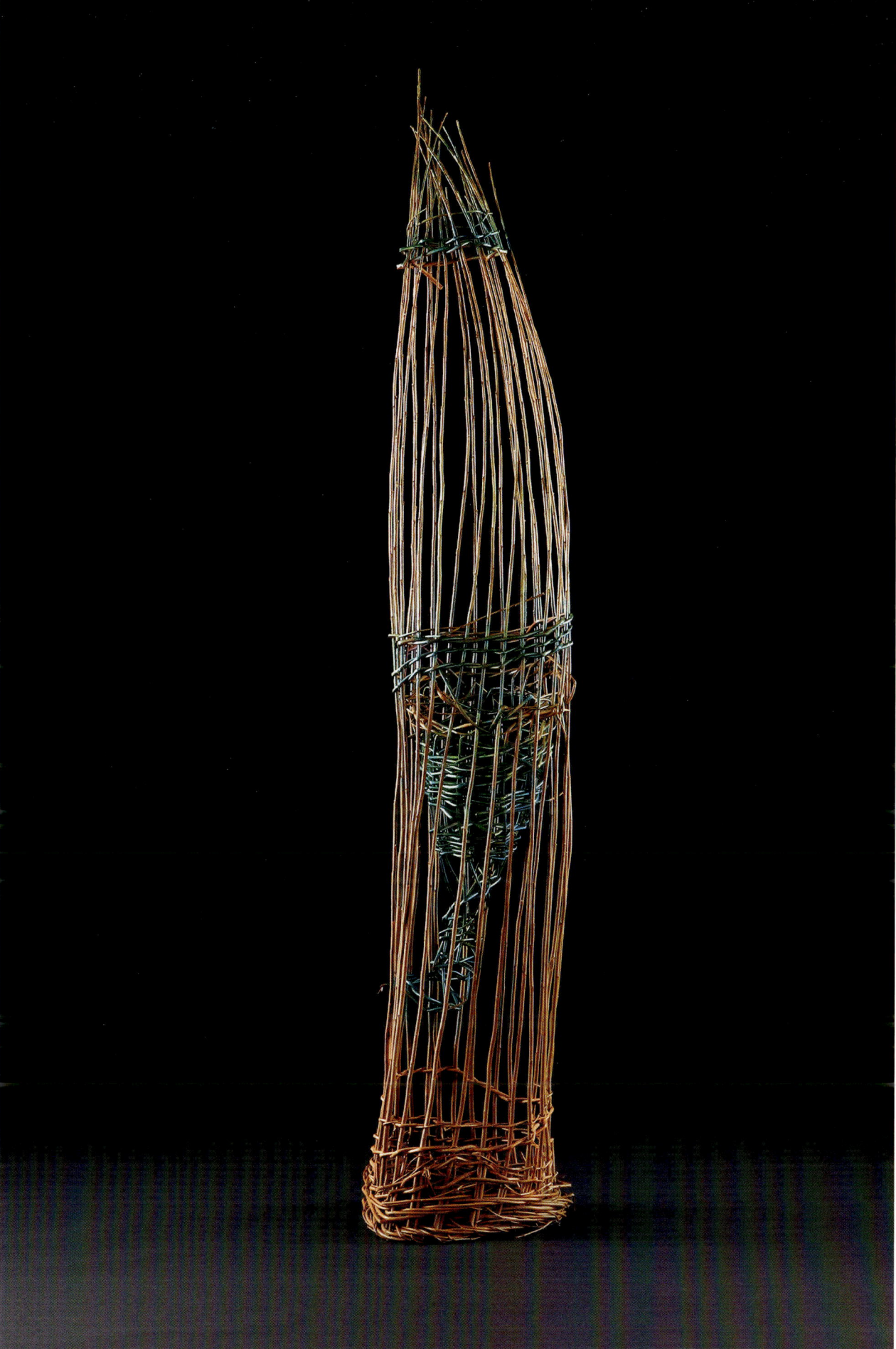

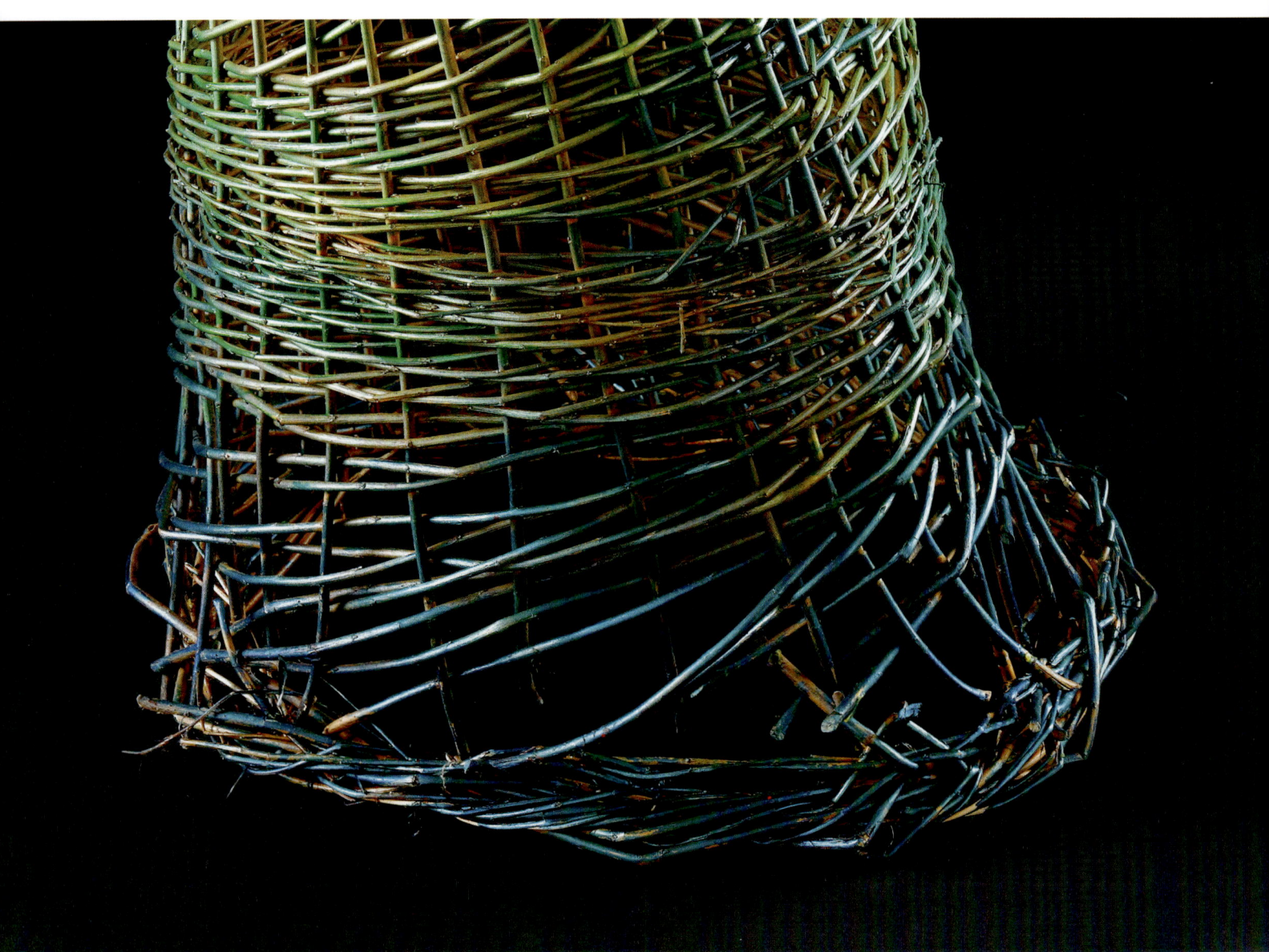

Shades of Green, 2008
twined willow, acrylic paint
214 × 38 × 38 cm

opposite: *Shades of Green*
(detail), 2008

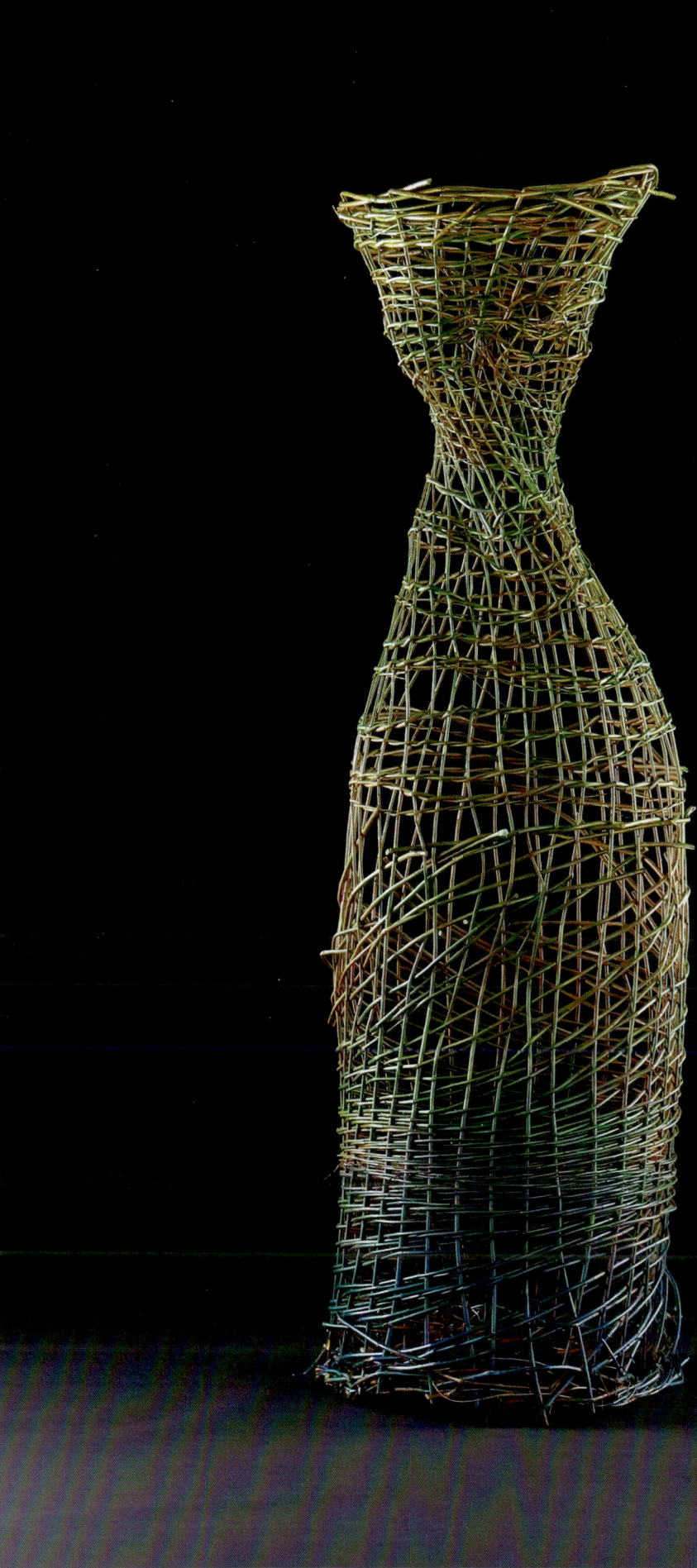

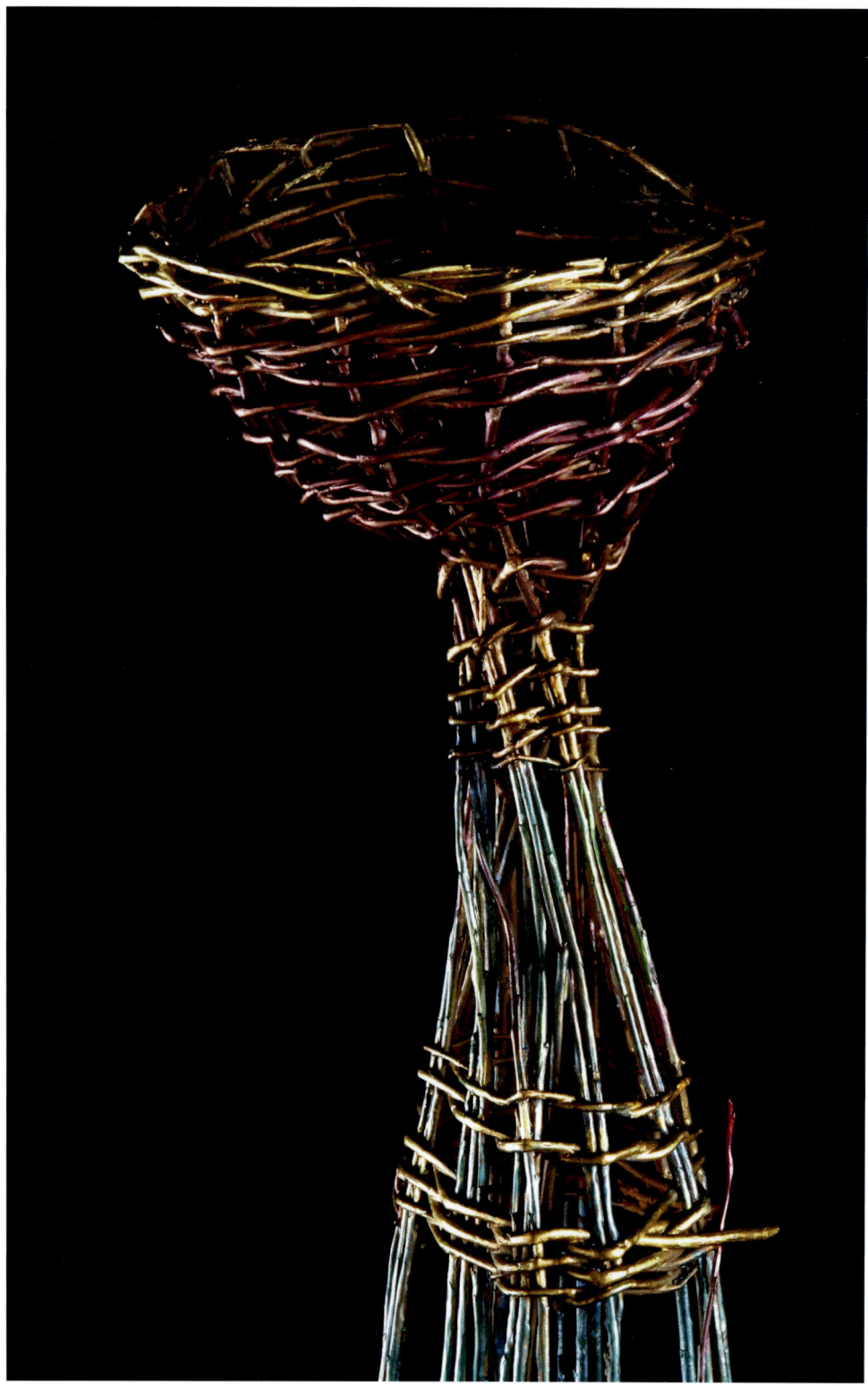

Timeless Spirit (detail), 2006
bronze, cast from twined willow,
acrylic paint
135 × 38 × 38 cm

opposite: *Timeless Spirit*, 2006

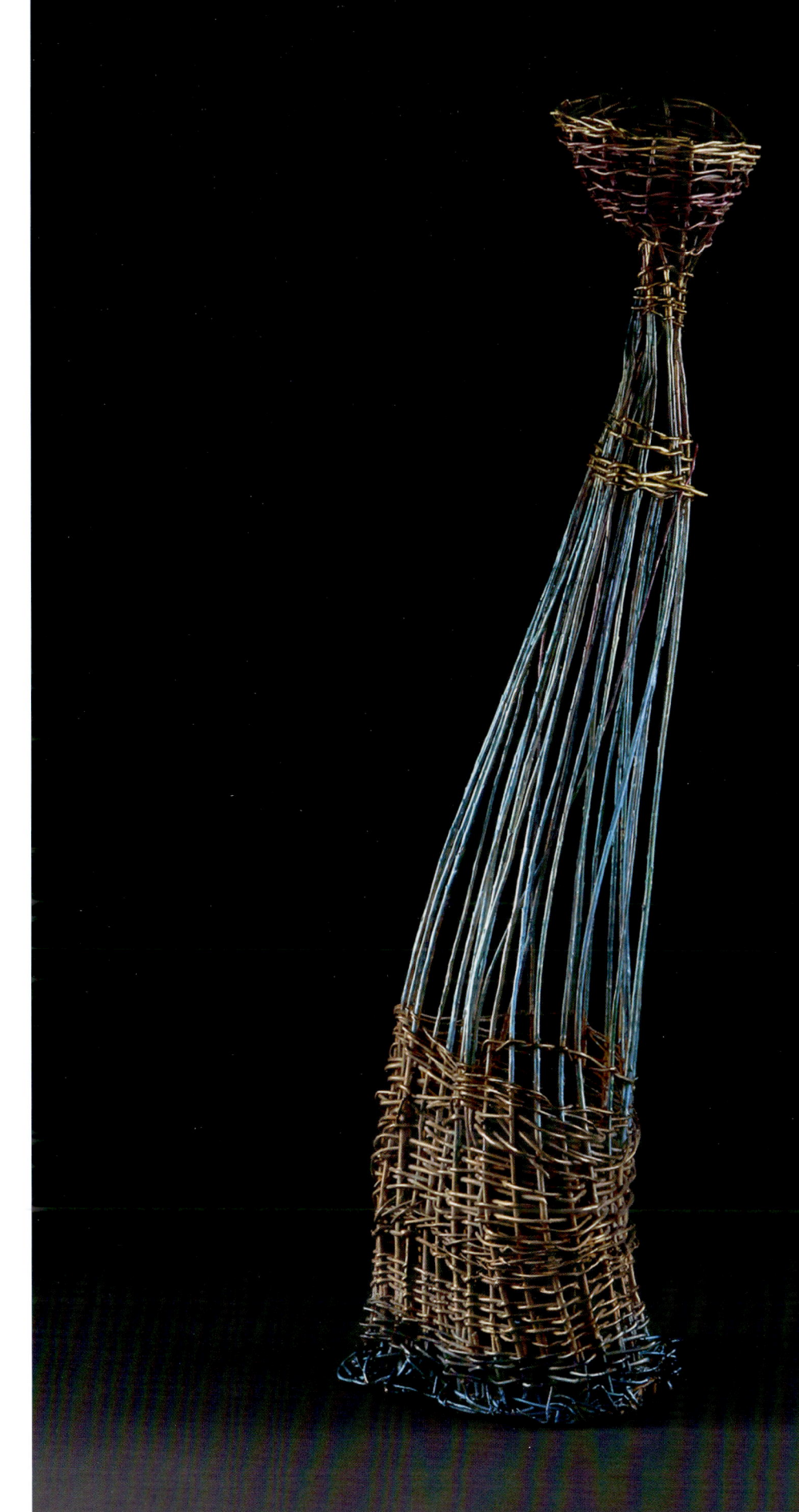

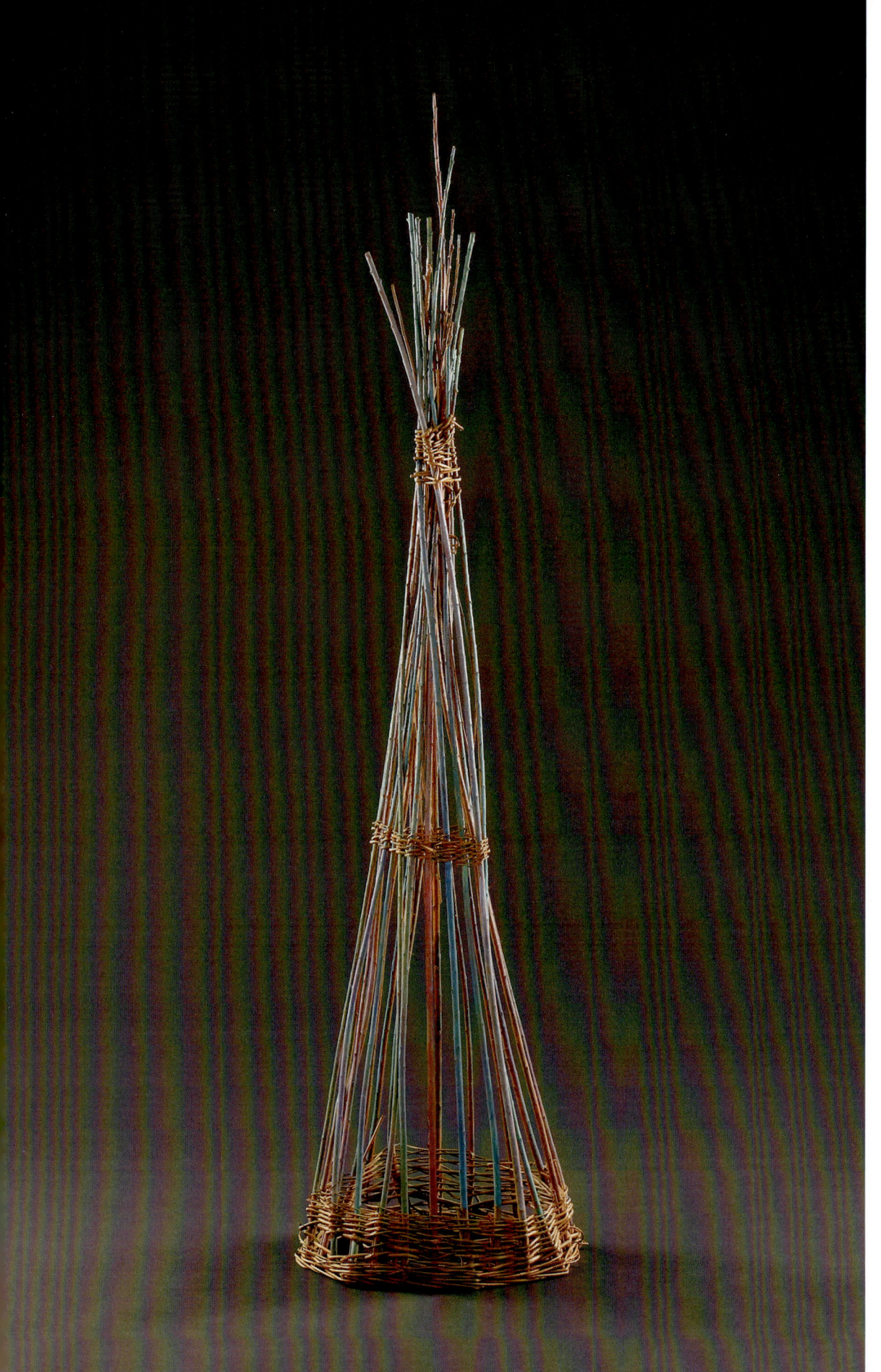

Symphony, 2007
twined willow, acrylic paint
170 × 41 × 45 cm

opposite: *Together Still*, 2013
patinated bronze, cast from
twined willow, acrylic paint
86 × 31 × 18 cm

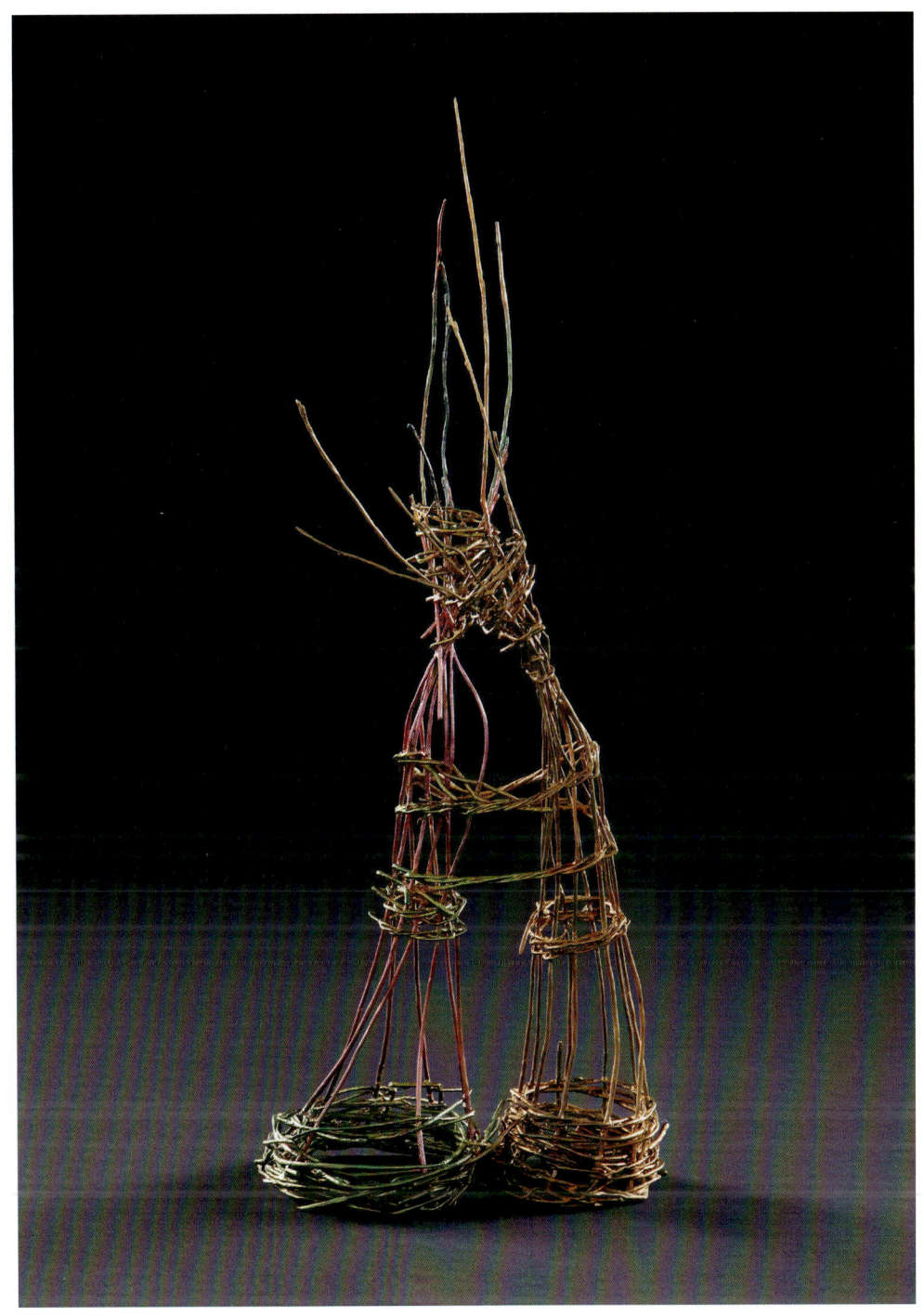

Caring in progress, 2010

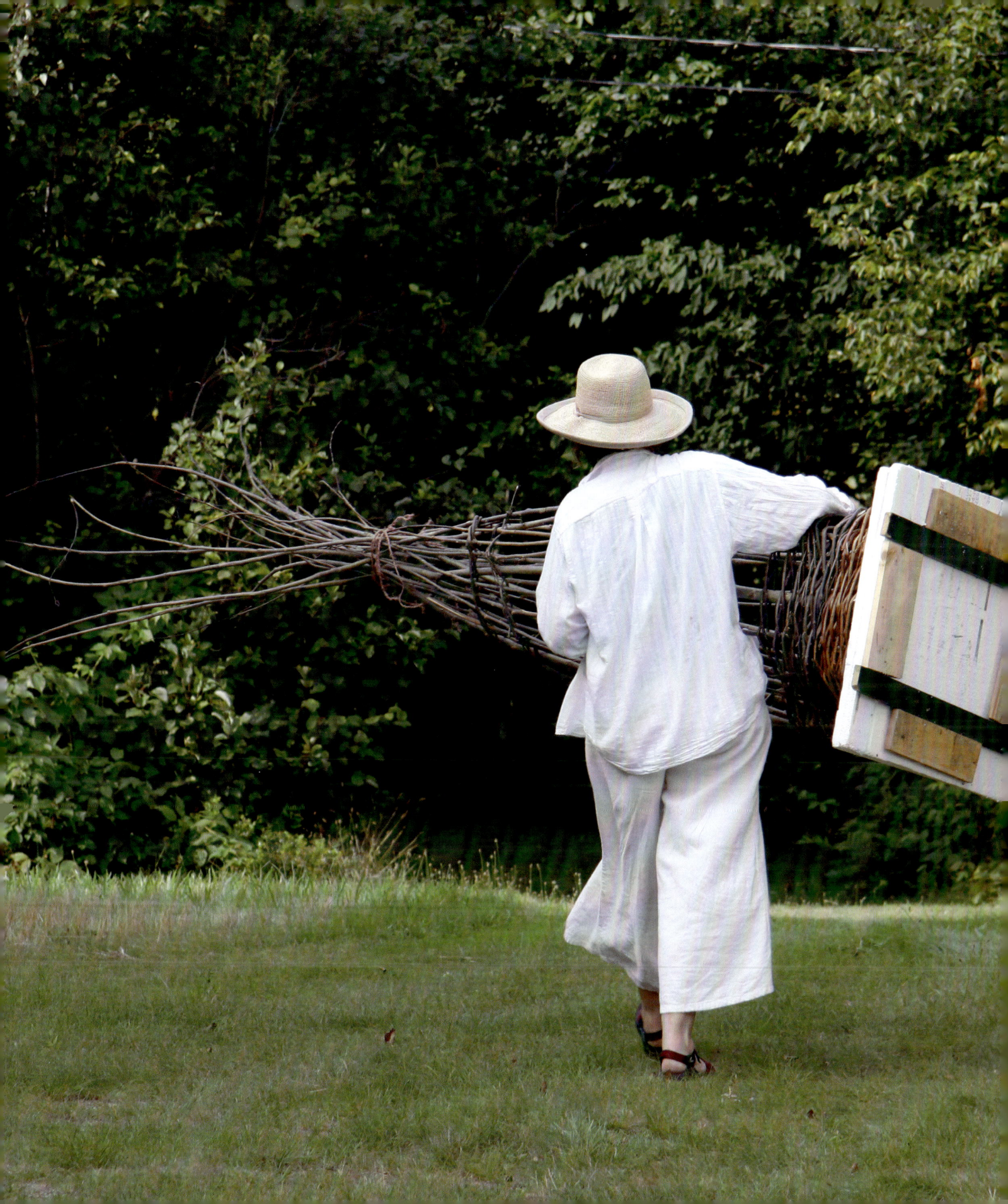

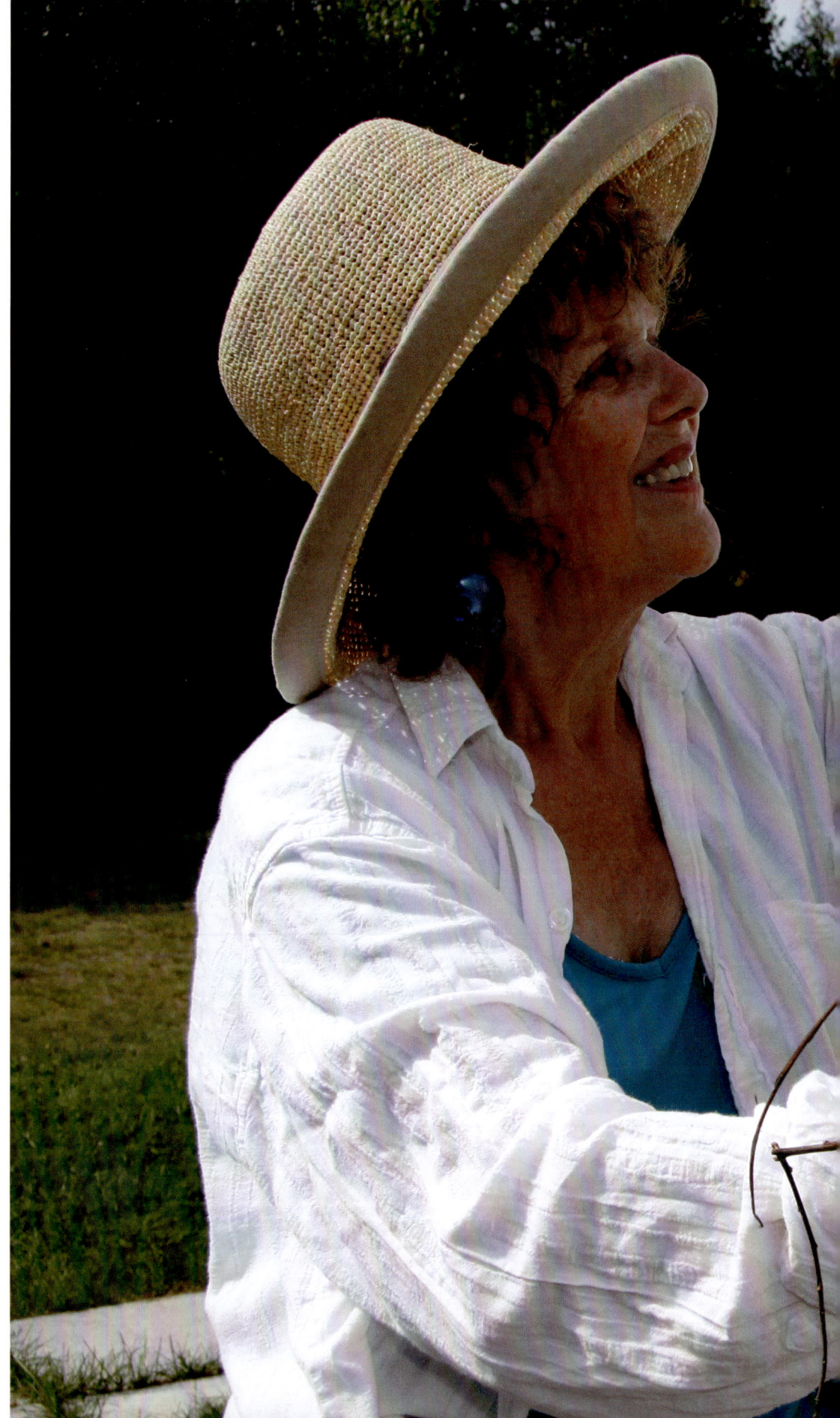

Caring in progress, 2010

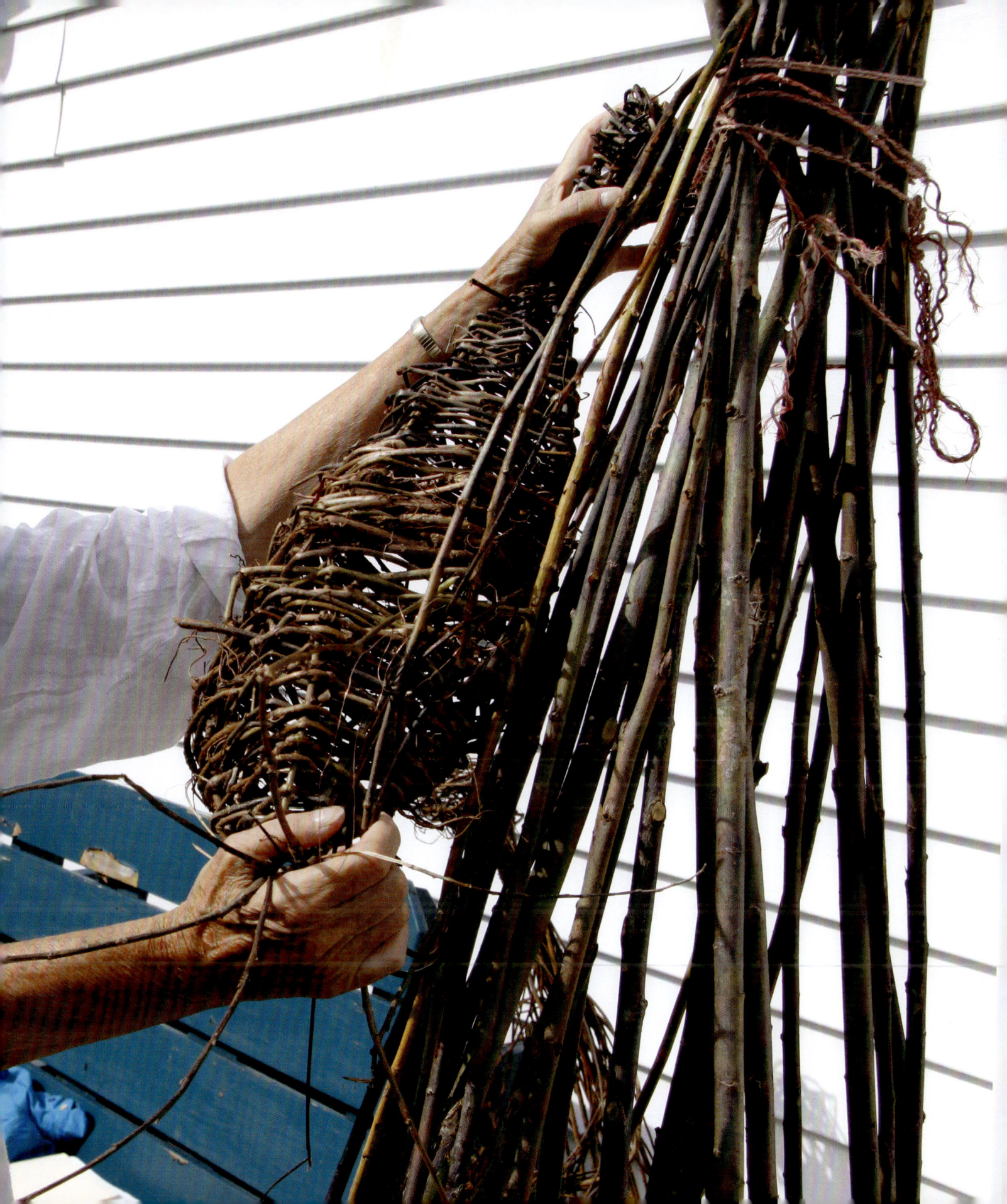

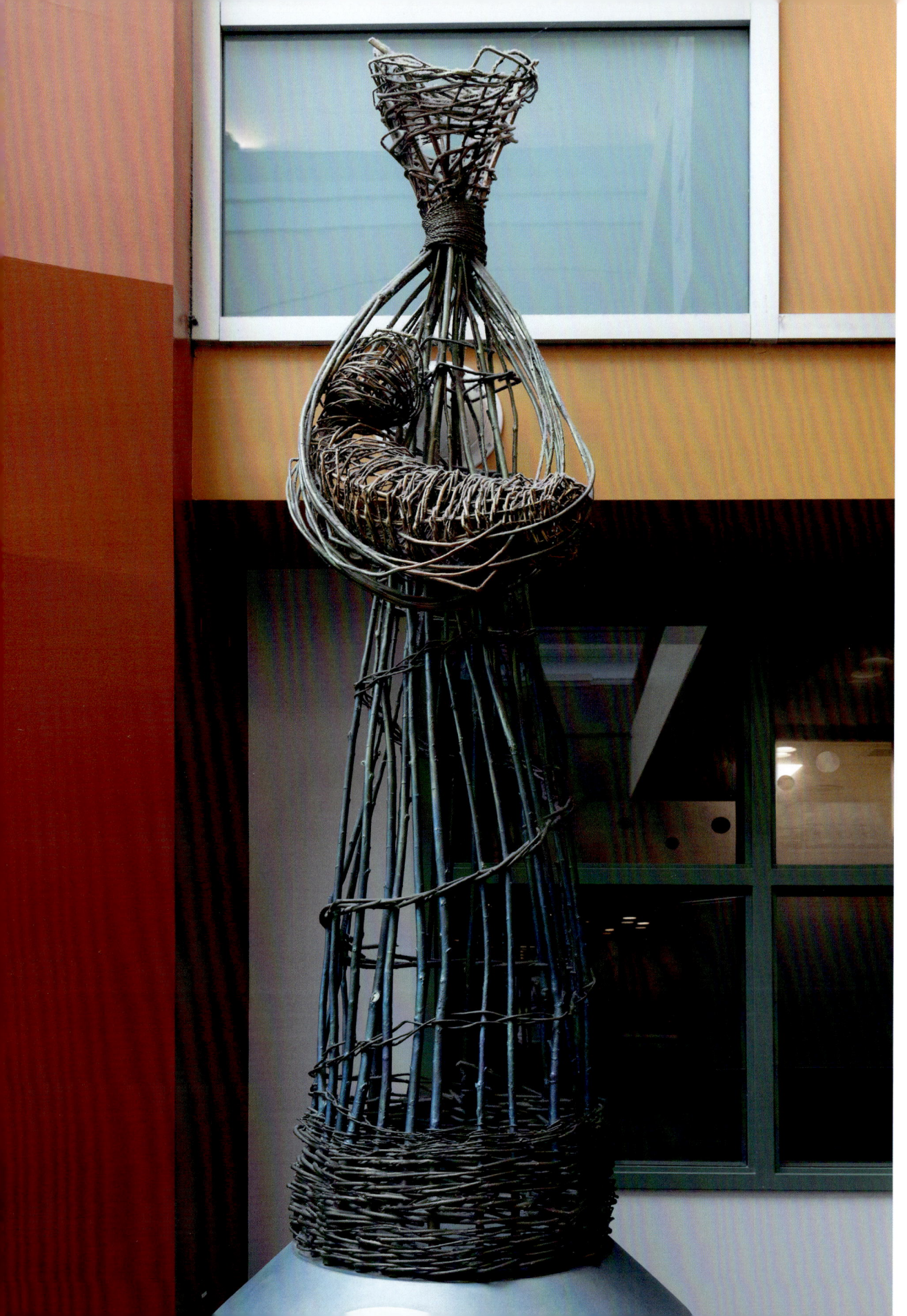

Caring

Caring is a sculpture of a person cradling a child, and it is a work very close to my heart. Through the years, I have created figures of mothers with children in various materials and sizes, and with a number of titles. Where they were once inspired by my own three children, they've been guided by thoughts of my beloved granddaughter Emma since her birth thirty years ago.

My daughter Laura had moved to Bermuda for an architectural internship, and I was visiting her when she went into labour. We boarded a bus while timing her contractions since Emma's father was at work with their one family car. He arrived later, before Emma was born, and we all celebrated her blessed arrival together. That day, I proudly became, and am still, her Momma Dawn. I visited Bermuda frequently until Emma and Laura returned to Canada in 1994. For one exceptional year, she and Laura lived with me in Dartmouth.

Today, Emma and I are usually at least two hours apart by car. She is married and pursuing a career in marine biology. But we speak every week, and she is a cherished inspiration in my life and work, especially *Caring*.

The creation of *Caring* began in 2009, when I was invited by Sarah Moore Fillmore, then curator of the Art Gallery of Nova Scotia, to submit a proposal for the one-hundred-year celebration of the IWK (Izaak Walton Killam) Health Centre in Halifax, Nova Scotia. The commissioning procedure is always an invigorating process. It is often the result of a multi-level competition and usually requires dialogue and compromise on both sides.

Dr. Alex Gillis and Dr. Richard Goldbloom spearheaded the selection committee. While I presume other artists were considered, my first presentation seemed to deeply resonate with them. From that moment onward, there was a lot of concentrated, determined work. I've always found these collaborations to be positive, some more than others. With

Caring, 2010
patinated bronze, cast from
twined willow, acrylic paint
244 × 48 × 48 cm
pedestal 60 × 91 × 91 cm
IWK Health, Richard Goldbloom
Pavilion, Halifax, Nova Scotia

Caring, it was a privilege to see the passion these esteemed pediatric surgeons and administrators had for the creative process.

I wove *Caring* from live willow growing along the ditches near my home in Little Harbour. Merle took great interest in the entire creation process. He helped me harvest the willow and was indispensable in packing up this massive work to send it off for bronze casting. I sketched a special base for fabrication by Mulgrave Machine, a company started by my late brother Robbie, now owned by his children, and still where I turn when I have a design best rendered in steel.

The whole commission took the better part of a year to complete. *Caring* now stands in the Richard B. Goldbloom Pavilion at IWK Health, as it's now called, where the sculpture was installed for the centenary celebration in 2010. The finished work is of a larger than life, four-metre-high figure cradling a baby. I specifically designed it to represent a caregiver of any gender or race. The face is coloured with a basic bronze patina, which not only reflects the colour of the original willow but also an ethnically neutral skin colour. The sculpture is meant to represent everyone with a child they love.

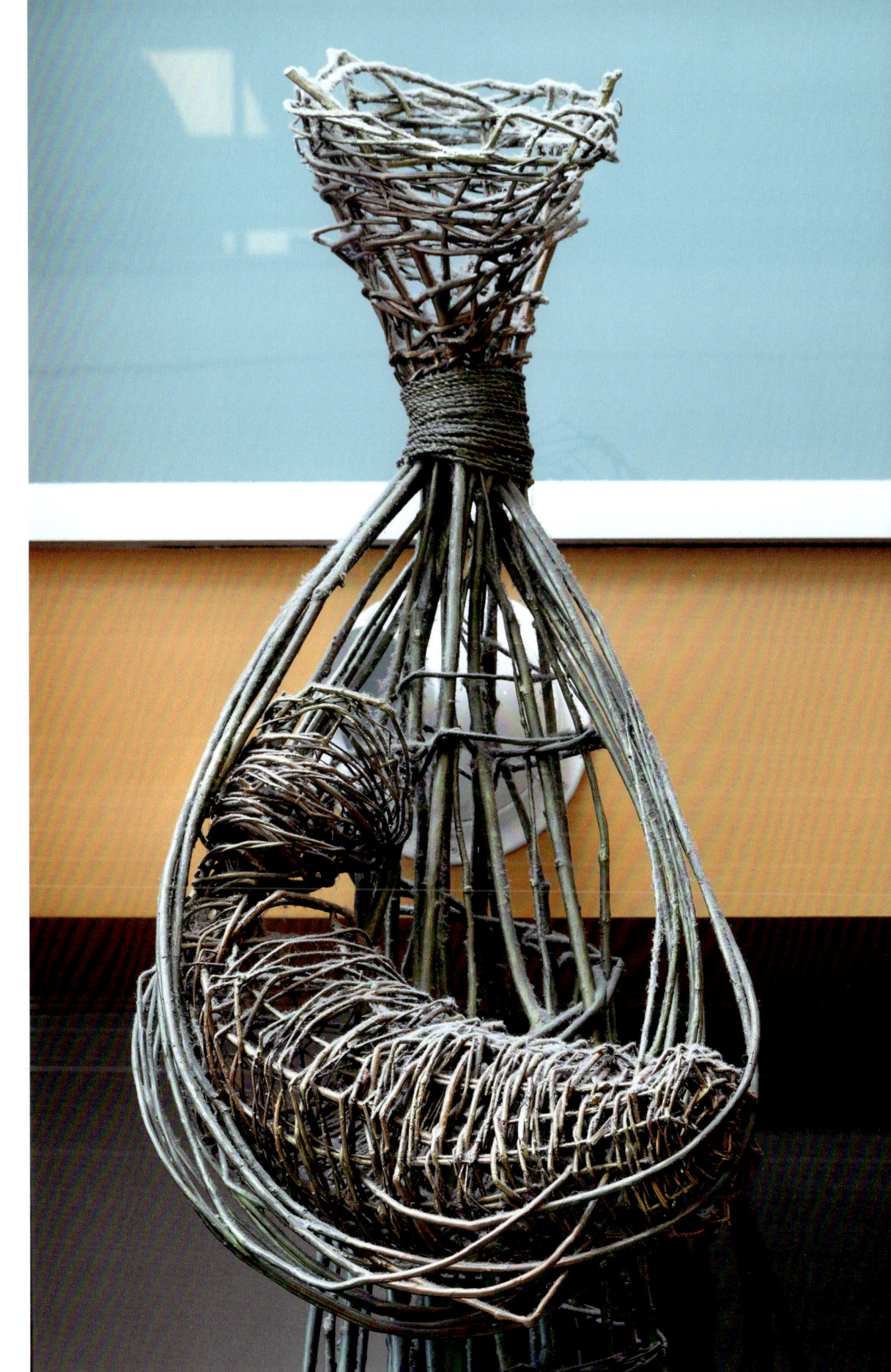

Caring (detail), 2010
patinated bronze, cast from
twined willow, acrylic paint
244 × 48 × 48 cm, pedestal
60 × 91 × 91 cm

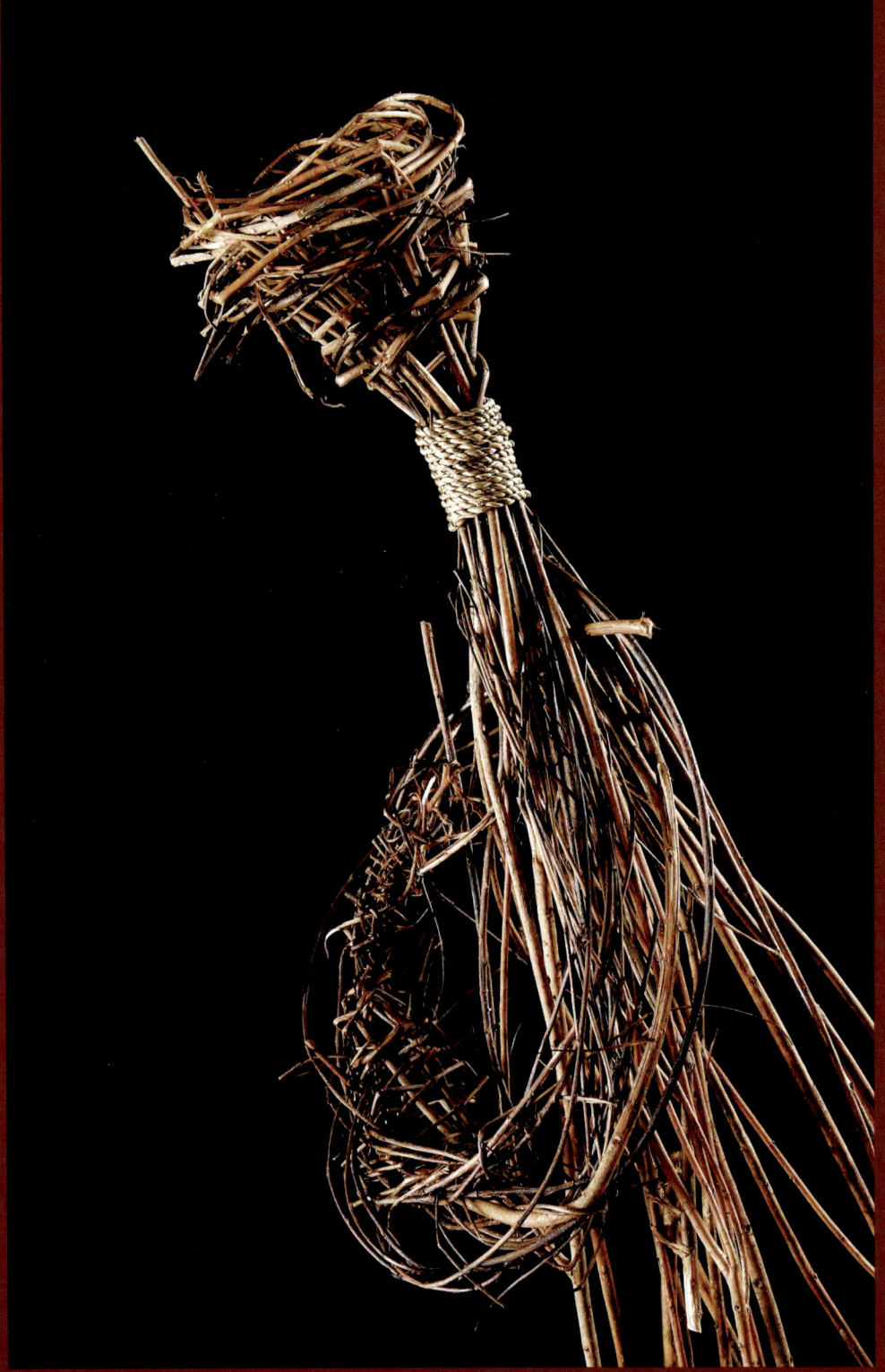

Mother and Child (detail), 2008
twined willow, seagrass
112 × 29 × 30 cm

opposite: *Care*, 2018
bronze, cast from twined willow,
seagrass
111 × 29 × 29 cm

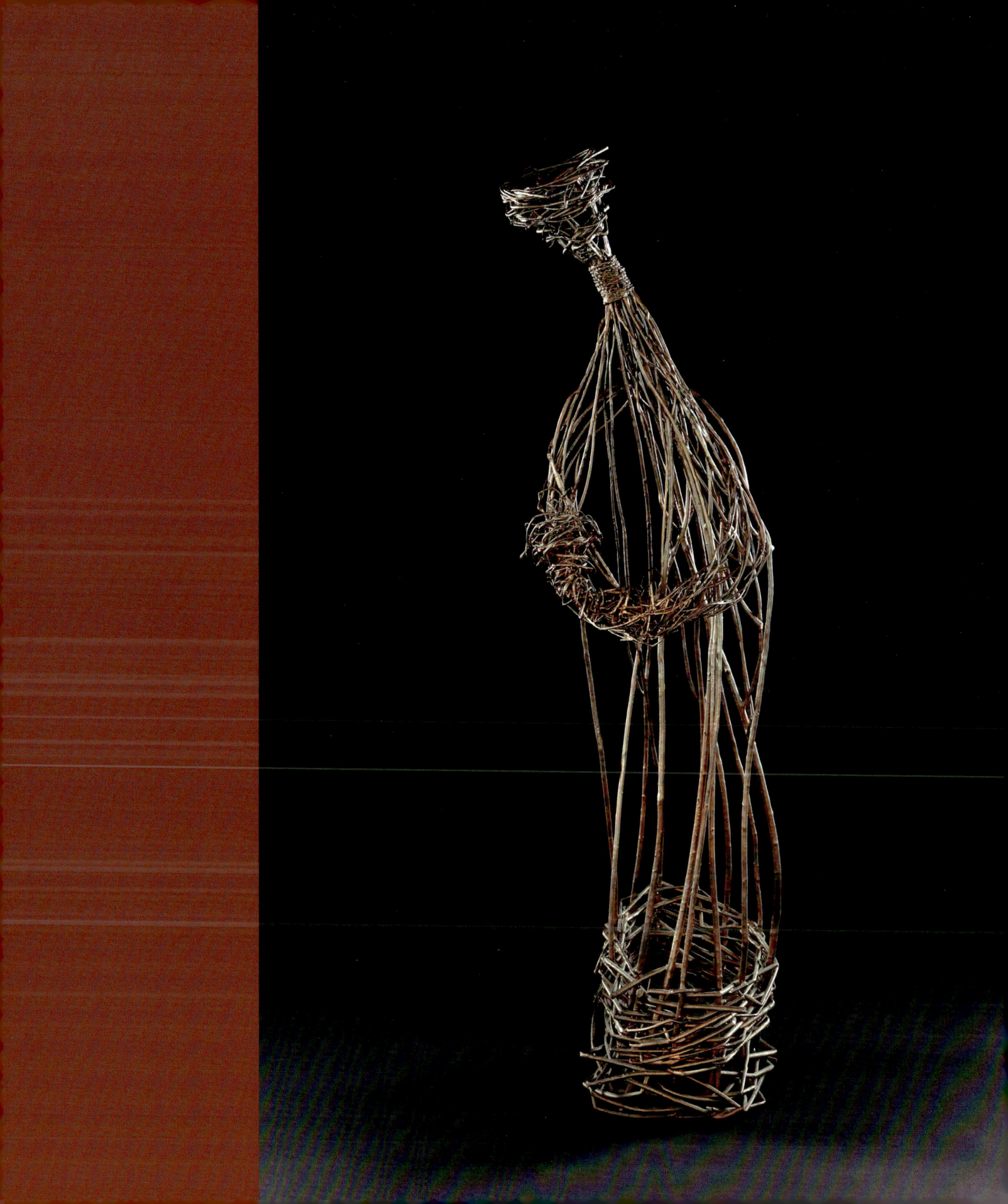

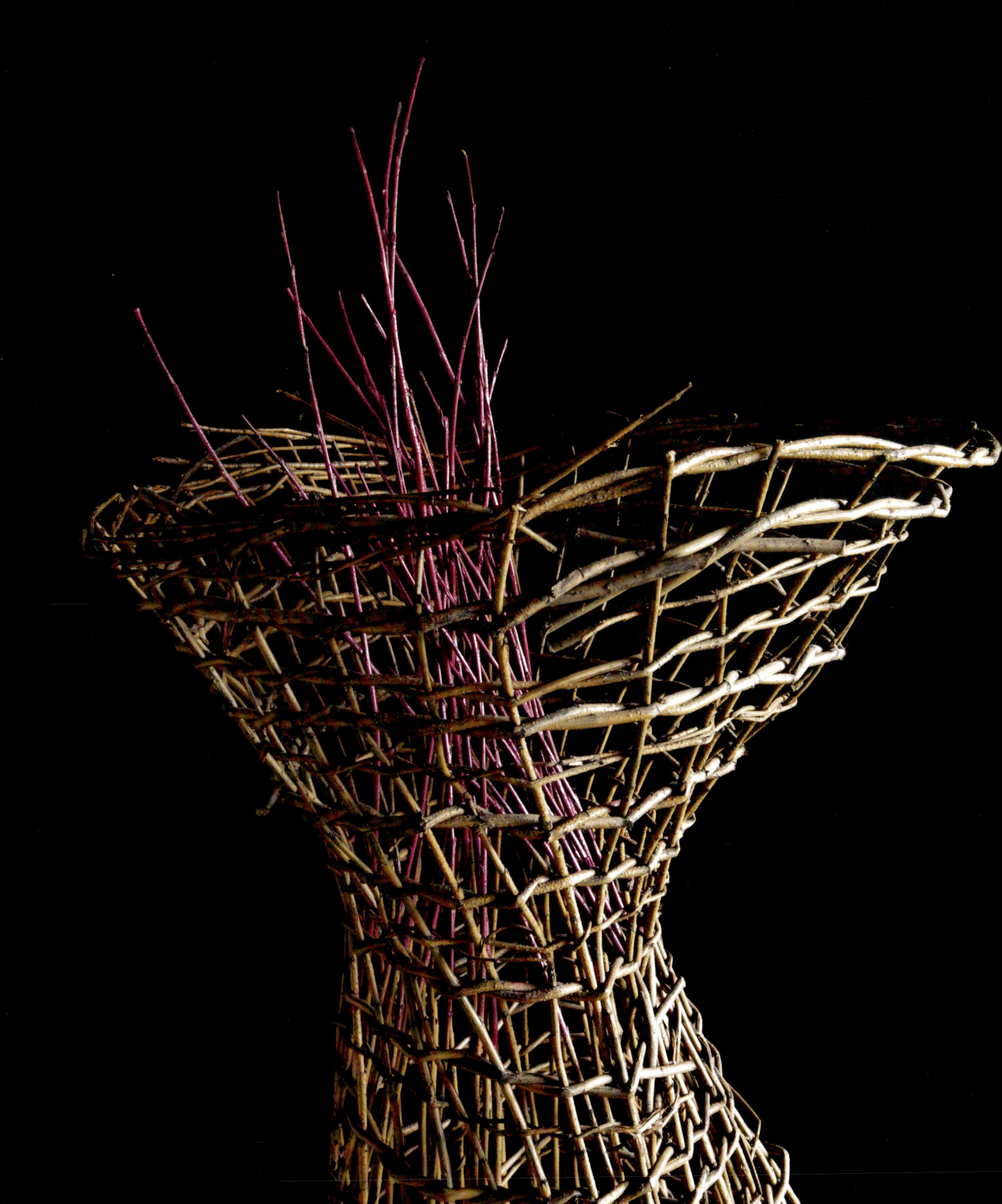

Spirits

During the dark days of April 2020, when terror raged in the small community of Portapique, Nova Scotia, I watched the news and felt something akin to trauma. A heavily armed killer, disguised as an RCMP officer and driving a mock police car, raged from Portapique to Enfield, leaving a trail of brutal mayhem.

When the horror finally ended with the murderer's takedown, twenty-two unique lives had been lost in the horrific thirteen-hour rampage. All residents of the province were stunned beyond belief and saddened by the bloodbath, but for the victims' loved ones, life would never be the same.

Two days later, I trudged to my studio with a heavy heart. I was committed to delivering work later that week, to the Craig Gallery in Dartmouth, for a virtual exhibition entitled *A Fortunate Adversity: COVID-19 Version*. The title now felt impossible. How could anything good come out of this tragedy? I went to the studio in search of relief. To unthink the horror. But as I tried to quiet my mind, I was drawn to stories of the lives ended too soon. As I had been doing for almost half a century, I poured my emotion into the work. The result was three commemorative sculptures representing three of the women lost that day.

Spirit of Joy represents Lisa McCully, who was described as "joyful and happy." In a social media post a few weeks before she died, Lisa sent a message to loved ones forced apart by the COVID-19 pandemic. "Here's a little goodnight song to all our friends and family. We miss you," McCully said cheerfully, holding a ukulele, her two young children sitting to either side. The forty-nine-year-old teacher then began to play and sing a heartwarming rendition of Eddie Vedder's "Tonight You Belong to Me." Her children sang along. All three then wished their viewers good night, smiling at the camera. For Lisa's spirit I symbolized her joy with rose-coloured fronds rising from a figure woven in willow.

Spirit of Joy (detail), 2020
twined willow, acrylic paint
165 × 64 × 55 cm

Spirit of Love symbolizes pregnant caregiver Kristen Beaton, who friends described as loving and kind. "Kristen's name may go down in history because of how she died but believe me, the way she lived is so much more amazing," one wrote. "While we were all staying home wondering what to get on our weekly grocery run, or what to watch on Netflix during this COVID-19 lockdown, she was out there every day, literally, putting her life in harm's way by her continued work for the Victorian Order of Nurses." For Kristen's spirit I added red, the colour of love, to the crown of the work, to her heart, and to her midsection where Kristen was bearing new life.

Spirit of Courage defines Heidi Stevenson, the RCMP officer who sacrificed her life to protect others. "She was just spectacular," retired RCMP sergeant Jerry Mayo told the *Chronicle Herald*. "Phenomenal with kids, with the elderly. Probably one of the best I've ever worked with." She has been described as a bright light whose shining example left this world a better place. Scarlet highlights on her spirit represent her courage and compassion.

The Craig Gallery itself was closed due to the pandemic, but their glazed showcase where the three works were displayed was lit and open to the Alderney Gate Mall. I hope the works help ensure that these women are forever remembered for their goodness rather than for the evil that took them.

Spirit of Joy, 2020
twined willow, acrylic paint
165 × 64 × 55 cm

120

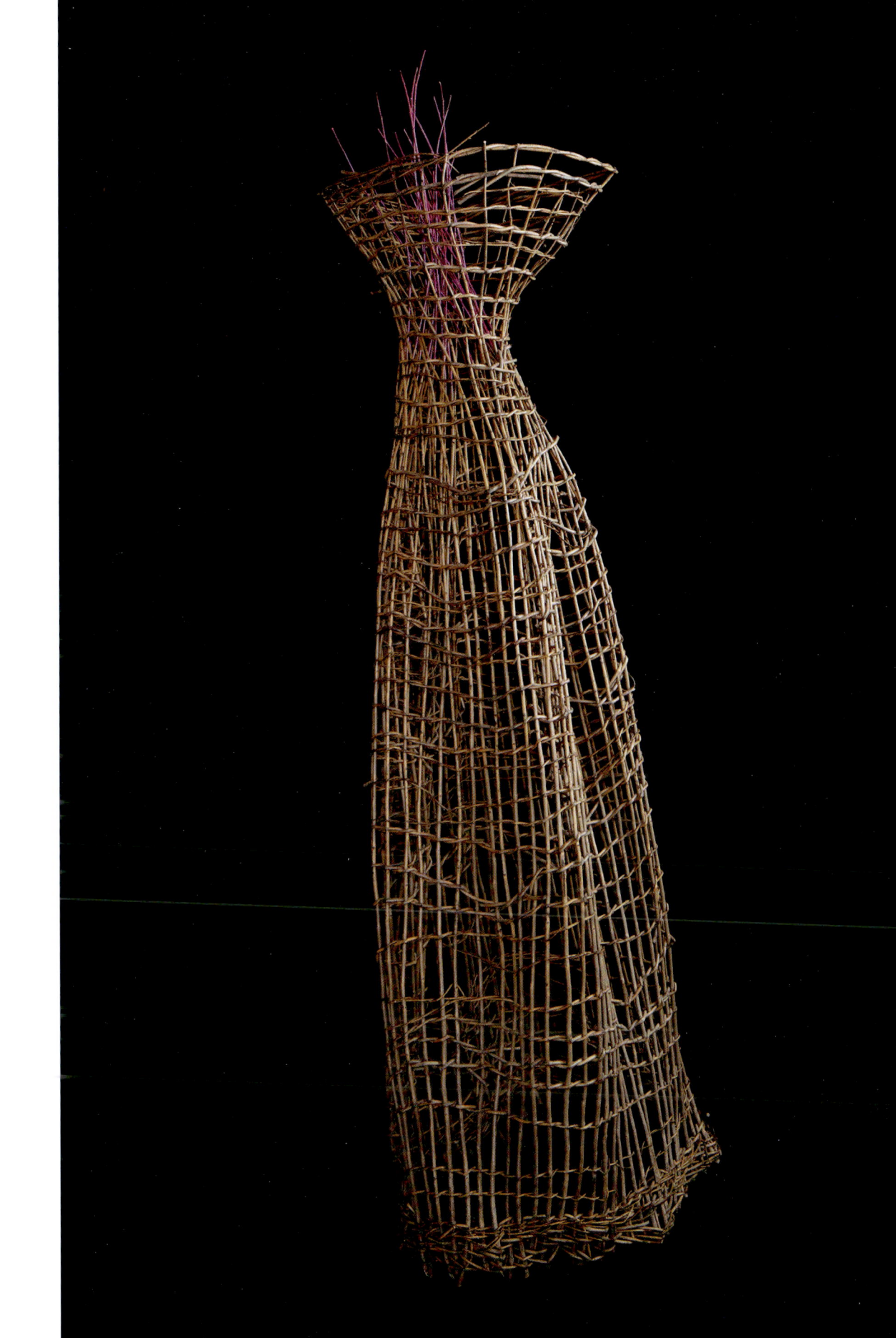

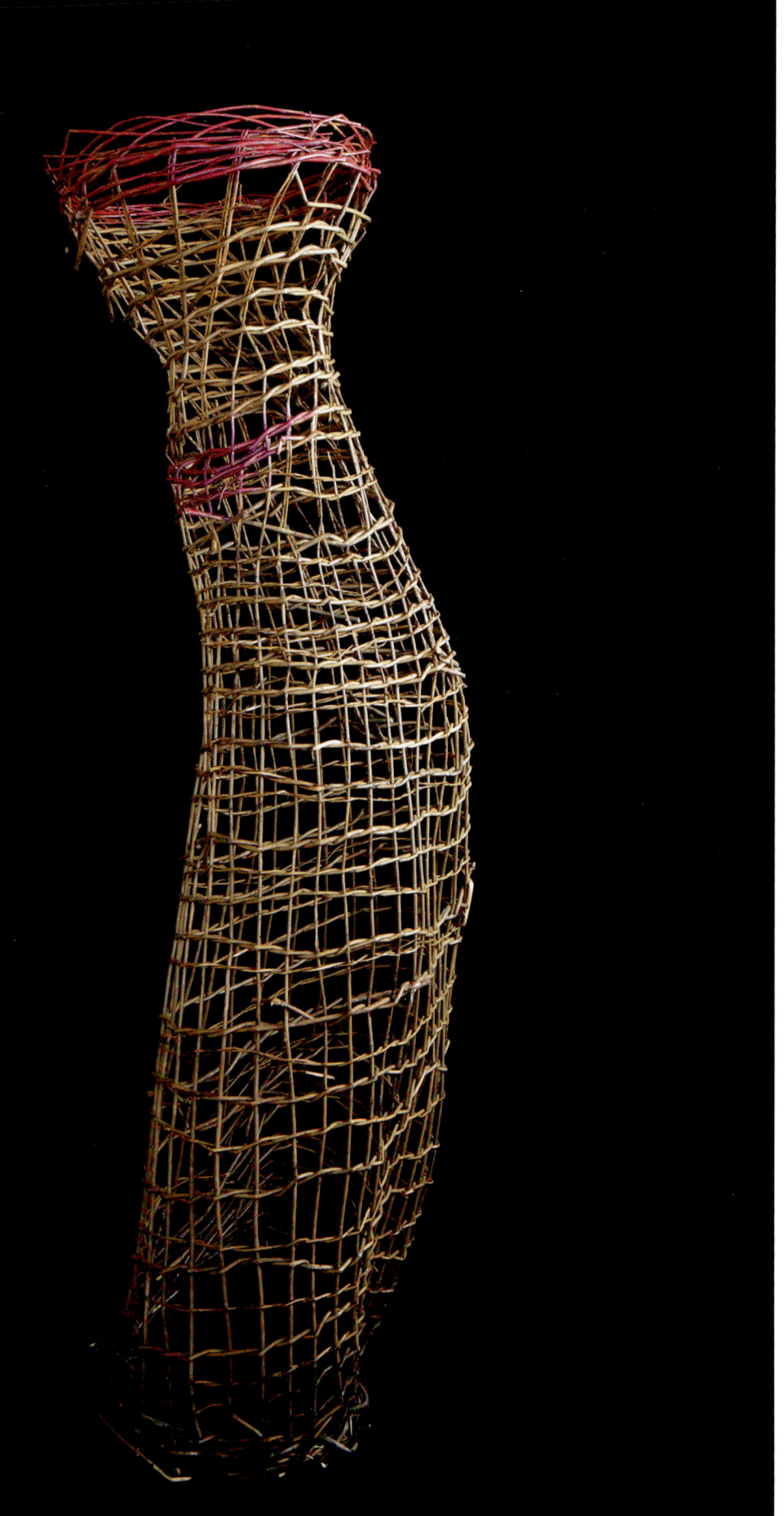

Spirit of Love, 2020
twined willow, acrylic paint
156 × 60 × 55 cm

opposite: *Spirit of Love* (detail), 2020

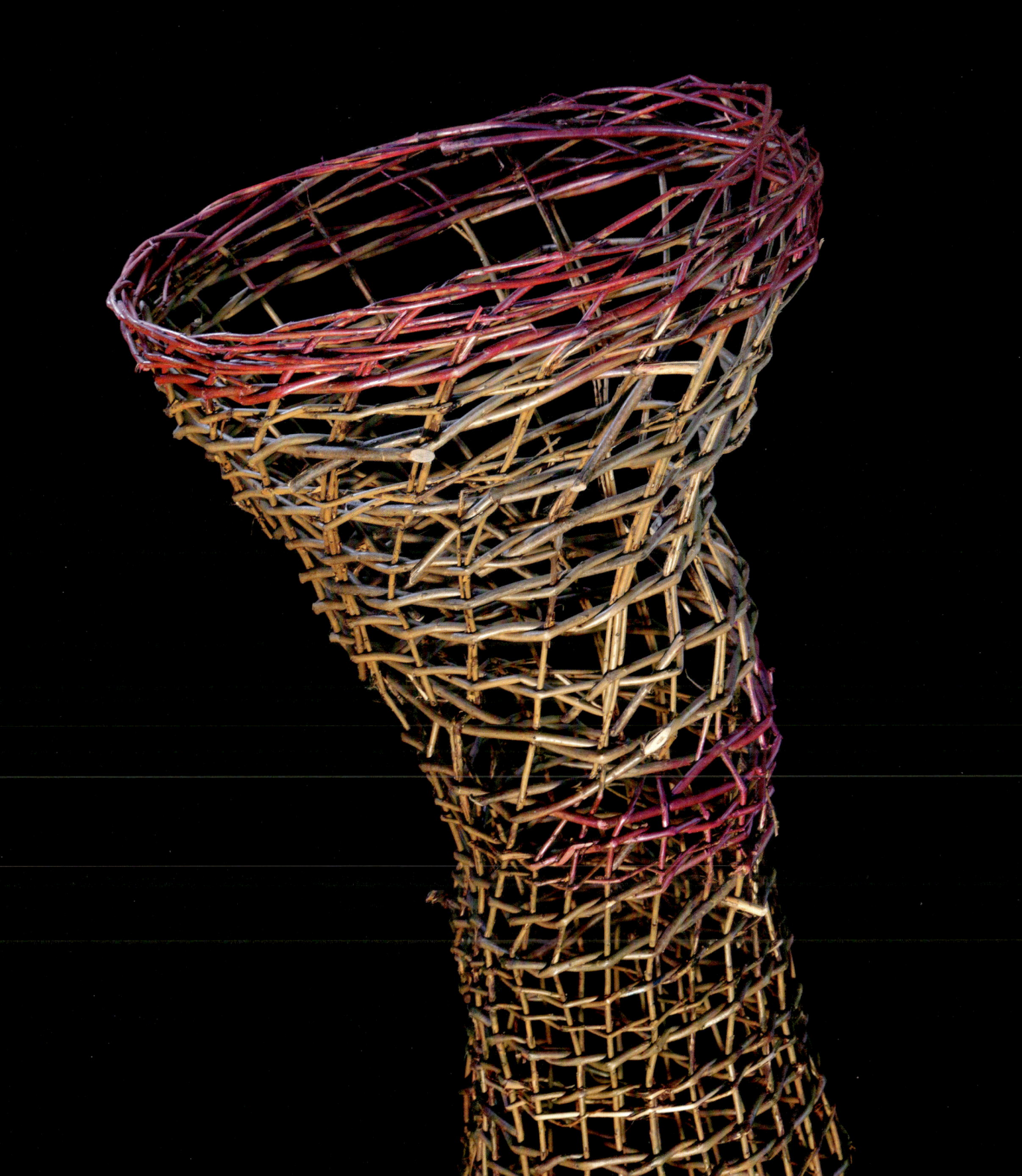

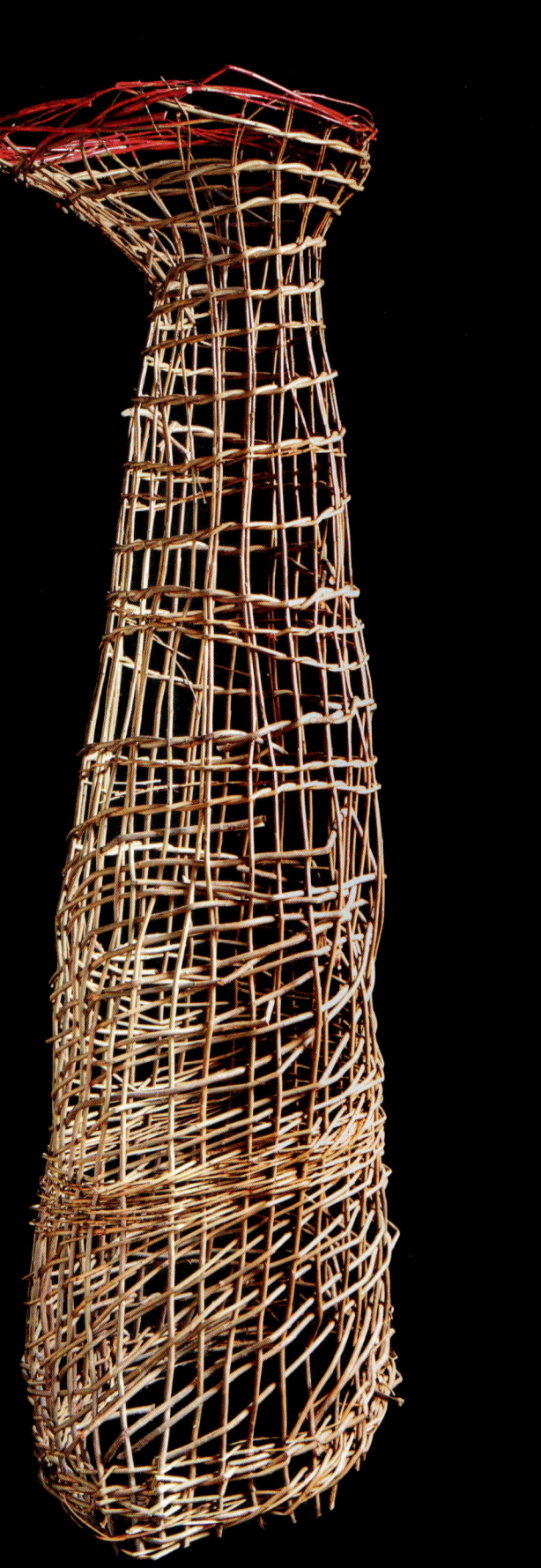

Spirit of Courage, 2020
twined willow, acrylic paint
153 × 62 × 40 cm

opposite: *Spirit of Courage*
(detail), 2020

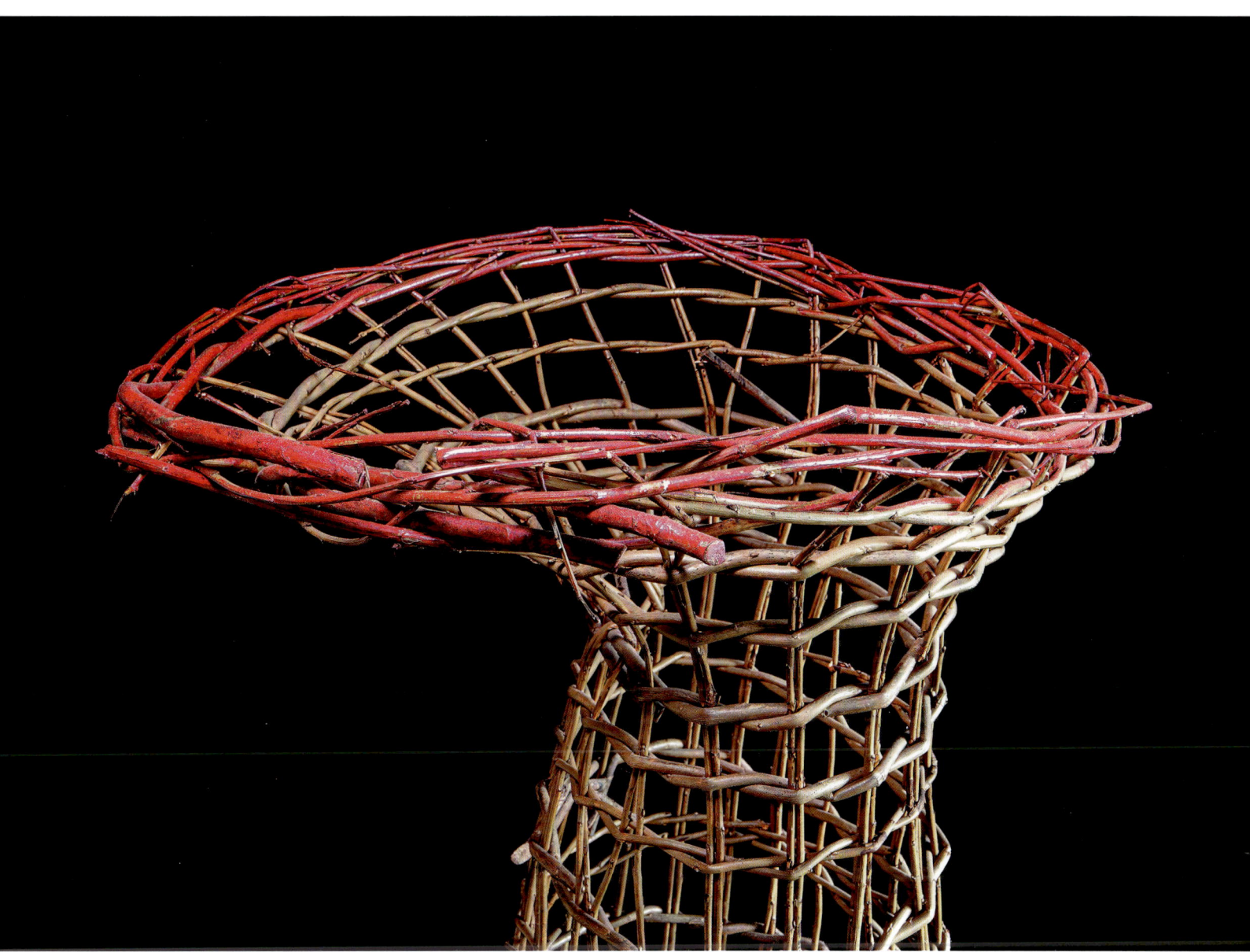

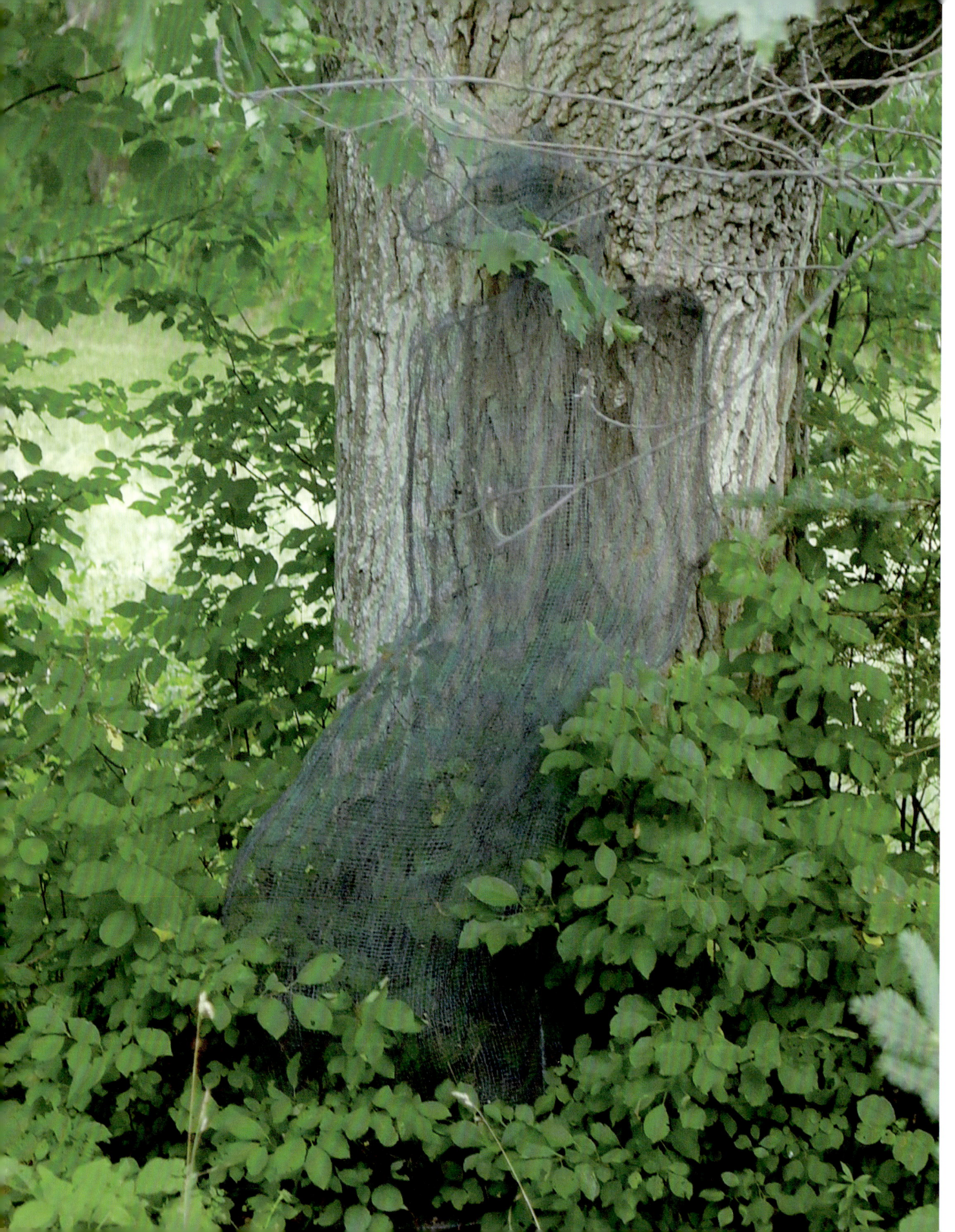

Lost

On a clear May afternoon in 2023, I strolled to the 185-year-old ancestral home on our property that has been my studio since 2006. As I rounded the corner to the verandah where several of my woven wire sculptures usually sit on benches, I stopped, dumbfounded. Instead of their familiar forms, I saw nothing. Feeling unsafe, I walked back to our house. I couldn't speak. I went into my office and didn't come out, or even tell Merle about the robbery, for hours.

I was missing six large figurative, woven copper wire sculptures. For forty years, when not on exhibition, these works had lived wherever I lived, taking up residence in my outdoor spaces. I wove them on a loom from wire, sculpted them into figures by hand, and had them electroplated to stiffen the wire so they held their shape. Some of the figures were also patinated to create a lovely verdigris finish.

While I absorbed the shock, I managed to identify the missing pieces. I found photographs of them and reported the theft to the authorities. I held little hope of recovering the works, as I suspected they were already being sold and melted down for their copper.

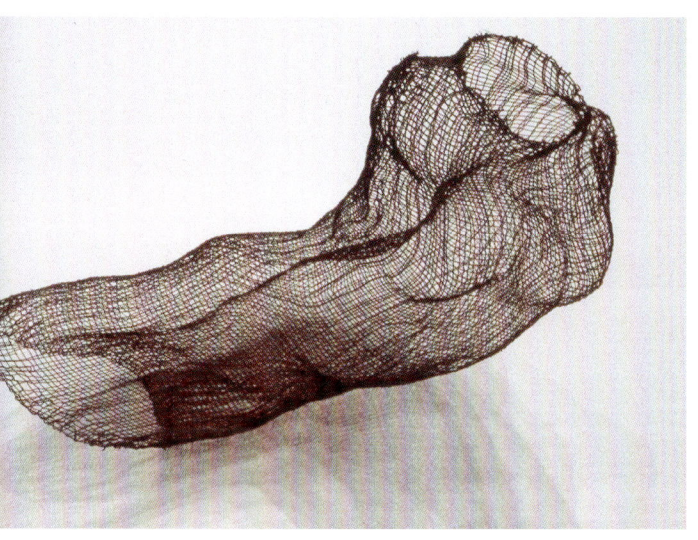

Female Torso, 1984
copper wire woven on loom,
electroplated, patinated
40 × 84 × 53 cm

opposite: *Unfinished Figure*, 2004
copper wire woven on loom,
patinated, welded copper
armature
251 cm high

Little did the thieves know that these sculptures were worth thousands of dollars.

I wrote to my children, and word spread like wildfire as my daughter Laura mounted a social media campaign to warn salvage yards and try to recover the sculptures. I was both surprised and heartened by the compassion shown by friends and strangers alike. I felt violated and disappointed but, honestly, I was not angry. These were just things. No one died or got hurt. I truly felt sad for the thieves. If they are hungry, I'm sorry. If they are addicted, I'm sorry. If they have no remorse, I'm still sorry.

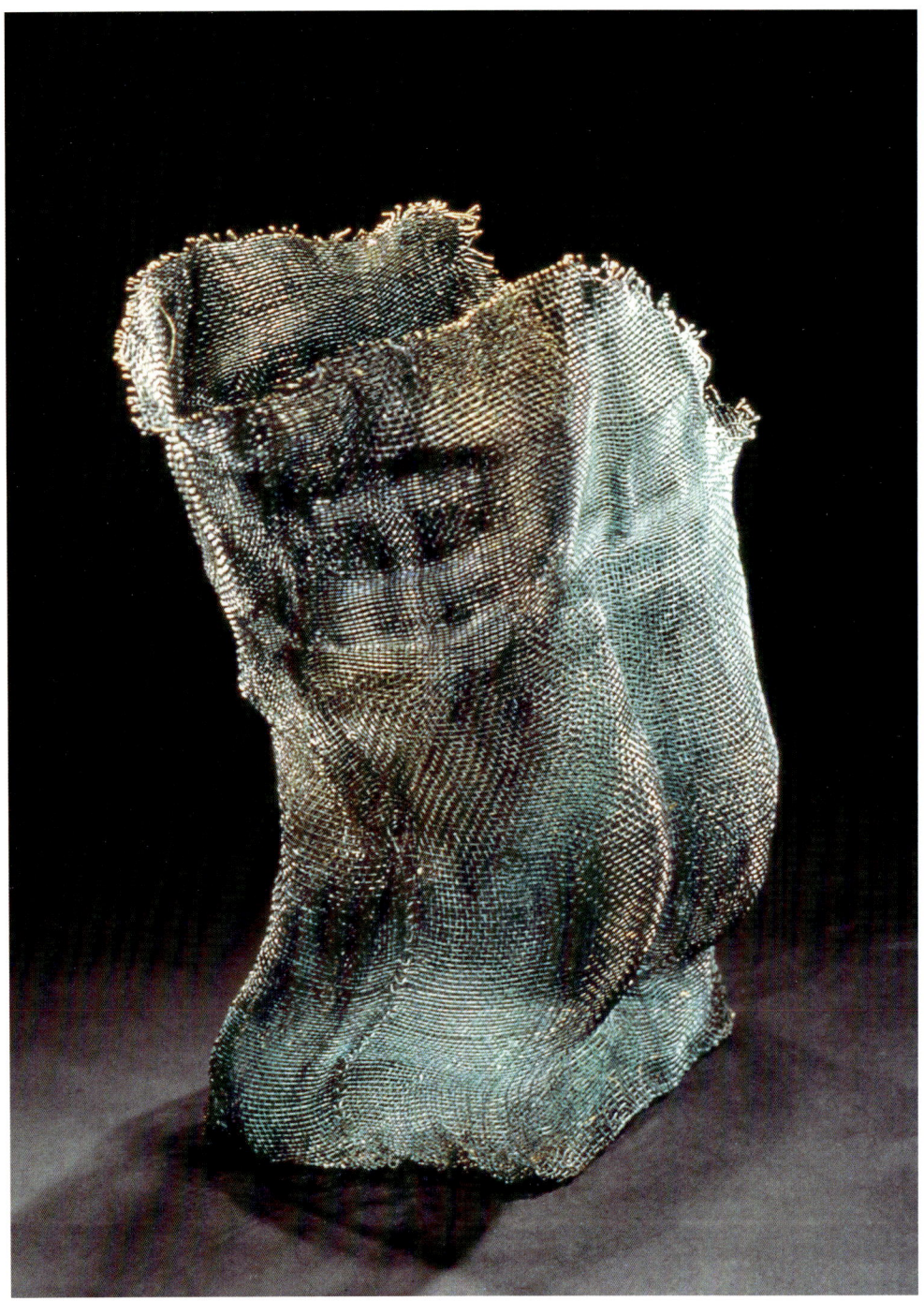

Male Torso, 1984
copper wire woven on loom,
sculpted, electroplated,
patinated
40 × 30 × 26 cm

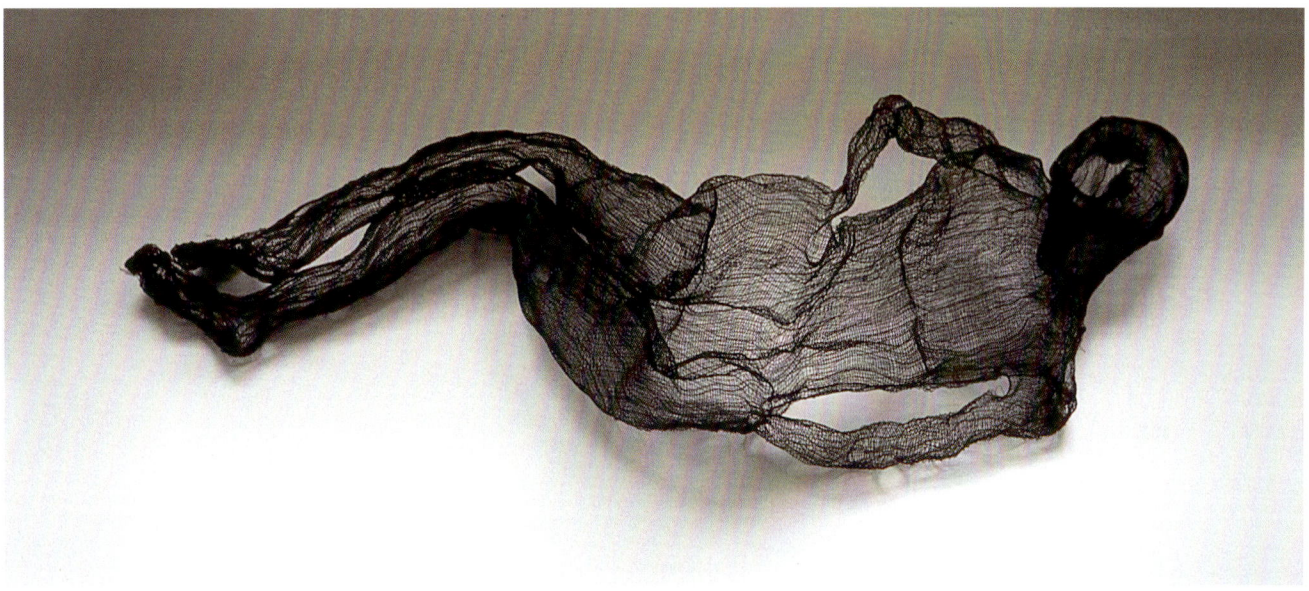

Turning Away, 1983
copper wire woven on loom,
electroplated, patinated
approx. 40 × 168 × 53 cm

The lost pieces have never been recovered. They had all been exhibited in years past, but there was one that was very important to me that I had hoped to include in an upcoming retrospective exhibition of my work. *Turning Away* was the only autobiographical piece I have ever done. It developed almost subconsciously during a difficult time at the end of my first marriage. When I finished forming it, I realized I had inadvertently sculpted a broken soul. I threw it down on the floor, looked at it and thought, "That's me." It was a dark piece. But it had a place in my body of work. Maybe this was fate's way of telling me it was time to put that work, and that time, behind me.

Almost fifty years ago, a rejection letter from an exhibition pointed out that the work might not be bad, but the photograph was not good enough to describe it. After that, I hired a professional to document my work. For twenty years, it was Peter Barss, and later, it was Bruce Murray. We would work together for hours to "stage" the work in the studio or in nature. It was exhausting — and hugely fun. Without those photo sessions, I would have no record of my stolen work!

Grecian Figure, 1990
copper wire woven on loom, sculpted,
electroplated, patinated
112 × 46 × 41 cm

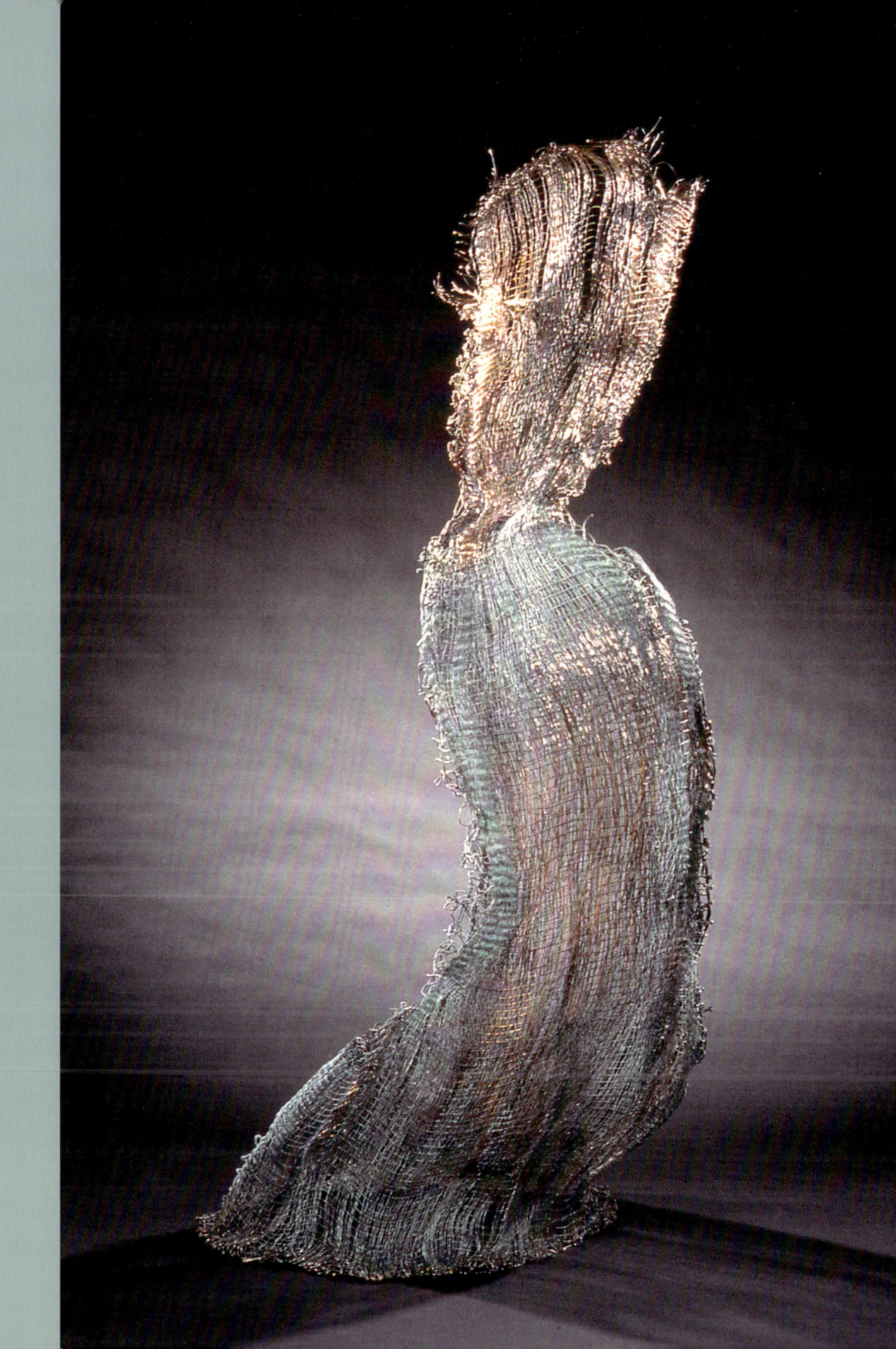

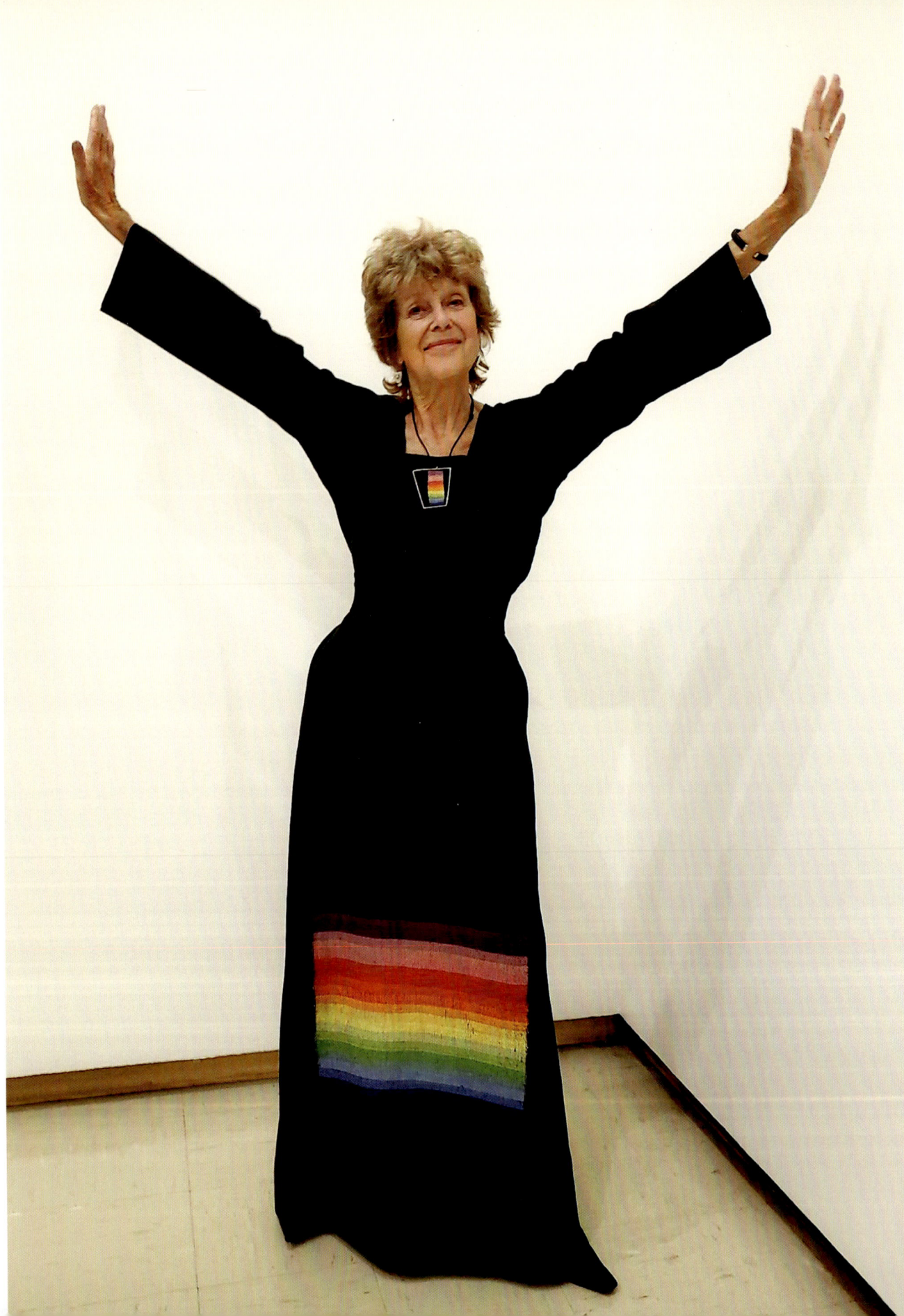

Bright Colours on a Dark Background

When Her Majesty Queen Elizabeth II visited Canada in 1976, my husband Scott and I were invited to three events. To mark the occasion, I decided to weave a multi-purpose outfit: a black dress with two aprons, meaning it could be worn three different ways. One version would simply be the black dress. Another would add a natural apron with lace. The third featured a black apron with brightly coloured stripes. This last was inspired by my vivid memory of that special dress my mother wore on our train trip to Montréal in the 1940s, with its "bright colours on a dark background."

The royal occasions themselves were a bit of a blur: a reception on the yacht *Britannia*, a luncheon at Government House in Halifax, and a reception at the Queen Elizabeth Hotel in Montréal. I had no expectation of making chit-chat with Her Royal Highness and Prince Philip. While exciting for me, the queen was duty-bound to receive the endless lines of curtsying and bowing strangers with their limp — or overzealous — handshakes, each one nervously mumbling "Your Majesty." It must have felt like the royal equivalent of grading widgets on an assembly line. Yet, for that brief moment, with each person, she always made direct eye contact. When I wore the striped apron, I'm sure I saw her eyes flick downward for a nanosecond to the brightly coloured rainbow!

A year later, I submitted the dress and aprons to a Nova Scotia Designer Crafts Council exhibition. While it was there, I had a phone call from Sheila Stevenson, the executive director of the council, who asked if the NSF (not for sale) label was absolute. She told me that Hart Massey (the son of Governor General Vincent Massey) and his cousin Geoffrey Massey (the son of the actor Raymond Massey) were travelling around Canada purchasing works to become part of the Massey Collection of Fine Crafts, which would both tour the country and become a permanent collection.

Black Dress and Rainbow Apron, 1973
hand-woven fine single-linen yarn

The Massey cousins wanted my dress, and furthermore, they did not like the value I had declared, which was $80 for the cost of the yarns. They wanted to pay $125 for each of the three pieces of the dress: a handsome $375 in 1976! Would I reconsider? I would, and I did, but the price was not what changed my mind. It was the recognition of inclusion in their national collection as a work of fine craft.

Eventually, after touring Canada and being featured in a book, the Massey Collection of Fine Craft was donated to the Canadian Museum of History in Hull, where it lay in storage for forty years.

Just before COVID-19 hit in 2020, Jane Tisdale, fine arts conservator at the Owens Art Gallery in Sackville, New Brunswick, had begun preparing an exhibition entitled *Warps, Heddles, Shuttles and Sheds: The Art and History of Weaving at Mount Allison University*. Borrowing from private and public collections, Jane obtained hundreds of woven works by Mount Allison alumni.

My daughter Laura and I went to see the exhibition when it opened in the summer of 2021. Seeing how the dress and aprons came alive on mannequins — hung at a perfect level for close viewing — felt like a reunion with a long-lost friend. "Wouldn't I love to slip into that dress for a moment!" I exclaimed. Unbeknownst to me, Laura, ever fearless, asked Jane. Jane consulted the Museum of History, and lo and behold, they granted permission for me to try on the dress before it was returned to storage — as long as we were very, very careful. *Yes!* In collections around the world, there are untold treasures like mine, buried in boxes and hidden from view. Applause for everyone who gives them the light of day and shares the joy they bring!

Jane arranged a space in the Owens, and Laura and a resident photographer captured the moment. No one was more surprised than I when the original hook-and-eye closure closed snugly without a stretch. It fit just right. I was instantly transported from being eighty-five years old to being thirty-nine again. I raised my arms to the sky in celebration.

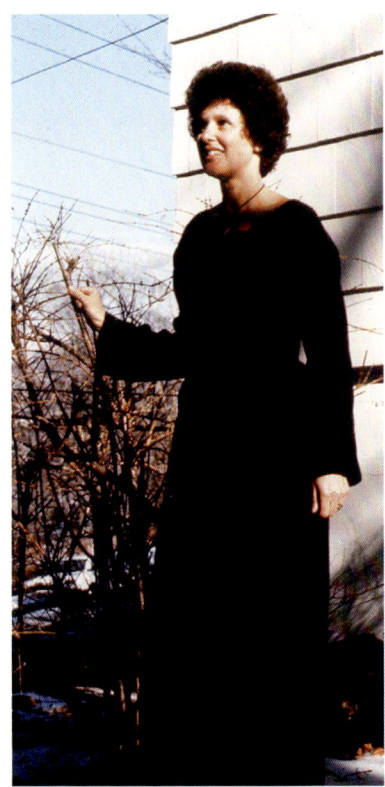

Black Dress, 1973
hand-woven fine single-linen
yarn

Black Dress with Finnish Lace Apron, and Two Belts, 1973
dress hand-woven of fine single-linen yarn; apron with
Finnish lace pattern woven of fine, natural, single-linen yarn

Detail of *Finnish Lace Apron*, 1973

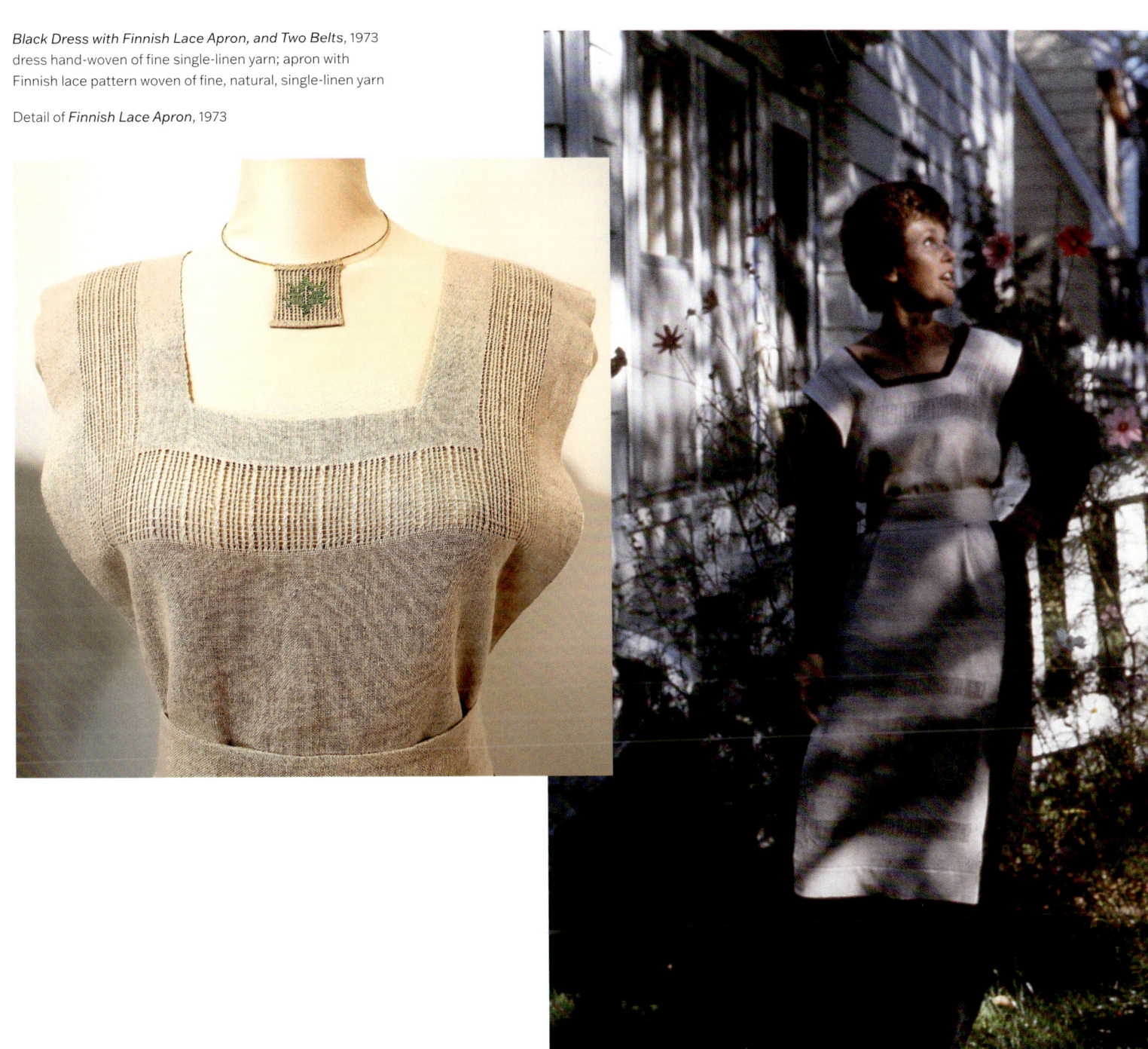

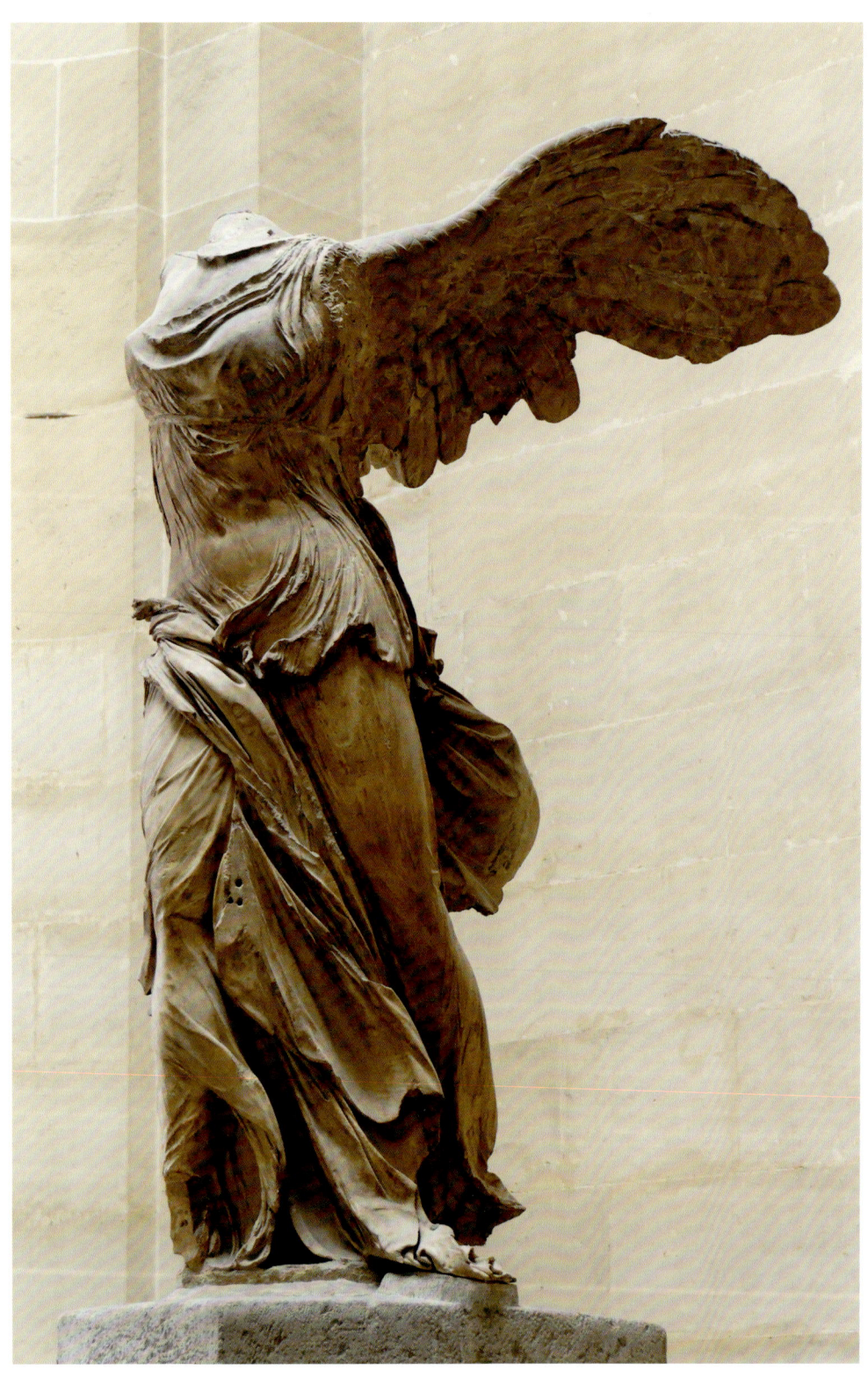

Winged Nike of Samothrace,
c. 190 BC
Louvre Museum, Paris
photo: Marie-Lan Nguyen

Muse

In the summer of 1959, my college roommate, Lorna, and I travelled around Europe on a Lambretta scooter for four months. A major highlight was the Louvre in Paris. In the world's largest museum, we indulged ourselves to the point of saturation and exhaustion. The experience was life-altering.

I saw the triumphant Greek sculpture Winged Victory of Samothrace during that first trip, but it was Leonardo da Vinci's *Mona Lisa* — the small, unobtrusive gem — that lingered in my mind.

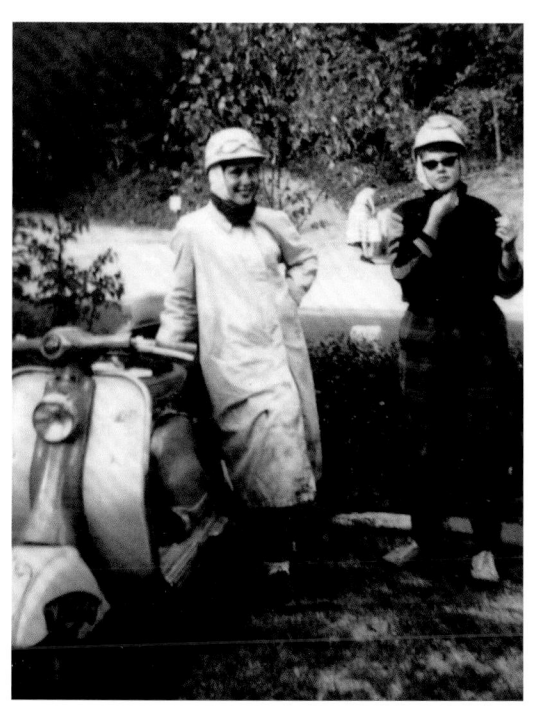

Lorna (left) and Dawn travelling in Italy, 1959 (photo: unknown)

On returning to the Louvre with Merle sixty years later, we decided to focus on particular areas to visit in depth, rather than trying to do it all and drowning in inspiration.

Suddenly, looming at the top of a grand marble staircase, I saw it. Winged Victory. I gasped, realizing: this sculpture had been living in my head and my heart since I first saw it in 1959 — for all my years of making sculpture. My muse. She was my unconscious, or maybe semi-conscious, source of inspiration for so many of my works, and I had not recognized her poignant influence till then. I whispered a prayer of thanks: *Thank you, unknown artist.*

Muse, the verb, means *to think about something carefully and thoughtfully.*

Muse, the noun, means *a state of deep thought or dreamy abstraction; a person who is a source of inspiration.*

Reflecting on my work, I realize that both the muse and the act of musing, have been central to my process for decades, ever since I sat on the staircase in my grandmother's home as a little girl, gazing through the prisms of the stained-glass windows, dreaming and creating.

It makes sense, then, that in 1993, when the Cultural Federations of Nova Scotia asked me to create awards for leaders in several categories of cultural activity, I returned to the concept of the muse. In mythology,

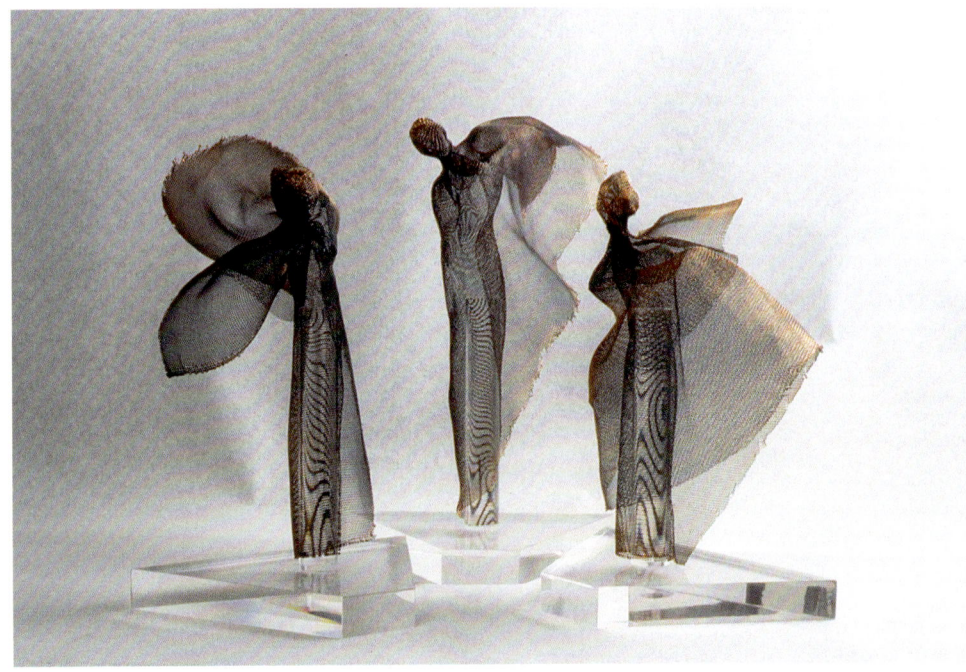

Muses, Cultural Life Awards, 1993
woven copper wire cloth, sculpted, electroplated, patinated, acrylic bases
38 cm high

opposite: *Muse Calliope*, 1994
woven copper wire cloth, sculpted, electroplated, patinated, cast bronze base
86 × 56 × 31cm

the muses were the inspirational goddesses of the arts and sciences. For the Cultural Federations' awards, I turned to Calliope (epic poetry), Euterpe (music), Terpsichore (dance and choral singing), Thalia (comedy), and Clio (history) to serve as muses for my creations.

The word "museum" comes from the Greek word *mouseion*, which means "shrine of the Muses," or any place dedicated to them. In 2005, I was invited to create a monumental outdoor sculpture at the International Sculpture Symposium at the Andres Institute of Art in Brookline, New Hampshire. As I drove to the place of my two-week artist residency, I pondered the fact that a museum is also a place *to muse*. And I recalled a childhood experience of being in a chapel in the woods at Camp Geddie, a summer camp in Merigomish, Nova Scotia. Trees surrounded an enclosure of benches, creating a serene cathedral-like space of contemplation. At the Andres Institute, this memory inspired me to create a room in the woods, bounded by trees, that I called *A Personal Museum*. I created a clearing and placed in the centre a long, flat rock for resting. Entry to the rounded enclosure was marked with two columns constructed of welded bronze rods and woven wire. The end result was a beautiful place to muse.

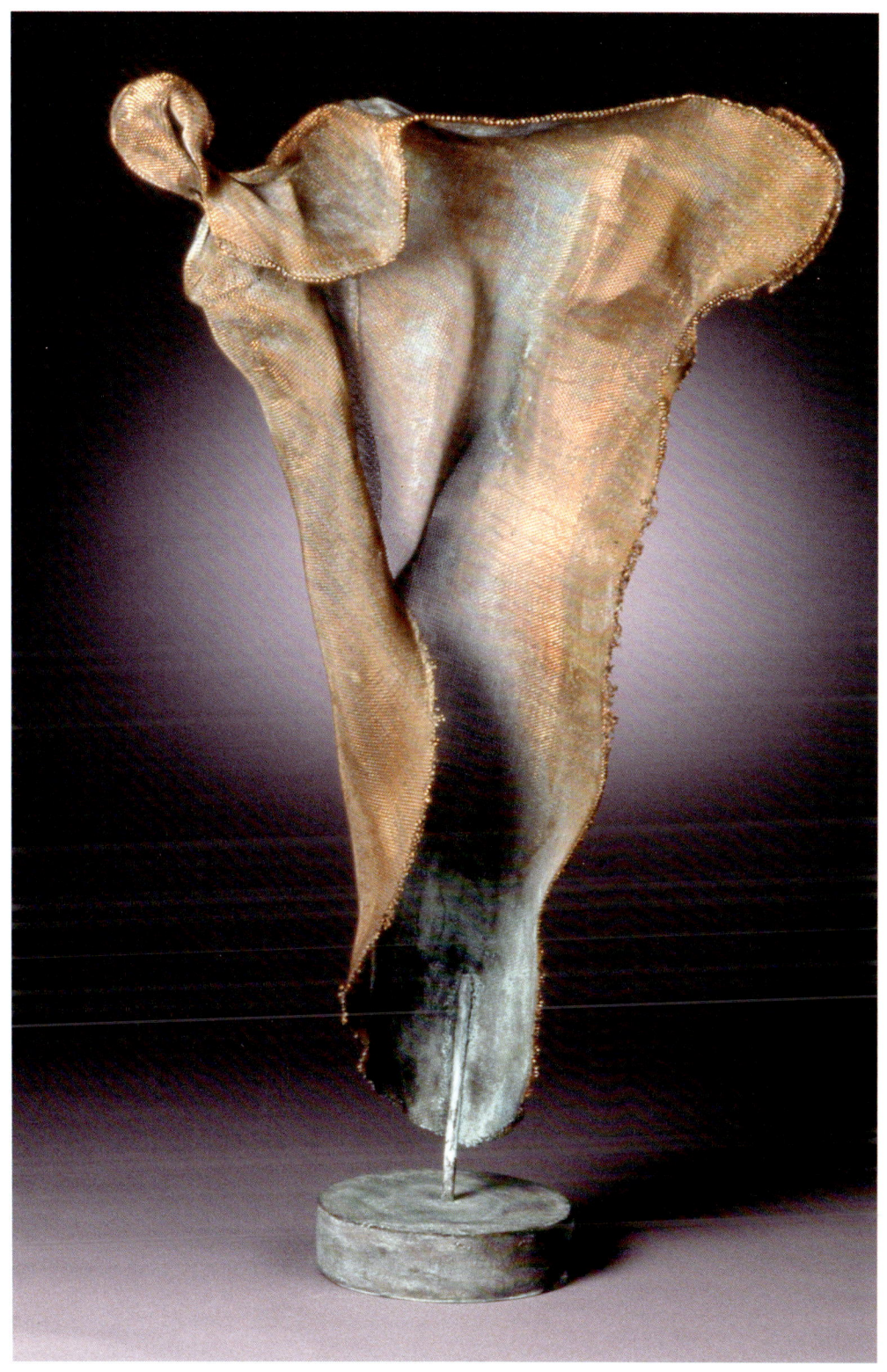

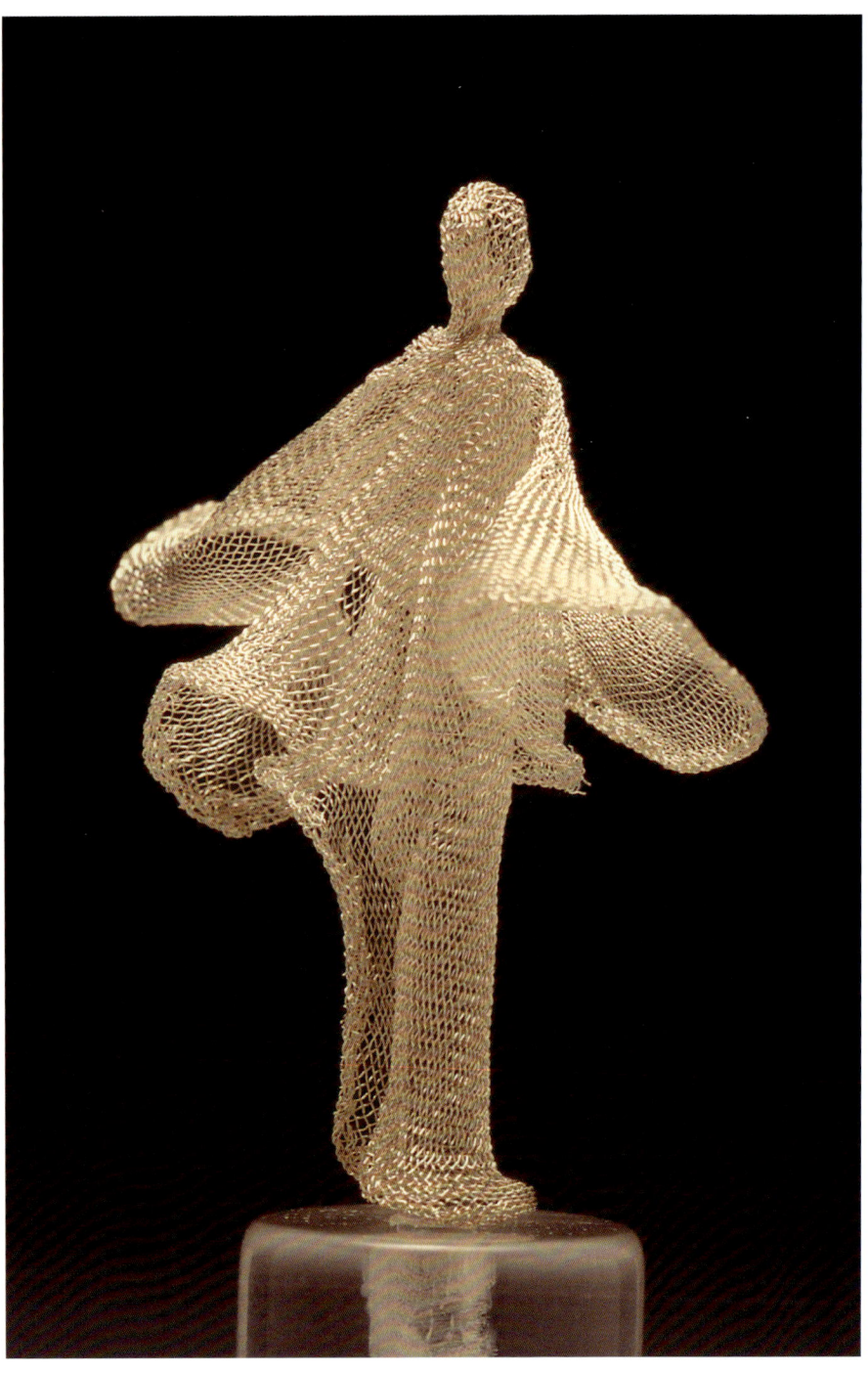

Miniature Silver Muse, 1993
woven fine silver wire, sculpted,
acrylic base
5 cm high

opposite: *Clio*, 1994
woven wire cloth, sculpted,
electroplated, patinated, cast
bronze base
86 × 56 × 30 cm

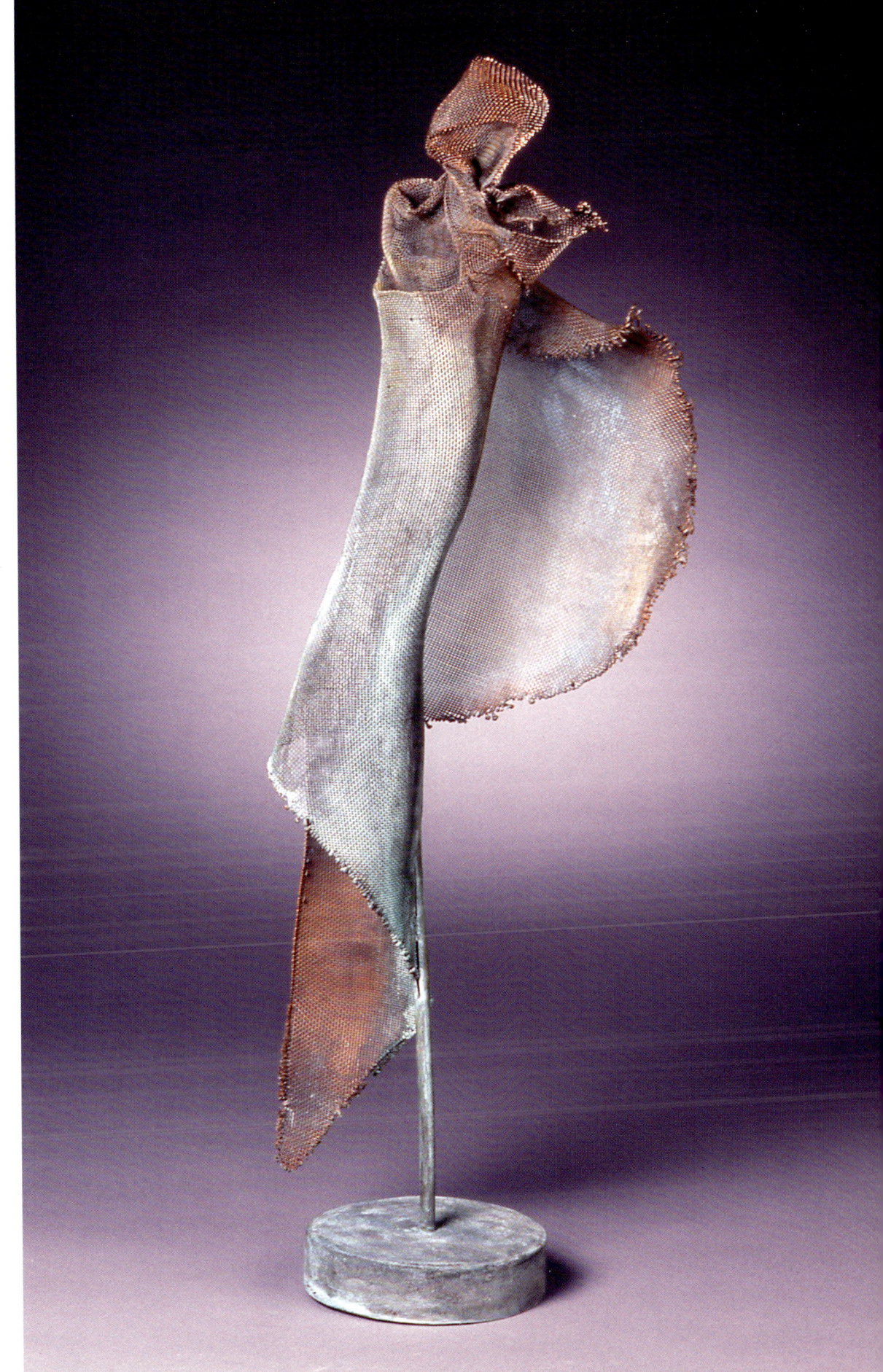

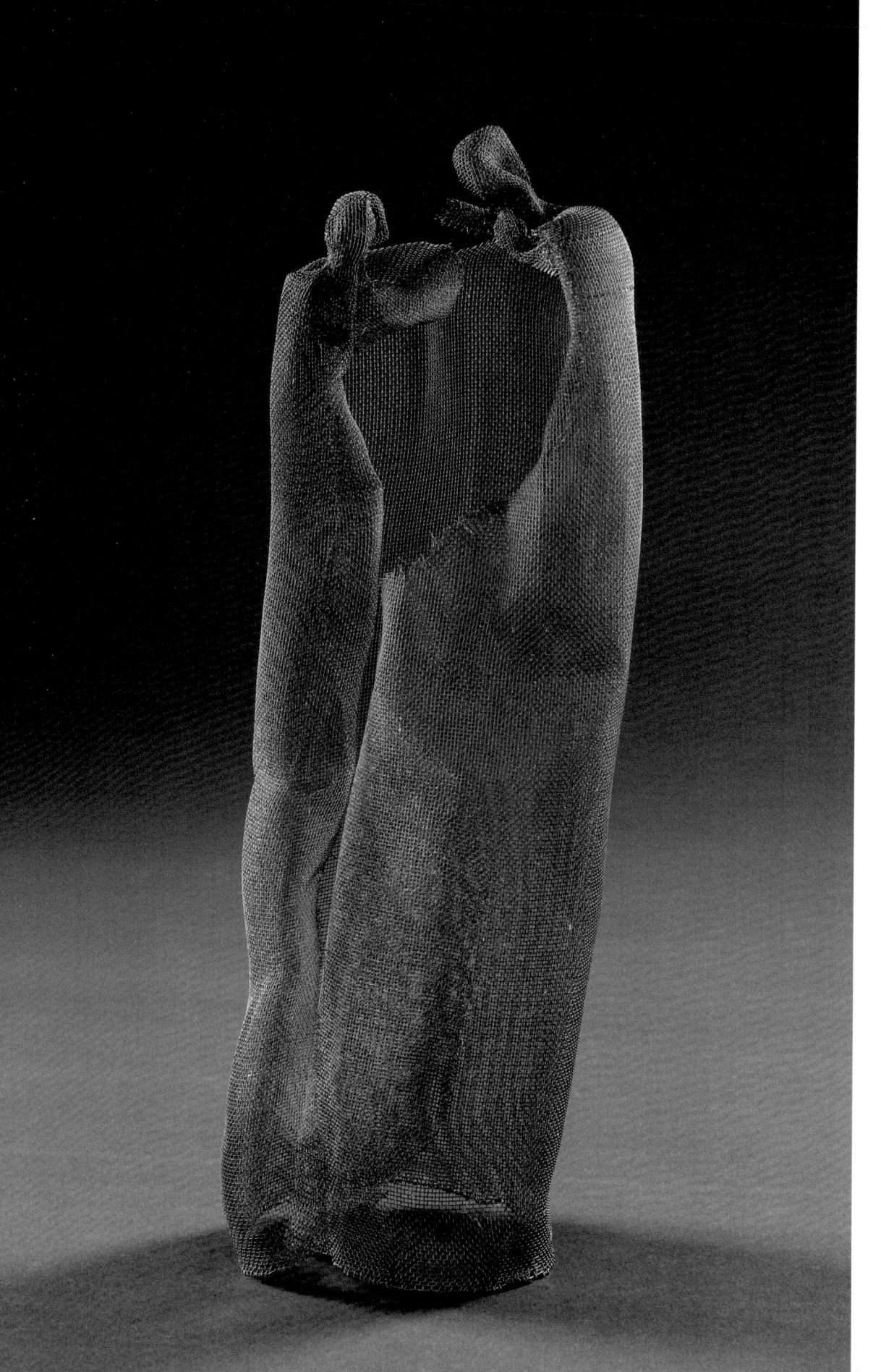

Soft Shadows, 2004
woven wire cloth, sculpted,
electroplated, patinated, acrylic
paint
34 × 14 × 10 cm

The concept of the muse returned to me in 2011, when Sackville, New Brunswick, commissioned a public sculpture to welcome visitors to their town hall. Placed on a low, embellished plinth that signifies the horizontal landscape of the Tantramar region, the figure represents a person enlightened through an encounter with art. I called it *Muse on the Marsh*.

In 2022, the concept of the muse inspired me when local artists were invited to propose artwork for the new Pictou Culture Hub, which would embrace both the existing deCoste Performing Arts Centre and the new Pictou-Antigonish Regional Library. I proposed a tall bronze sculpture called *MUSE!* I added the exclamation point to the title because I like to think of it as a call to action, even a lively command! The sculpture will stand at the front entrance of the hub as an invitation to engage with all its cultural offerings. Whether you are coming to read a book, attend a play, listen to music, see an art show, talk or hear a talk, perform or attend a meeting, the hub will provide spaces "to think carefully about things" and "to be inspired." In essence, to muse!

Even though the cost of casting my woven work in bronze has become prohibitive, I boldly suggested a two-metre-high bronze statue. (At eighty-seven, I'm in my "now or never" era!) I was delighted to win the commission.

In anticipation of the honour, I had been working for months on the body of a large muse-like work in twined willow. Finding an indoor space to finish it presented a problem. In the mid-1970s, I had worked on two large-scale commissions in an unfinished basement space with little natural light. And now, fifty years later, in the midst of winter, I completed *MUSE!* on a horizontal table in an unfinished basement with little natural light. It's full circle, but I'm delighted to still be creating — to still be guided by the muse.

As I write this, *MUSE!* has just been shipped to the foundry for the months-long process of having its delicate willow burned away and replaced with enduring bronze. My greatest wish is that someday, someone may round the corner — just as I did that fateful day in the Louvre — and be stopped in their tracks when they see *MUSE!* And they will be inspired to gaze, think, connect, create, feel…and muse.

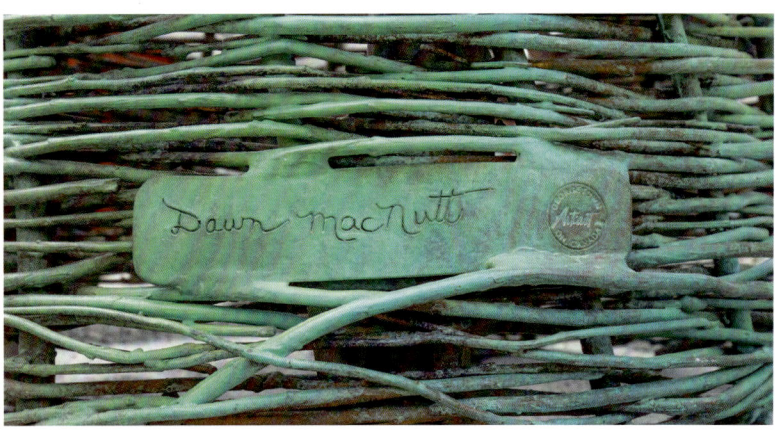

above and opposite: *MUSE!*, 2024
patinated bronze cast from woven willow,
acrylic paint, crowned with gold leaf,
granite base
244 × 122 × 84 cm
Pictou, NS

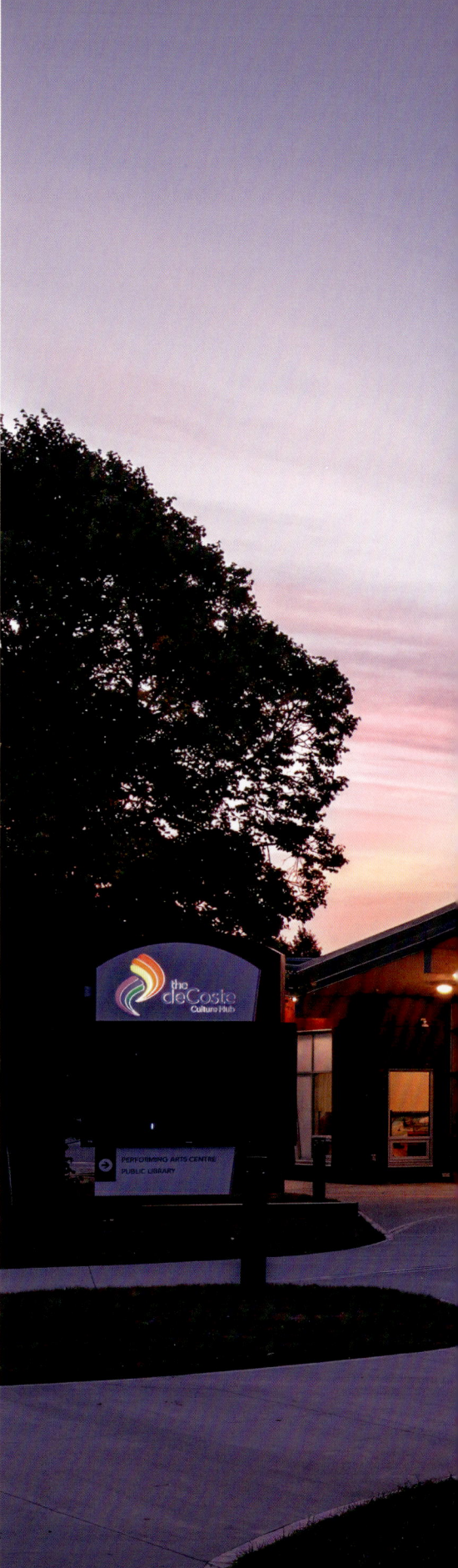

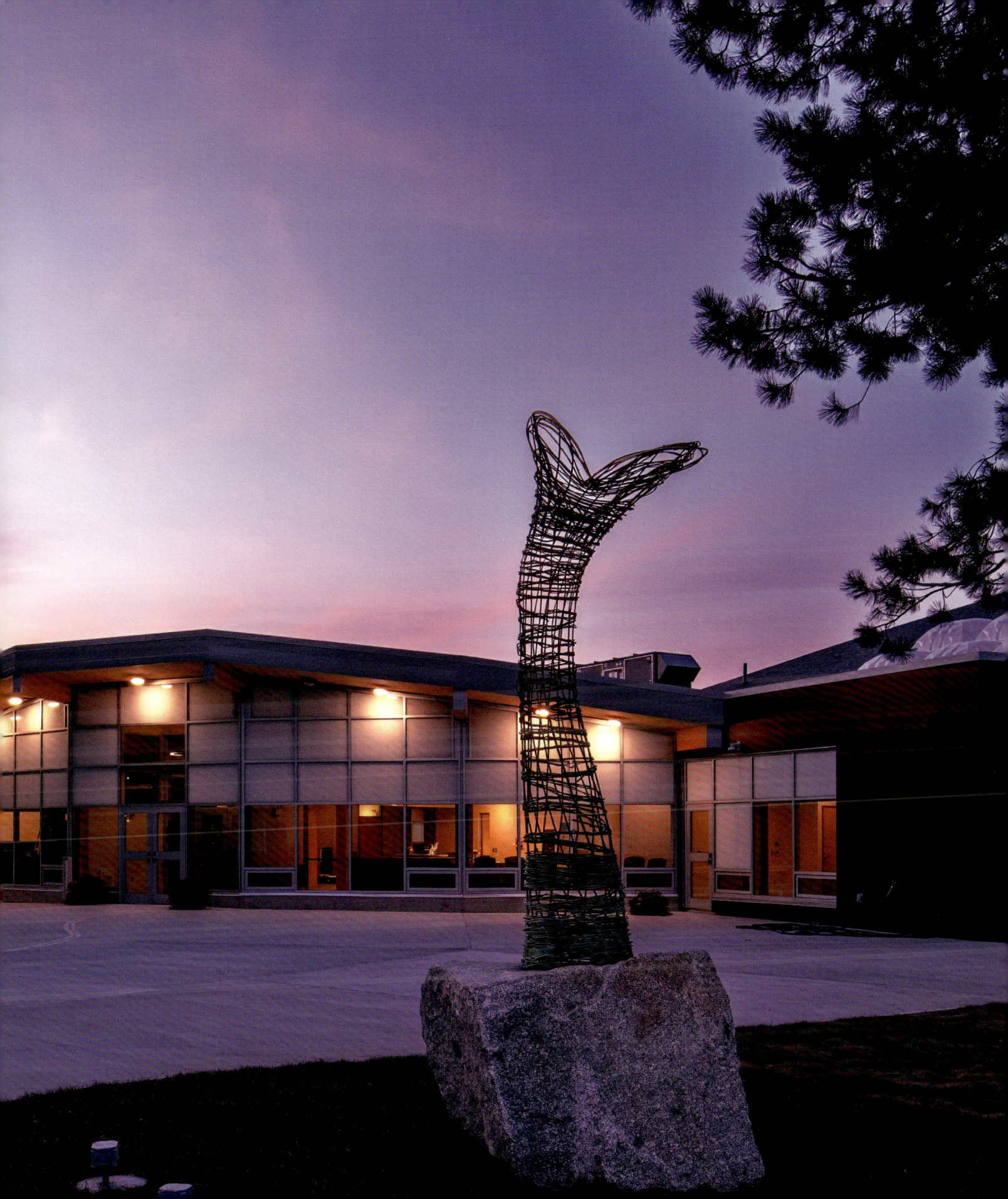

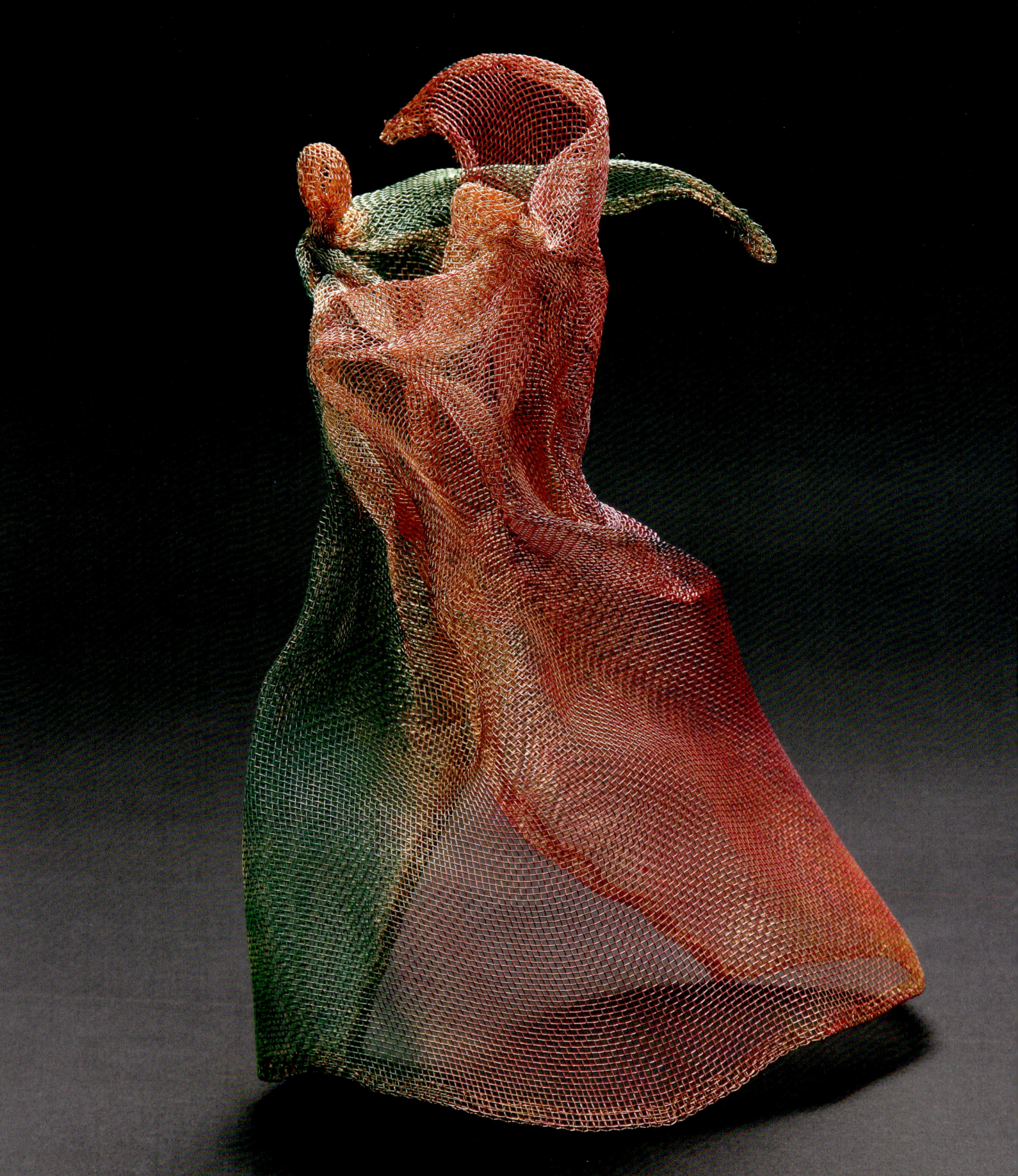

Acknowledgements

This book would not exist if it weren't for writer Margaret McGee Kashmir. She suggested it and encouraged me throughout its creation. She "interviewed" me and recorded my stories, some of them difficult. When she asked what my focus was, I replied, "My work is what best reflects my life experiences."

I am indebted to those who have affected me and constantly informed my work. Only a few of their names are sprinkled throughout this book. The Honourable Margaret Norrie McCain has been an advocate and pillar of strength supporting this project. Her heartfelt encouragement of my writing sustained me through the process. Thanks to Ramona Lumpkin, who first suggested I approach the MSVU Art Gallery for an exhibit. Maxine Krawczyk has been an angel. She is a visual researcher and meticulous organizer who works magic quietly and efficiently. She confronted my overwhelming archive of photographs, many in outmoded slide format, and made sense of it all. I'm thankful to have shared some stories with family (Jamie, Laura, Clive, and Emma) and trusted friends Margaret-Ellen Disney and Emily Falvey, whose responses motivated me. Most importantly, my husband, Merle, supported my absence in the kitchen and garden department! He not only grew the food but also often prepared it while I twined willow and navigated the elusive skills of computerized writing. And kudos to the photographers who contributed to this book, especially Peter Barss, Bruce Murray/VisionFire, and Gerry Farrell.

I am grateful to the former director of MSVU Art Gallery, Laura Ritchie, for her early work organizing a retrospective exhibition in tandem with this publication. A huge thanks to Melanie Colosimo, director of MSVU Art Gallery, who teamed up with Emily Falvey, director/curator of the Owens Art Gallery at Mount Allison University, to develop the book in association with the show. Thanks also to Andrea Terry, director of StFX Art Gallery, for hosting the show in Antigonish,

Dance, Dance, Dance, 2013
woven wire cloth, sculpted, acrylic paint
33 × 24 × 22

147

Timeless Form, 1996
twined willow
213 cm high

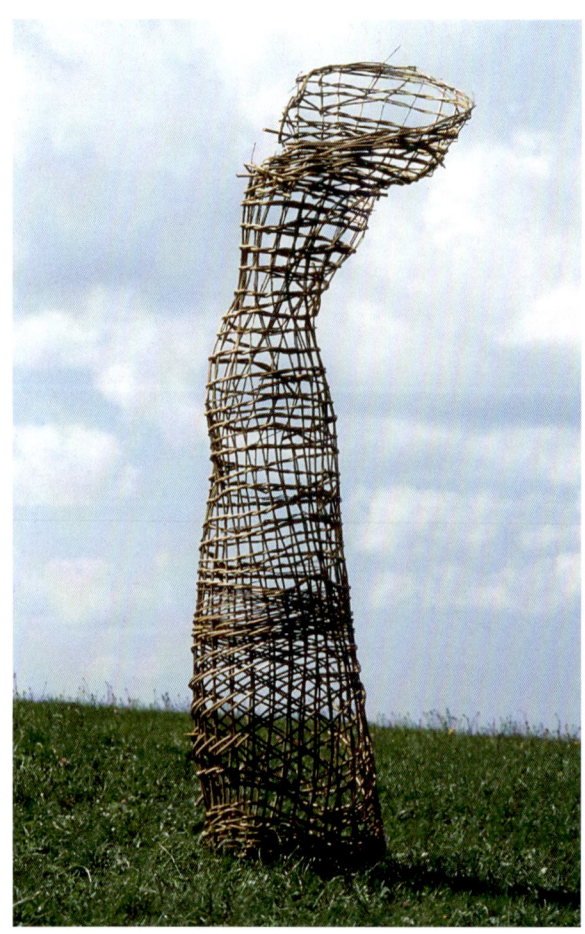

a welcome opportunity to exhibit close to home! Finally, I would like to thank Goose Lane Editions for supporting this book, especially Alan Sheppard, managing editor, and Julie Scriver, creative director, who gave me gentle encouragement from the beginning; and Alison Taylor, editor, who respectfully brought order to my uninhibited writing style.

Free Spirit, 2009
twined willow, acrylic paint
142 × 38 cm

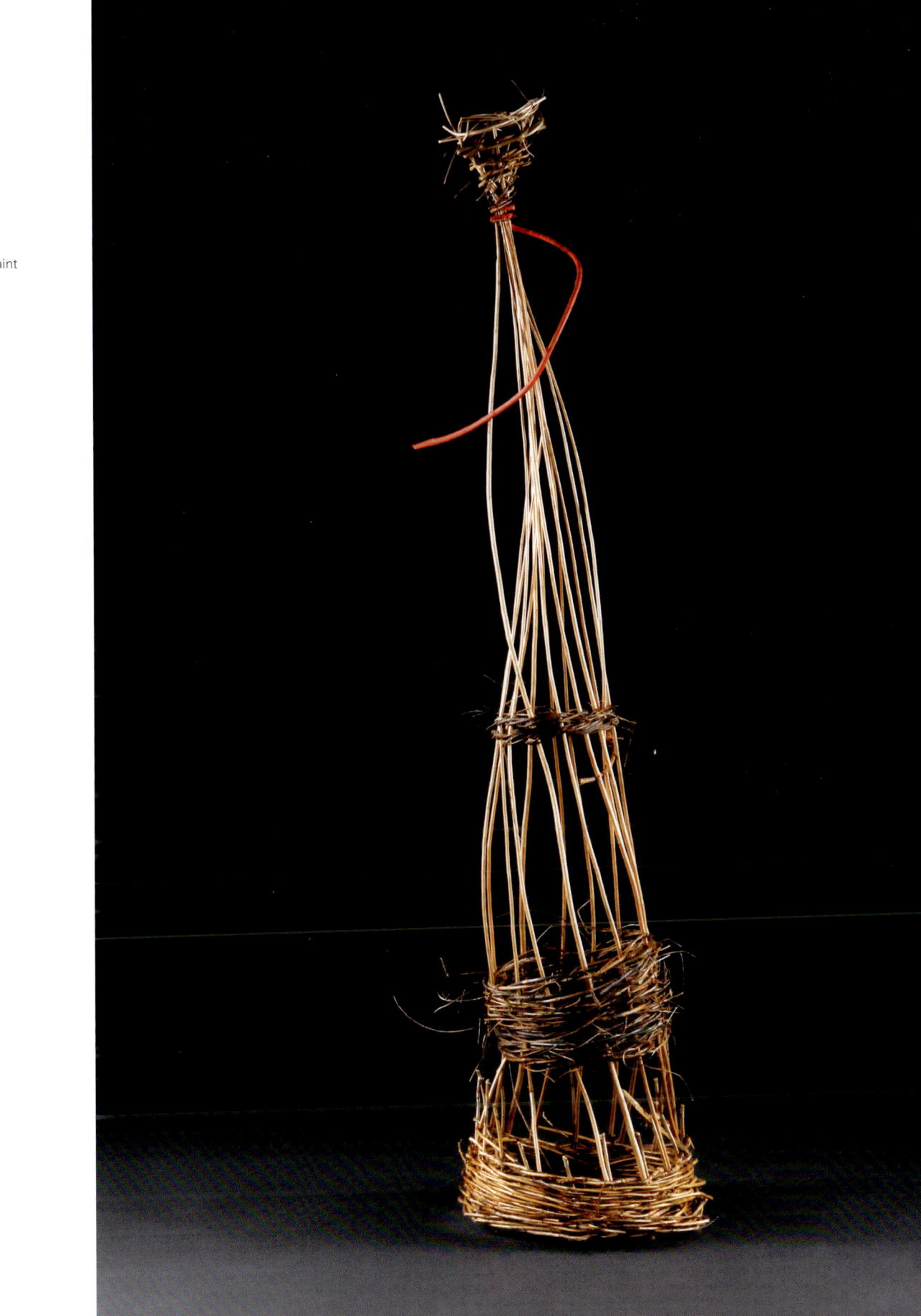

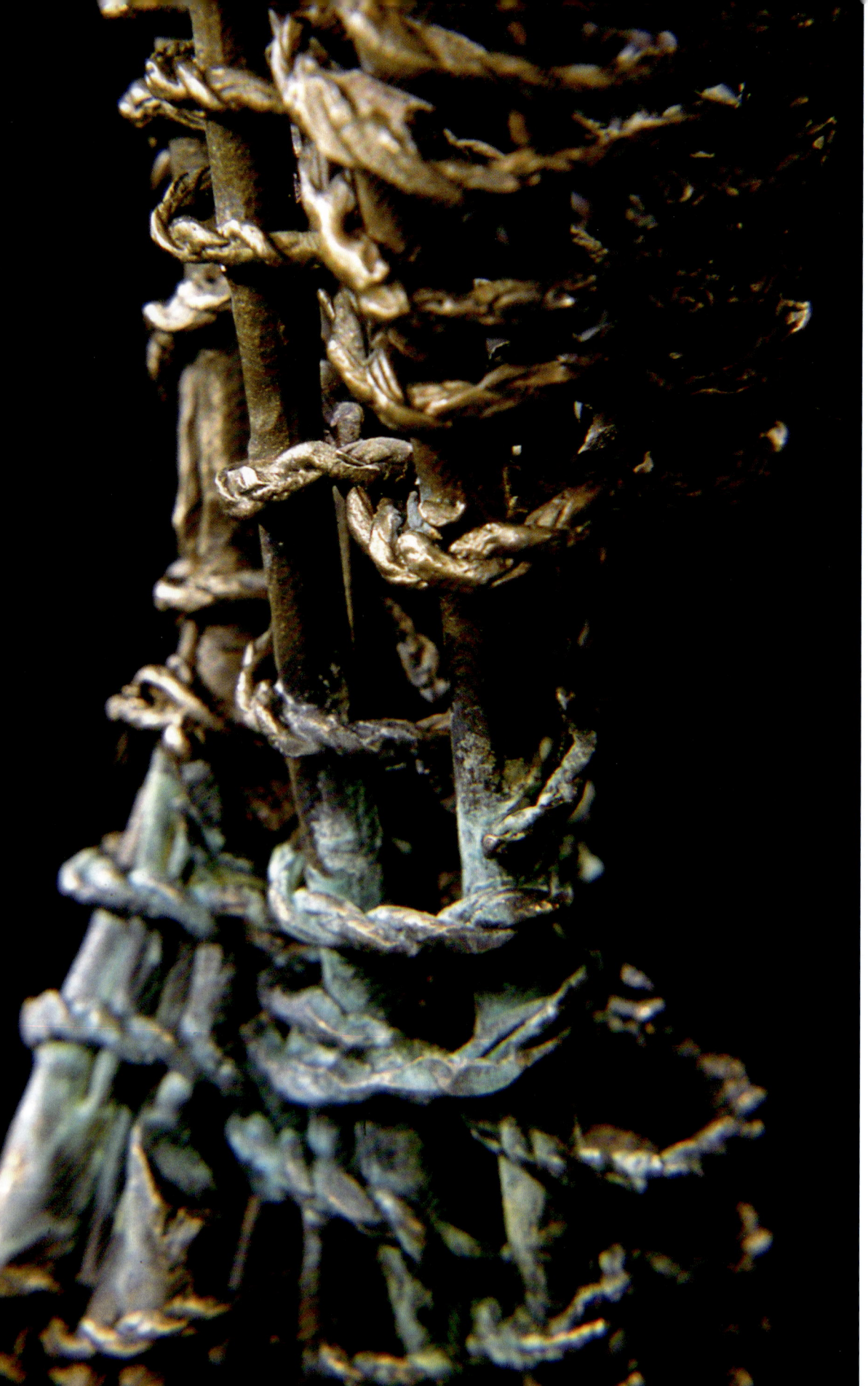

Bronze (detail), 2010
patinated bronze, cast from
twined willow, acrylic paint
dimensions variable

List of Works

All works collection of the artist unless otherwise noted. Images courtesy of the artist unless otherwise noted.

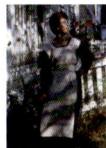

Black Dress with Finnish Lace Apron and Two Belts, 1973 (pp. 134, 135)
dress hand-woven fine single-linen yarn; apron with Finnish lace pattern woven of fine, natural, single-linen yarn
Collection of the Canadian Museum of History, artifact number: 83-170.1-.5
(photo: Sondra MacLeod)

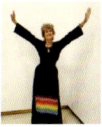

Black Dress and Rainbow Apron, 1973 (p. 132)
hand-woven fine single-linen yarn
Collection of the Canadian Museum of History, artifact number: 83-170.1-.5
Image courtesy of the Owens Art Gallery, 2021
(photo: Laura MacNutt)

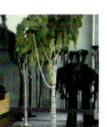

Once Upon a Time, 1975 (pp. 38–39, 40)
hand-spun, naturally dyed wool on linen warp
122 × 152 cm
Collection of the Dartmouth General Hospital
Image courtesy of the Owens Art Gallery
(photo: Roger J. Smith)

Trees and Other Things, 1978 (p. 43)
hand-spun, naturally dyed wool, woven on loom; fleece sculpted and hung from a yarn-wrapped, welded steel armature
214 cm high
Collection of Andy Lynch, the Estate of Lorna Gillis, and Shaun MacLean
(photo: Michael Hillis)

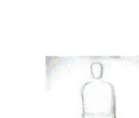

Tangled Garden, 1979 (p. 16)
felted, dyed fleece, plied wool yarn, hand-spun, naturally dyed, needle-woven flowers
25 × 20 × 2.5 cm
Collection of Joan Carlisle-Irving
(photo: Michael Hillis)

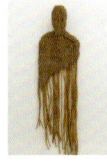

Man in a Kimono, 1980 (p. 49)
graphite on paper
28 × 21 cm

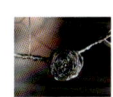

Presence, 1981 (p. 25)
twined seagrass over hemp rope
243 × 76 × 10 cm
Collection of the Nova Scotia Art Bank
Image courtesy of the Owens Art Gallery
(photo: Roger J. Smith)

Silver Thaw, 1981 (p. 14)
wrapped and melted silver wire
20 × 10 × 12.5 cm

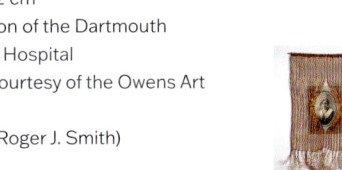

Anna Reid's Daughter, 1982 (p. 22)
copper wire double-woven on loom with embedded photograph
51 × 12 cm
(photo: David Dahms)

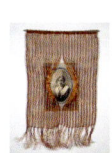

Thicket, 1982 (p. 45)
copper wire woven on loom, sculpted, wrapped branches electroplated, patinated
56 × 33 × 48 cm
Private collection
(photo: Bruce Murray, VisionFire)

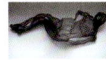

Turning Away, 1983 (p. 129)
copper wire woven on loom, electroplated, patinated
approx. 40 × 168 × 53 cm
stolen in 2023
(photo: Peter Barss)

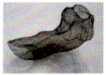

Female Torso, 1984 (p. 127)
copper wire woven on loom, electroplated, patinated
40 × 84 × 53 cm
stolen in 2023
(photo: Peter Barss)

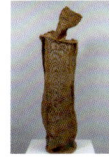

Giacometti, A Kindred Spirit, 1984 (p. 57)
seagrass and copper wire, welded metal armature
174 × 60 cm
MSVU Permanent Art Collection
Image courtesy of MSVU Art Gallery
(photo: Steve Farmer)

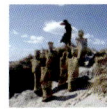

Kindred Spirits, 1984 (pp. 1, 16, 53, 55, 57)
seagrass woven on copper wire warp loom, sculpted, welded metal armature
dimensions variable
Individual works reside in various collections
(photos: Peter Barss)

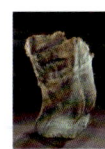

Male Torso, 1984 (p. 128)
copper wire woven on loom, sculpted, electroplated, patinated
40 × 30 × 26 cm
stolen in 2023
(photo: Peter Barss)

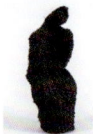
Man in Black Coat, 1984 (p. 66)
twined dyed sisal and copper wire
24 × 11 × 10 cm
(photo: Peter Barss)

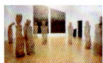
Woven Forms, 1984 (pp. 12-13)
welded, wrapped metal armature
dimensions variable
and *Rhythms*, 1984 (pp. 12-13)
loom-woven wool tapestry
304 × 304 cm
Images courtesy of MSVU Art
Gallery
(photo: David MacKenzie)

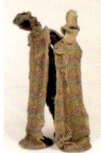
Vulnerability, 1986–1994 (p. 63)
seagrass woven on copper wire
warp loom, sculpted, welded metal
armature, intentionally left outside
to deteriorate over several years
183 × 186 cm
(photo: Peter Barss)

Fine Silver Trees, 1987 (p. 44)
fine silver woven on loom,
cast silver base
20 cm high
Collection of Sandra Hickey
(photo: Marianne Fraser)

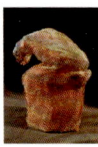
Anguish, 1988 (p. 67)
copper wire woven on loom,
sculpted, electroplated, oxidized
23 × 10 × 10 cm
(photo: Peter Barss)

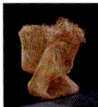
Embrace, 1988 (p. 60)
copper wire woven on loom,
sculpted
18 × 15 × 8 cm
(photo: Peter Barss)

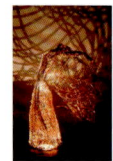
Spirit of Freedom, 1988 (p. 21)
copper wire woven on loom,
sculpted, electroplated, oxidized
28 × 23 × 23 cm
Collection of the Estate of Mary
Sparling

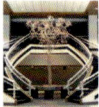
Together We Stand, 1989–1990
(pp. 18, 19)
stainless steel wire woven
on loom, branches wrapped,
hung from the ceiling; leaves
hand-cut from Moonbeam and
Eclipse fabric, aluminized knitted
polyester attached to the tree with
fine wrapped stainless steel
610 × 457 × 457 cm
Commissioned by QEII Health
Sciences Foundation for Halifax
Infirmary
Moved to Citadel High School in
2008

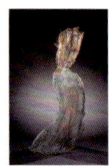
Grecian Figure, 1990 (p. 131)
copper wire woven on loom,
sculpted, electroplated, patinated
112 × 46 × 41 cm
stolen in 2023
(photo: Peter Barss)

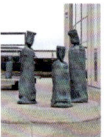
Kindred Spirits, 1990 (p. 58–59)
patinated bronze, cast from woven
fisherman's ropes
dimensions variable
Collection of Halifax Regional
Municipality
(photo: Keely Hopkins)

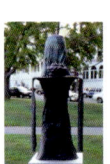
Vytaeimo, 1991 (p. 70)
bronze, cast from bread and fabric
142 × 61 × 61 cm
Collection of Halifax Regional
Municipality

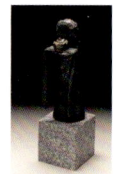
Vytaeimo, maquette, 1991 (p. 73)
bronze, cast from bread and fabric
19 cm high
Collection of the estate of Olya
Williams
(photo: George Georgakakis)

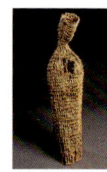
Courage, 1992 (p. 76)
bronze, cast from twined
inflorescence and twined paper
48 × 12 × 12 cm
Collection of Hon. Margaret Norrie
McCain
(photo: Peter Barss)

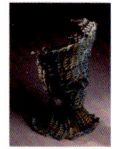
Requiem, 1992 (p. 69)
bronze, cast from twined paper
50 × 48 × 49 cm
Collection of Mulgrave Machine
Works

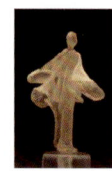
Miniature Silver Muse, 1993
(p. 140)
woven fine silver wire, sculpted,
acrylic base
5 cm high
(photo: Peter Barss)

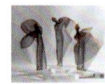
Muses, Cultural Life Awards, 1993
(p. 138)
woven copper wire cloth, sculpted,
electroplated, patinated, acrylic
bases
38 cm high
Various private collections
(photo: Peter Barss)

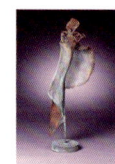
Clio, 1994 (p. 141)
woven wire cloth, sculpted,
electroplated, patinated, cast
bronze base
86 × 56 × 30 cm
Private collection
(photo: Peter Barss)

152

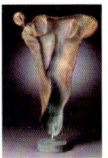

Muse Calliope, 1994 (p. 139)
woven copper wire cloth, sculpted,
electroplated, patinated, cast
bronze base
86 × 56 × 31cm
Collection of Interlude Spa
(photo: Peter Barss)

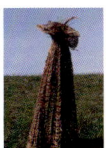

Timeless Form, 1995 (p. 4)
twined willow and seagrass
135 × 64 × 64 cm
Collection of Margaret and David
Fountain
(photo: Peter Barss)

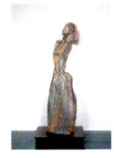

Transcendence, 1995 (p. 74)
copper wire woven on loom,
sculpted, electroplated, patinated
165 × 61 × 56 cm
Corporate collection
Image courtesy of the Woodlawn
Foundation
(photo: unknown)

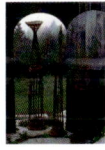

Caryatid and *Timeless Forms*,
1996 (p. 78)
twined willow
dimensions variable
Image courtesy of Prow Gallery
(photo: Peter Barss)

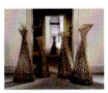

Draped Forms, 1996 (p. 80)
twined willow and seagrass
140–170 cm high
Collection of the Art Gallery
of Nova Scotia
(photo: Peter Barss)

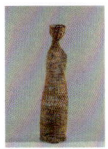

Timeless Figure, c. 1996 (p. 30)
twined willow and seagrass
162 × 40 × 23 cm
Collection of the Owens Art
Gallery, Gift of the Artist
(photo: Roger J. Smith)

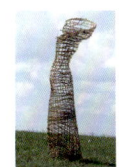

Timeless Form, 1996 (p. 148)
twined willow
213 cm high
Private collection
(photo: Peter Barss)

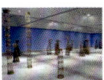

All the Ancients Walk Inside Us,
1997 (p. 82)
twined willow
150–305 cm high
Image courtesy of the Art Gallery
of Nova Scotia

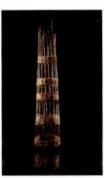

Column, 1997 (p. 85)
twined willow
172 × 13 × 13 cm
(photo: Peter Barss)

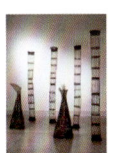

Columns and *Timeless Forms*,
1997 (p. 81)
twined willow
150–305 cm high
(photo: Peter Barss)

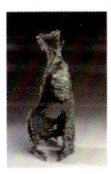

Vigil, 1999 (p. 91)
bronze, cast from twined willow
40 × 30 × 30 cm
Collection of Taiya Barss
(photo: Peter Barss)

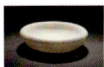

Bowl, 2000 (p. 92)
Parian marble
5 × 19 × 19 cm
(photo: Peter Barss)

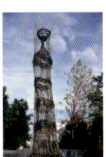

Sentinel, 2002 (p. 95)
bronze, cast from woven willow
and grapevine
431 cm high
Created on-site and at the
Pyramid foundry for the Okanagan
Thompson International Sculpture
Symposium, Kelowna, BC

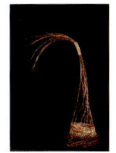

Recovery, 2004 (pp. 26, 27)
twined and wrapped English willow
and seagrass
120 × 74 × 50 cm
MSVU Permanent Art Collection
(photo: Bruce Murray, VisionFire)

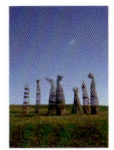

*Return to Delo*s, 2004 (pp. 2–3)
Timeless Forms series,
1995–2002
twined willow and seagrass
and *Timeless Figure* (centre),
c. 1996
bronze, cast from twined willow
140–170 cm high

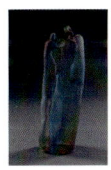

Soft Shadows, 2004 (p. 145)
woven wire cloth, sculpted,
electroplated, patinated, acrylic
paint
34 × 14 × 10 cm
(photo: Bruce Murray, VisionFire)

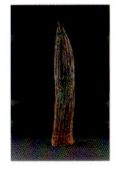

Spirit Within, 2004 (pp. 98, 101,
back cover)
twined willow, acrylic paint
158 × 33 × 28 cm
(photo: Bruce Murray, VisionFire)

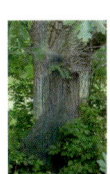

Unfinished Figure, 2004 (p. 126)
copper wire woven on loom,
patinated, welded copper
armature
251 cm high
unfinished, stolen in 2023

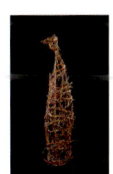

Motherhood in Willow, 2005
(p. 36)
twined willow and grapevine
106 × 31 × 31 cm
(photo: Peter Barss)

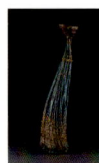

Timeless Spirit, 2006 (pp. 104, 105)
bronze, cast from twined willow, acrylic paint
135 × 38 × 38 cm
Collection of Hon. Margaret Norrie McCain
(photo: Bruce Murray, VisionFire)

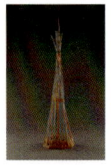

Symphony, 2007 (p. 106)
twined willow, acrylic paint
170 × 41 × 45 cm
Collection of Hon. Margaret Norrie McCain
(photo: Bruce Murray, VisionFire)

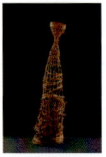

Walk in Peace, 2007 (p. 86)
twined willow and grapevine
147 × 40 cm
(photo: Bruce Murray, VisionFire)

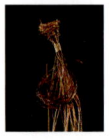

Mother and Child, 2008 (p. 116)
twined willow, seagrass
112 × 29 × 30 cm
(photo: Bruce Murray, VisionFire)

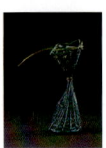

Robin, 2008 (p. 156)
patinated bronze, cast from twined willow, acrylic paint
46 × 40 × 19 cm
Collection of the Nova Scotia Art Bank
(photo: Bruce Murray, VisionFire)

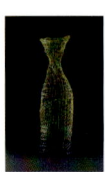

Shades of Green, 2008 (pp. 102, 103)
twined willow, acrylic paint
214 × 38 × 38 cm
(photo: Bruce Murray, VisionFire)

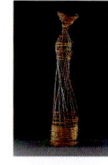

Summer Stroll, 2008 (pp. 8, 9)
twined willow, acrylic paint
150 × 40 × 40 cm
(photo: Bruce Murray, VisionFire; browngrotta arts)

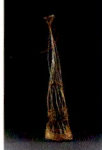

Free Spirit, 2009 (pp. 6, 149)
twined willow, acrylic paint
142 × 38 cm
(Photo: Bruce Murray, VisionFire)

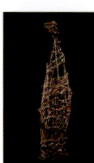

Motherhood in Bronze, 2009 (p. 37)
patinated bronze
106 × 31 × 31 cm
(photo: Peter Barss)

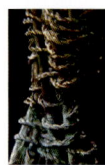

Bronze, 2010 (p. 150)
patinated bronze, cast from twined willow, acrylic paint
dimensions variable
(photo: Peter Barss)

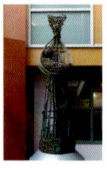

Caring, 2010 (pp. 108–9, 110–11, 112, 115)
patinated bronze, cast from twined willow, acrylic paint
244 × 48 × 48 cm, pedestal 60 × 91 × 91 cm
Collection of IWK Health, Richard Goldbloom Pavilion
(photo: Keely Hopkins)

Against All Odds, 2013 (p. 10)
twined willow, acrylic paint
92 × 75 × 40 cm
(photo: Bruce Murray, VisionFire)

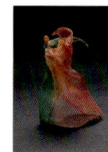

Dance, Dance, Dance, 2013 (pp. 146, 155)
woven wire cloth, sculpted, acrylic paint
33 × 24 × 22
Collection of Laura MacNutt
(photo: Bruce Murray, VisionFire)

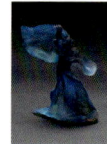

Rhapsody in Blue, 2013 (p. 158)
woven wire cloth, electroplated, oxidized, acrylic paint
40 × 30 × 20 cm
Private collection
(photo: Bruce Murray, VisionFire)

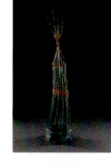

Summer, 2013 (p. 157)
twined willow, acrylic paint
135 × 38 × 38 cm
Courtesy of Gallery 78
(photo: Bruce Murray, VisionFire)

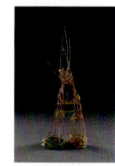

Together Still, 2013 (p. 107)
patinated bronze, cast from twined willow, acrylic paint
86 × 31 × 18 cm
Private collection
(photo: Bruce Murray, VisionFire)

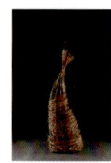

From the Land, 2015 (p. 87, front cover)
twined willow and grapevine
202 × 87 × 52 cm
(photo: Bruce Murray, VisionFire)

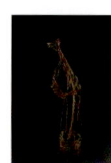

Care, 2018 (p. 117)
bronze, cast from twined willow, seagrass
111 × 29 × 29 cm
(photo: Bruce Murray, VisionFire)

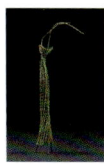

Echoes of the Past, 2018 (pp. 28, 29)
bronze, cast from twined willow
and seagrass
69 × 38 × 13 cm
Private collection
(photo: Bruce Murray, VisionFire)

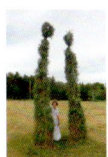

He and She Out Standing in the Field, 2018 (p. 97)
living willows
431 cm high
(photo: Merle Pratt)

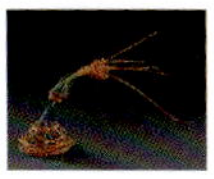

Moving Forward (2), 2018 (p. 35)
twined willow, acrylic paint
20 × 42 × 8.7 cm
(photo: Bruce Murray Vision Fire)

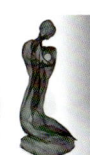

Invincible Summer, 2019 (p. 65)
copper woven wire cloth, sculpted,
electroplated, and patinated
68 × 20 × 36 cm
Collection of Margaret Kashmir
(photo: Sharjeel Kashmir)

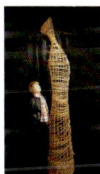

Jack, Larger than Life, 2020
(pp. 50, 51)
twined willow
324 × 51 × 51 cm
Collection of the LongHouse
Reserve

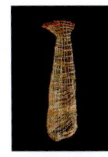

Spirit of Courage, 2020 (pp. 124, 125)
twined willow, acrylic paint
153 × 62 × 40 cm
(photo: Gerry Farrell)

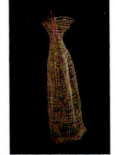

Spirit of Joy, 2020 (p. 118, 121)
twined willow, acrylic paint
165 × 64 × 55 cm
(photo: Gerry Farrell)

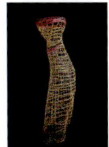

Spirit of Love, 2020 (pp. 122, 123)
twined willow, acrylic paint
156 × 60 × 55 cm
(photo: Gerry Farrell)

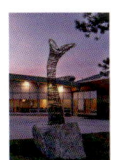

MUSE!, 2024 (pp. 144–45)
patinated bronze cast from woven
willow, acrylic paint, crowned with
gold leaf, granite base
244 × 122 × 84 cm
Collection of the Town of Pictou
(photo: Gerry Farrell)

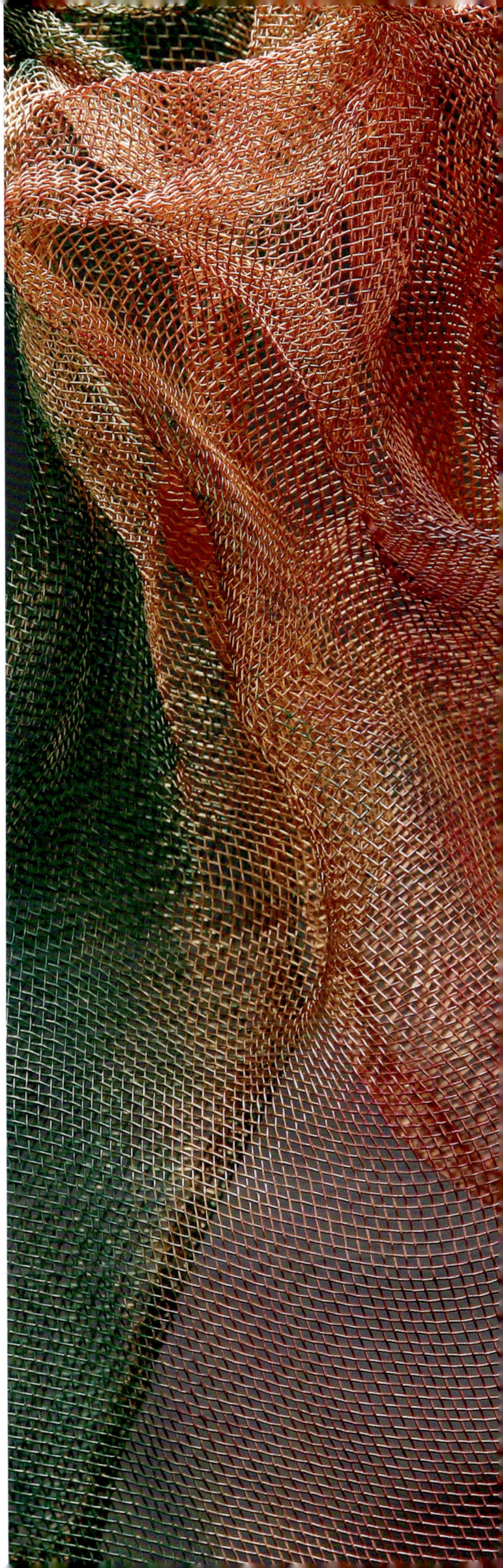

Dance, Dance, Dance (detail), 2013

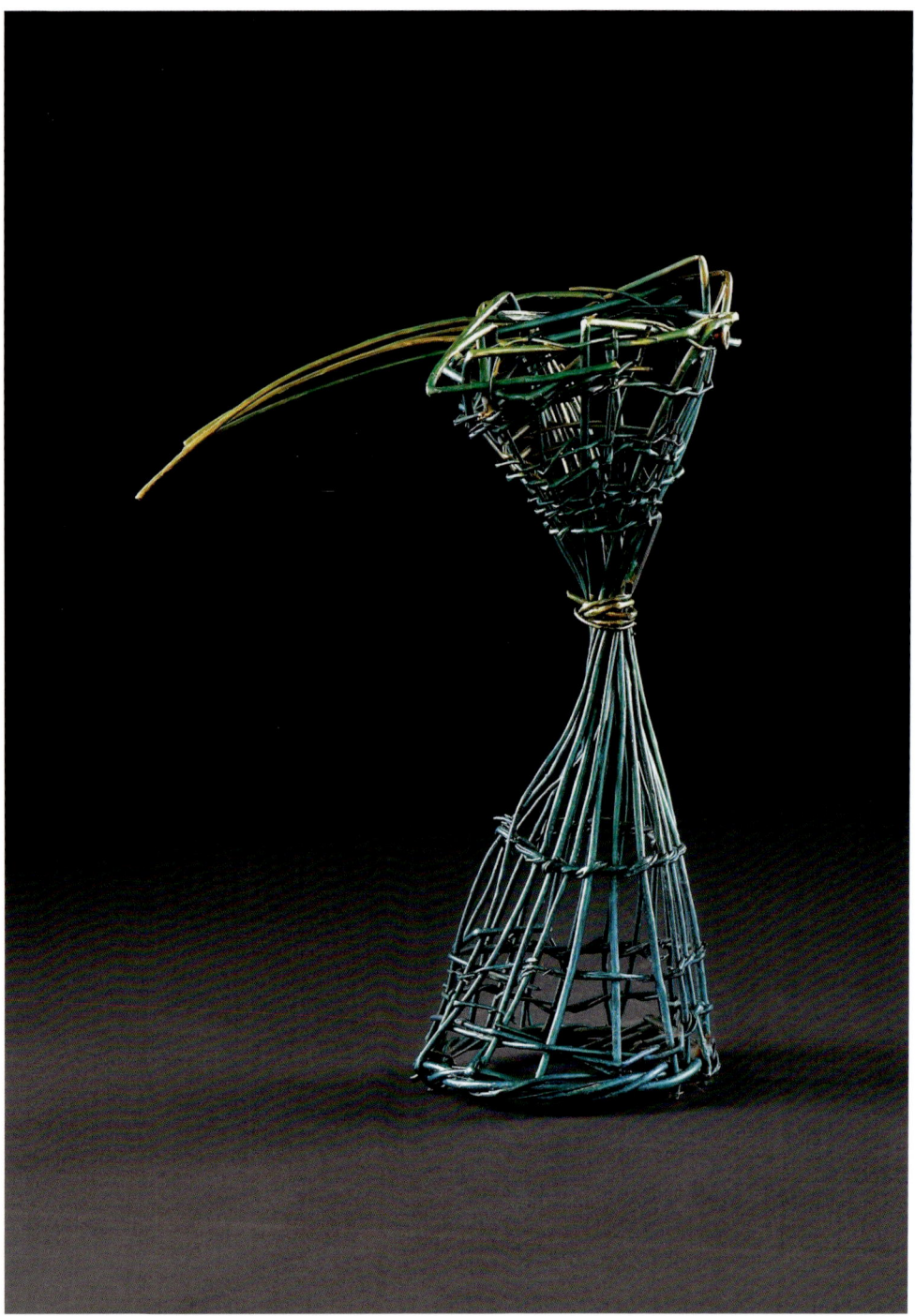

Robin, 2008
patinated bronze, cast from
twined willow, acrylic paint
46 × 40 × 19 cm

opposite: *Summer*, 2013
twined willow, acrylic paint
135 × 38 × 38 cm

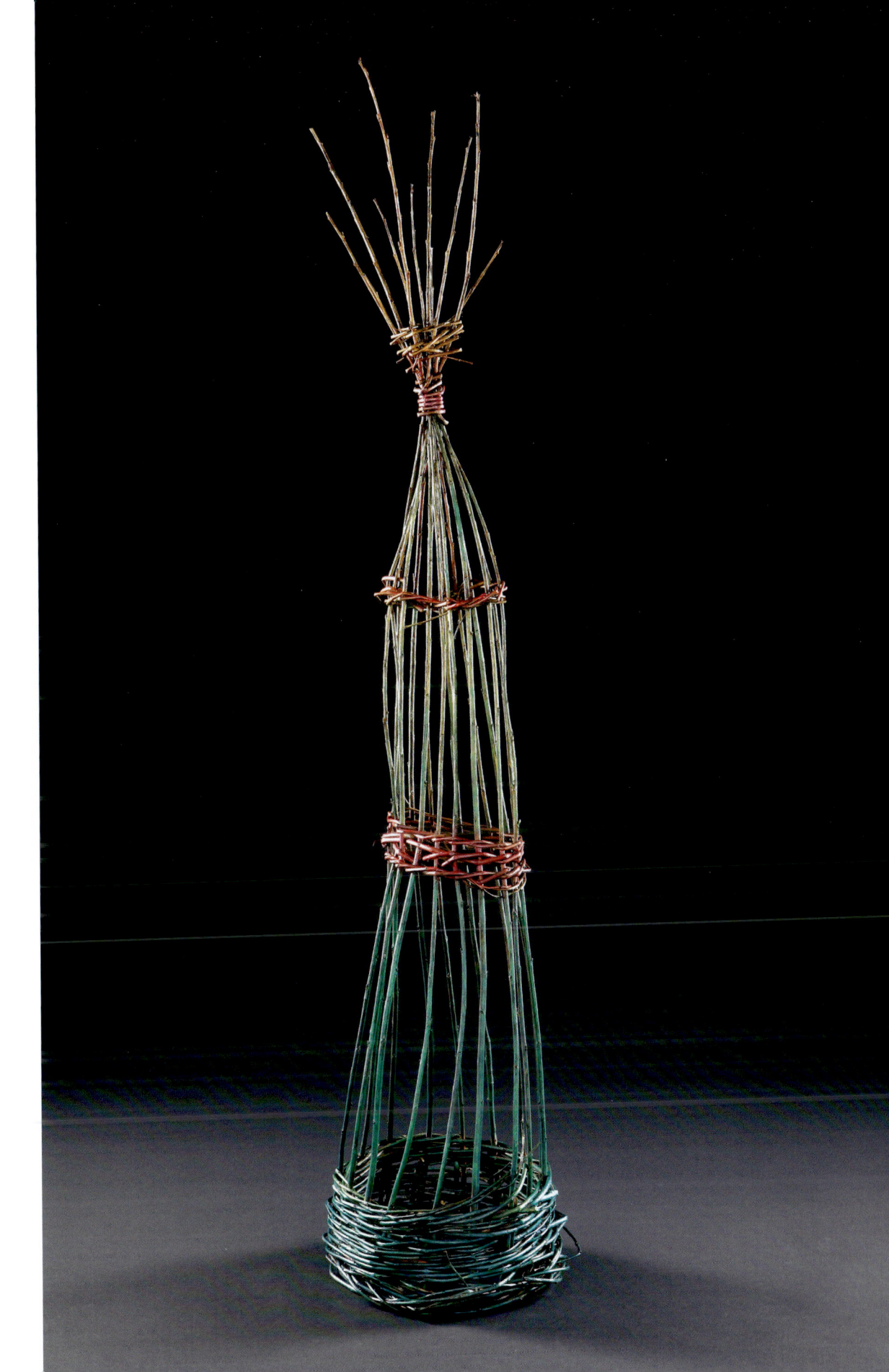

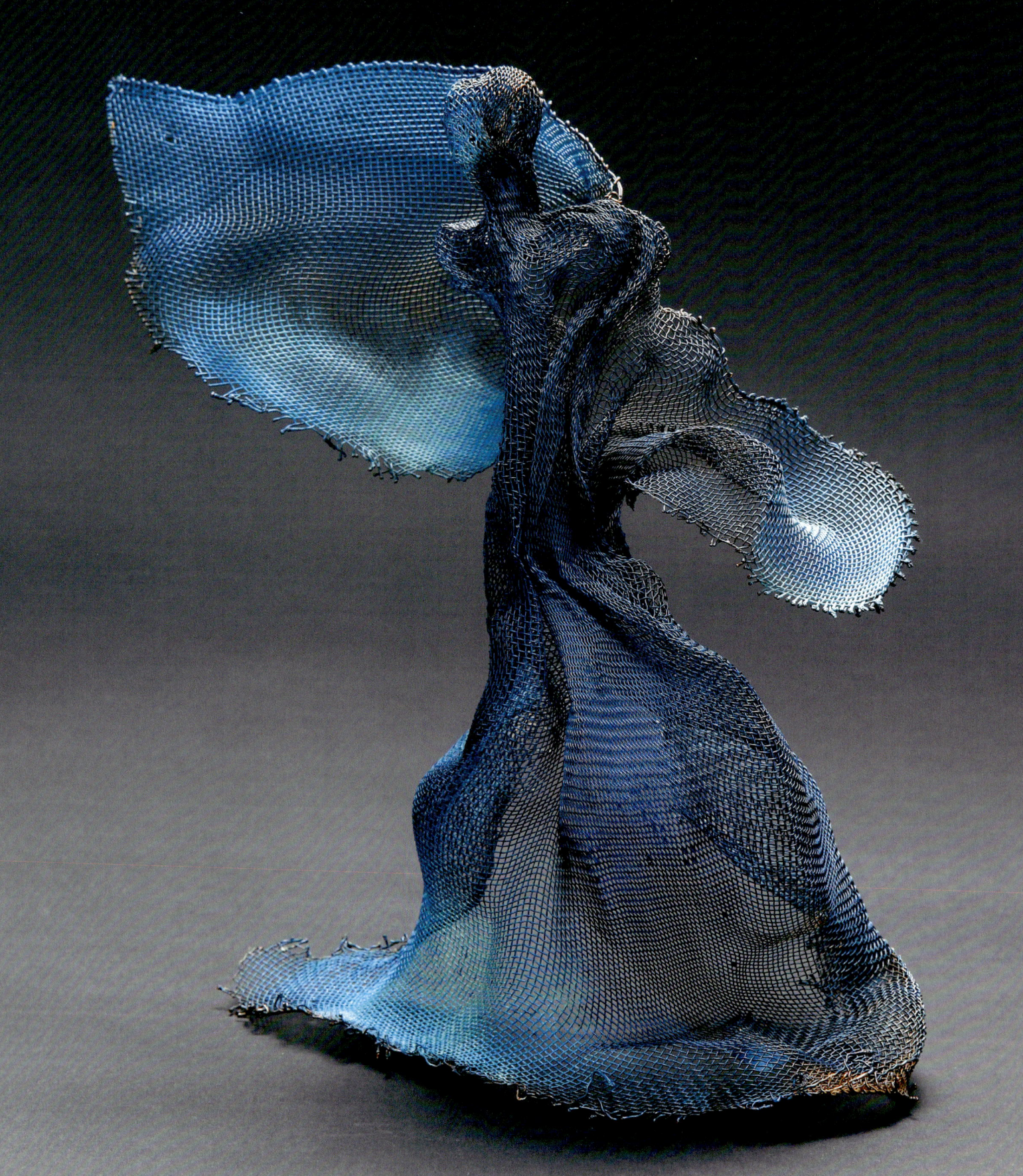

About the Artist

Dawn MacNutt's work is most often inspired by her lifelong love of the human condition, what she describes as "the beauty of human frailty."

Interpreting universal human form, or architectonic column-like forms, she generally works with natural materials. There is continued interest in her life-size willow works cast into bronze for outdoor installations and sculpture gardens.

She remarried in 2007 and came to live in rural Pictou County, Nova Scotia, where, coincidentally, she was born. As she and her husband worked to restore the old house on the property into the studio in which Dawn now works, the deed revealed that the structure was built in 1838 by her great-great-great-grandfather, Alexander James Reid. As she created in this ancestral space, looking out to the rural landscape of the woods, so near the ocean, her work took on new layers of joy and peace.

Dawn MacNutt obtained a bachelor of arts (art and psychology) in 1957 from Mount Allison University, New Brunswick. In 1970, she obtained a master's degree in social work from Dalhousie University, Halifax, Nova Scotia. She was inducted into the Royal Canadian Academy of the Arts in 2008. In 2005, she was honoured with a Doctorate of Humane Letters by Mount Saint Vincent University and in 2014 with a Doctorate of Laws by Mount Allison University.

As well as her exhibition and commission work, she is a longstanding member of the International Sculpture Center; CARFAC (Canadian Artist Representation); Craft Nova Scotia; Visual Arts Nova Scotia; and Creative Pictou County. She served as a national director on the Canadian Craft Council from 1983–1987 and her work is held in numerous collections including the MSVU Art Gallery, Halifax; the Art Gallery of Nova Scotia, Halifax; the Owens Art Gallery, Sackville; the Museum of Arts and Design, New York; Rideau Hall, Ottawa; and the Canadian Museum of History, Ottawa.

Rhapsody in Blue, 2013
woven wire cloth, electroplated,
oxidized, acrylic paint
40 × 30 × 20 cm

Edited by Alison Taylor.
Copy edited by Paula Sarson.
Cover and page design by Julie Scriver, Goose Lane Editions.
On the cover: (front) *From the Land*, 2015, twined willow and grapevine,
202 × 87 × 52 cm (photo: Bruce Murray, VisionFire); (back) *Spirit Within*, 2004,
twined willow, acrylic paint, 158 × 33 × 28 cm (photo: Bruce Murray, VisionFire).

Library and Archives Canada Cataloguing in Publication

Title: Timeless forms / Dawn MacNutt.
Names: MacNutt, Dawn, 1937– author, artist. | Mount Saint Vincent University Art
Gallery, publisher.
Identifiers: Canadiana 20240438981 | ISBN 9781894518826 (hardcover)
Subjects: LCSH: MacNutt, Dawn, 1937– | LCSH: Sculptors—Nova Scotia—Biography |
LCSH: Textile artists—Nova Scotia—Biography. | LCSH: Creation (Literary, artistic,
etc.) | LCGFT: Autobiographies. | LCGFT: Essays.
Classification: LCC NB249.M267 A2 2025 | DDC 730.92—dc23

Printed in Canada by Friesens.
10 9 8 7 6 5 4 3 2 1

MSVU Art Gallery
Mount Saint Vincent University
166 Bedford Highway
Halifax, Nova Scotia
CANADA B3M 2J6

Owens Art Gallery
Mount Allison University
61 York Street
Sackville, New Brunswick
CANADA E4L 1E1

We would like to acknowledge that Mount Saint Vincent University is located in
Kjipuktuk (Halifax) and Mount Allison University is located in Sikniktuk, both part
of Mi'kma'ki, the unceded ancestral territory that remains the homeland of the
Mi'kmaq Nation. This territory is covered by the Covenant Chain of Treaties of
Peace and Friendship signed between 1725 and 1779. These treaties are affirmed
by the Supreme Court of Canada and recognize Indigenous Title, which is embedded
in both the 1763 Royal Proclamation and in section 35(1) of the 1982 Constitution
Act. The treaties are living agreements that establish the rules for an ongoing treaty
relationship between nations. We pay respect to the knowledge embedded in the
Mi'kmaw custodians of the lands and waters and to the Elders, past, present,
and future.